Read the Reviews

Bottom Line™ provides a clear roadmap for increasing share-
authors detail the advantages of the theory but also show how
ted — with enormous benefits — by several different compa-
les can apply to any business that realizes the importance of
ips with its various constituents.
EO, COO, CFO or CPO, you should read this book, before
do."

llkamp, Former Vice Chairman, Daimler-Chrysler
ner, Ripplewood Holdings, LLC
boration Management, LLC

ransform your purchasing department into a strategic supply
ration that adds value up and down the supply chain? *Straight*
e™ can help you make that transformation. It's a book that
-class case examples with the accumulated insight of four of the
chasing pros. And here's the bonus: It's practical, down to earth,
ble."

, Editor, Supply Chain Management Review

demonstrate with vivid, real-life examples the impact procure-
the top and bottom line. They have provided an easy-to-follow
nsforming procurement into the value-driving force that it can
pany. *Straight to the Bottom Line*™ is a must-read for senior
or procurement professionals wanting to increase the impact of
nt organization."

Breves, Chief Procurement Officer, Alcoa

and procurement have been moving from a simple negotiation
ategic interface with external resources. Procurement moved from
ment (dealing with discounts) to supply management (dealing
ization of supplier relationship: innovation, capacity...).
he Bottom Line™ highlights these new, valuable perspectives. The
as, facts, trends, practices and this is all about procurement. Senior
ives, as well as senior procurement leaders, should give this book
n."

acia, Director
an Institute of Purchasing Management (E.I.P.M)
for Purchasing, www.eipm.org

STRA..
TO T
BOTTOM.

AN EXECUTIVE'S
WORLD CLASS SUPP

"An important read for executive and sourcing and supply chain leaders. Significant insights are provided into critical issues and the strategies required for achieving sourcing and supply chain excellence and how such excellence contributes to top and bottom line performance. Company examples clearly demonstrate successful strategies.

"In addition, Chapter 9, "Transformation: Making Sure the Changes Stick," provides unusual clarity about what companies must do to both sustain and improve sourcing and supply chain performance and resulting overall company performance. Leading-edge strategies and practices, based on the authors' broad-based knowledge and experience, provide useful transformation roadmaps throughout.

"A hard-hitting book that provides guidance to executive leaders about what their companies should do to gain sustainable competitive advantage through sourcing and supply chain excellence."

Robert M. Monczka, Ph.D., Director,
Strategic Sourcing and Supply Chain Strategy Research,
CAPS Research
Distinguished Research and ISM Professor,
W.P. Carey School of Business Supply Chain Management
Arizona State University

"*Straight to the Bottom Line*™ offers an insightful analysis on the strategic yet pragmatic approach to supply management. This must-read book on organizational design presents a multidimensional outlook on successfully implementing a supply transformation in your organization."

Anthony Nieves, C.P.M., CFPM
Senior Vice President – Supply Management
Hilton Hotels Corporation

"*Straight to the Bottom Line*™ is the definitive work on the application of contemporary practice and principles of procurement/supply base management. Every CEO, CFO, CPO and their boards who are interested in increasing shareholder value need to read this. When they're done, they should make this required reading for their management and procurement teams.

"The authors clearly demonstrate their wealth of experience in this work. It's the most comprehensive treatise I've read on the practice and profession of procurement/supply base management. This should be required reading for all procurement professionals, CPOs, CFOs and board directors. I'd like 50 copies upon publication (with volume discount of course)."

Dick Conrad, Senior VP, Global Operations Supply Chain
Hewlett-Packard

"Since the industrial revolution, resources such as managerial talent, research, and engineering have been focused on improving productivity and efficiency in production processes to achieve competitive advantage. Rudzki, Smock, Katzorke, and Stewart make the case that investments in supply management resources are long overdue.

"Most businesses buy more goods and services than they add in internal value to a product or service. The rising technological complexity of products and the globalization of supply chains only adds to the imperative that firms manage their spend with a strategic plan that recognizes the value of partnering with suppliers for mutual advantage. *Straight to the Bottom Line*™ lays out the roadmap taken by the most talented procurement executives in America, supply management superstars, who made major contributions to large multinational corporations that were under intense pressure to improve the bottom line."

Dan Meckstroth, Chief Economist and Purchasing Council Director
Manufacturers Alliance/MAPI

"I interact with varying levels of executives every day and can truly say that *Straight to the Bottom Line*™ has as much value to the supply management executive and practitioner as it has to the C-level suite. The authors clearly have their battle scars and have done an admirable job in sharing the do's and don'ts of executing a supply management transformation.

"The numerous case studies of the good, the bad, and the ugly of supply management efforts, told in the mind and voice of the CPO, should be invaluable to senior executives and practitioners alike. For companies who want to not just be efficient, but also effective, in their journey to World Class Supply Management, this book should prove to be an invaluable resource."

Pierre Mitchell, Director, The Hackett Group

"*Straight to the Bottom Line*™ is a comprehensive, readable guide to creating a game-changing supply chain for a company of almost any size. The authors demonstrate how a company can elevate its procurement, manufacturing, engineering and other functions into an innovative supply chain organization that has genuine, bottom-line strategic value. They employ a wide range of interesting, real-life examples that illustrate their key points and provide proof that the strategies work! Their depth of knowledge and their enthusiasm for the consequence of a well-managed supply chain will be appreciated by those of us in the supply chain world, and will help people throughout business more fully understand the incredible power of this pivotal function."

Joe Carson, Chief Procurement Executive, Lucent Technologies

"The combined efforts of three veteran supply management pros and a talented journalist who deeply understands the supply management terrain have produced the best book that I have ever read on the value of superior supply management. The real-life examples described in this book accurately describe the reality of purchasing and supply management, both good and bad — the Stallkamp/Lopez comparison in Chapter 10 ("Automotive Purchasing: A Tale of Two Spenders") is a perfect example.

"Simply put, *Straight to the Bottom Line*™ is a must-read not only for procurement/supply management pros, but also for the many business people who need to better understand the vast untapped potential of strategic supply management."

Kevin R. Fitzgerald, Vice President, Supply Management Research
The Aberdeen Group, Inc.

"*Straight to the Bottom Line*™ is as starkly practical, as no-nonsense as its title indicates. No theory here. The book's authors have done what they write about and they've done it exceedingly well. They are consummate professionals at the top of their game. And their game happens to be procurement and supply chain management. They each have helped transform major companies using the tactics and strategies spelled out here. This is like a boxing book written by Dempsey, Louis and Ali. Strong praise? *Straight to the Bottom Line*™ lives up to it.

"The book is truly unique because it succeeds in addressing the problems and concerns of C-class executives, plus procurement management and their teams — virtually everybody in a company who is focused on dramatically improving today's business performance. Read it and learn. Your suppliers, your customers and your competitors certainly will."

Jack O'Connor, Publisher Emeritus, Purchasing Magazine

CO-PUBLISHED WITH

Purchasing
THE MAGAZINE FOR CHIEF PROCUREMENT OFFICERS AND SUPPLY CHAIN EXECUTIVES

SUPPLYCHAIN
MANAGEMENT REVIEW

STRAIGHT TO THE BOTTOM LINE™

AN EXECUTIVE'S ROADMAP TO WORLD CLASS SUPPLY MANAGEMENT

ROBERT A. RUDZKI • DOUGLAS A. SMOCK

MICHAEL KATZORKE • SHELLEY STEWART, JR.

Foreword by
Paul Novak, C.P.M., A.P.P.
Chief Executive Officer
Institute for Supply Management™

J.ROSS
PUBLISHING

Copyright ©2006 by Rudzki, Smock, Katzorke, Stewart

ISBN 1-932159-49-5

Printed and bound in the U.S.A. Printed on acid-free paper
10 9 8 7 6 5 4 3 2 1

Library of Congress Cataloging-in-Publication Data
Straight to the bottom line : an executive's roadmap to world class supply
management / by Robert A. Rudzki ... [et al.].
  p. cm.
Includes bibliographical references and index.
ISBN 1-932159-49-5 (hardcover. : alk. paper)
  1. Industrial procurement—Management. I. Rudzki, Robert A., 1953–
HD39.5.S76 2005
658.7—dc22   2005022400

Phone: (954) 727-9333
Fax: (561) 892-0700
Web: www.jrosspub.com

Table of Contents

Foreword

You may remember the movie *Patton*, in which George C. Scott portrayed General Patton. In a critical part of the movie, the American forces under Patton's command were engaged in a battle with General Rommel's forces in North Africa. In a surprise maneuver, the American forces prevail. Scott, portraying Patton, yells out, "Rommel, you magnificent bastard, I read your book!"

If you want to stay ahead of your competitors, then you need to read *Straight to the Bottom Line*™. I doubt that another book exists that explains more clearly the contribution that supply management can make to corporate success. But wait! This book also explains how to achieve that success.

Today's businesses are often surprised to learn how much of the revenue dollar is spent on goods and services — not just on direct materials in manufacturing, but on all goods and services including in nonmanufacturing businesses as well. The numbers range from 30 to 70%. Yet many companies still focus only on prices and on the tactical act of buying.

This book shows why that shortsighted view of focusing on prices leaves a competitive advantage open to your competitors. If I were in charge of supply management at your company, I would ask every member of senior management to read this book. If I were a member of your senior management, I would ask my chief of supply management to read this book. Then I would have a report, presentation, and discussion of what we are doing and, more importantly, what we are not doing and why. I suspect you will have the talent in your organization to do what is in the book, but you will find that the awareness and the resolve from senior management have been lacking.

Two clichés come to mind. The first is it takes a buck to make a buck. We find that when supply management is used to its full potential, each buck spent generates a return of 5 to 10 *times* the investment. That's right — a *multiple* of 5 to 10 times the investment you make in supply management. The second is a paraphrase of Benjamin Franklin: "a penny saved is a penny earned." Well, that is only true if you don't inadvertently spend the penny somewhere else. The book makes clear that senior management needs to verify the savings and then take control of them. Failure to control savings, and whether or not they are spent elsewhere, may be the largest lost opportunity in business today.

Then there is the issue of how supply management should be organized. Should it be centralized or decentralized? You will find an excellent discussion of the pros and cons in this book.

Finally, besides offering a roadmap to achieving great and sustainable results, *Straight to the Bottom Line™* is a good read!

Paul Novak, C.P.M., A.P.P.
Chief Executive Officer
Institute for Supply Management™

Preface

One of the most significant developments in Western business in the past 15 to 20 years has been the rising importance of purchased materials and services. Until recently, companies were inward focused: they produced most of what they sold and made little effort, in most cases, to tap external technology and innovation. That changed dramatically as global economics shifted, big-box customers emerged, and new management styles exposed glaring weaknesses in the traditional American and European approach of relegating "purchasing" to inferior corporate status, often in a back room of a local plant.

The crash of high-tech economies in 2000 and then the economic fallout of September 11, 2001 created a new imperative for executive management. In this book, we call that imperative *supply transformation*. Part I of *Straight to the Bottom Line™* outlines the opportunity (Chapter 1) and then provides a quick 10-question checklist (Chapter 2) to assess where you are right now. Part II of the book (Chapters 3 through 9) outlines the necessary steps to achieve a supply transformation, including appropriate goal setting, role of the supply organization within a company, selection of the right leader, a recommended corporate structure, the importance of measurement, and expectations. The four co-authors, who collectively have more than 60 years of purchasing experience, also provide advice on how to make a transformation stick and the role that new software can play in solving some of the knottiest problems, such as achieving enterprise-wide coverage of all spending opportunities.

Straight to the Bottom Line™ is an executive roadmap to supply transformation. Parts I and II were written as a fast read on supply transformation for busy C-level executives who never may have had much exposure to purchasing or supply management.

Part III outlines alternative approaches to supply management, including a detailed look at a line of attack favored by too many corporate executives: supplier confrontation through mandated price reductions. The most successful organizations today are creating long-term collaborations with suppliers, an approach successfully used by Chrysler in the 1990s. Today, companies such as Procter & Gamble are taking that approach to a new level and achieving significant competitive advantage. Part III also contains a best-in-class example (at United Technologies) of how executive management involvement can yield billion-dollar savings through a single program. Practical applications are also given for the latest in technology implementations, including bid optimization and outsourcing of procurement services.

For those executives who want a deeper dive on the key elements of the "new" supply management, Part IV contains 11 chapters that describe best practices ranging from strategic sourcing and contract management to low-cost-country sourcing and supplier diversity.

The appendices contain profiles of many of the leading software vendors, consultants, and outsourcing service providers that specialize in procurement and supply management.

Additional resources relating to this book are available from the Web Added Value™ Resource Center at www.jrosspub.com and from www.straighttothebottomline.com.

Acknowledgments

The creation of a book, particularly through the collaboration of four individuals, requires the acknowledgment of input and assistance of all types from a wide variety of people and organizations. It will be clear through the reading of this book that we are indebted to many mentors in a wide variety of corporations for helping us to shape our collective thoughts on supply transformation. No listing could be complete, but for the sake of brevity, we acknowledge the particular leadership of Gene Richter and Tom Stallkamp for creating a foundation for a new way to approach "purchasing." We thank Nancy Richter for providing access to Gene's speeches and presentations for use in this book. Information about a scholarship fund established in Gene's name can be found at www.richterfoundation.org.

We also acknowledge those leading-edge contemporary practitioners who shared their ideas with us to advance the cause of better business management. They include, in particular, Richard A. Hughes, Vice President of Global Purchases at Procter & Gamble, and Kent Brittan, Vice President of Supply Management at United Technologies Corp.

We also received encouragement from a wide variety of business executives, both inside and outside of procurement. Their interest in this book was an important motivation for us.

Finally, we thank the many friends, associates, and family members who gave us specific advice, moral support, proofreading, or other counsel which carried us through the project.

About the Authors

Robert A. Rudzki is President of Greybeard Advisors LLC, a firm that assists enterprises to improve their financial performance. He is also a director of a privacy and security software company and an advisory board member of several companies. Previously, Bob was senior vice president and chief procurement officer at Bayer Corp., where he led a nationally recognized transformation effort. Prior to that, he was an executive at Bethlehem Steel Corp., which he led to recognition by *Purchasing* magazine as a Best Places to Work and a top-quartile ranking in a best-practices survey of 160 global corporations. In the course of his career, he has held various executive management positions, with finance, accounting, procurement and logistics, business development, and P&L responsibility. Bob can be reached at rudzki@greybeardadvisors.com.

Douglas A. Smock is Editorial Director of GlobalCPO.com, an online source of procurement analysis and best-in-class practices. Previously, he was editor-in-chief of *Purchasing* magazine. During his tenure at *Purchasing*, the magazine received five national awards for editorial excellence from the American Society of Business Press Editors. No other publication in this field had ever won even one of these awards. During his career, he also served as chief editor of *Plastics World*, associate publisher of *Modern Mold and Tooling* at McGraw-Hill, and staff writer for the *Pittsburgh Post-Gazette*. He founded and produced the *Urethanes Report* and

High-Tech Molding newsletters and has won or supervised staffs that earned three Jesse Neal awards, one of the most prized awards in the industry, which recognizes editorial excellence in independent business publications. Doug can be reached at dsmock@globalcpo.com or dasmock@yahoo.com.

Mike Katzorke is Vice President Supply Chain Management with Smiths Aerospace. Prior to joining Smiths in December 2003, he was senior vice president of supply chain management at Cessna Aircraft Co., which he led to a Medal of Professional Excellence award from *Purchasing* magazine in 2003. His career also includes Sperry, Motorola, Honeywell, and AlliedSignal. Mike has participated in and led the application of the Malcolm Baldrige, lean manufacturing, and Six Sigma tools in integrated improvement processes at three Fortune 100 companies. He designed and initiated the rollout of supply chain management at AlliedSignal as corporate director of materials and at Cessna. Mike can be reached at mkatzorke@smiths-aerospace.com or mkatzorke@worldnet.att.net.

Shelley Stewart, Jr. is Vice President of Supply Chain at Tyco, where he is responsible for $19 billion in spend and leads cross-divisional sourcing teams. He is also responsible for promoting best practices across the company's supply chain organization, through the use of technology such as e-sourcing tools. Prior to joining Tyco, he was senior vice president of supply chain management at Invensys plc, headquartered in London. In this position, he provided leadership for the strategic sourcing of $4.6 billion and had overall responsibility for lean operational excellence. Before joining Invensys, Shelley was vice president of supply chain management with the Raytheon Co., following 18 years with United Technologies Corporation, where he held numerous senior-level supply chain and operational positions. Shelley can be reached at sstewart@tyco.com or shelstew@aol.com.

™Web
Added
Value

Free value-added materials available from
the Download Resource Center at www.jrosspub.com

At J. Ross Publishing we are committed to providing today's professional with practical, hands-on tools that enhance the learning experience and give readers an opportunity to apply what they have learned. That is why we offer free ancillary materials available for download on this book and all participating Web Added Value™ publications. These online resources may include interactive versions of material that appears in the book or supplemental templates, worksheets, models, plans, case studies, proposals, spreadsheets and assessment tools, among other things. Whenever you see the WAV™ symbol in any of our publications, it means bonus materials accompany the book and are available from the Web Added Value Download Resource Center at www.jrosspub.com.

Downloads available for *Straight to the Bottom Line™: An Executive's Roadmap to World Class Supply Management* include a PowerPoint presentation that further explores the link between supply management and improved ROIC, a lost opportunity calculator that enables the user to quantify the impact of "maverick buying," and a client survey to assess the view of internal clients regarding your supply management activities.

I

Executive Assessment

Pre-transformation

1

The Opportunity

It is not the biggest nor the strongest nor the most intelligent that will survive. It is the species most adaptable to change.

—Charles Darwin,
author of *The Origin of the Species*

An incremental annual investment of $20 million can save $1 billion over a three-year span.

That's not theory. That's happening at a $40 billion North American–based manufacturing company today. The incremental investment is in people and technology: the real payoff is in working smarter by managing supply-side costs more effectively.

Most companies, even some of the most glittering among the Fortune 1000, do a poor job of managing external costs. That concept was relegated to the purchasing function, which in turn was shoved in the back office and treated like the Siberia of corporate culture. In smart companies today, purchasing is a holistic part of corporate function and strategy and is not treated like a stand-alone function. Nor are engineering, manufacturing, logistics, and sales. They are all marshaled to address a company's cost structure — as well as its top-line growth.

Smart companies tap the power of their supply base not only for best-in-class technological innovation but also for supply chain improvements that can dramatically improve return on invested capital (ROIC) through actions to improve revenues, reduce costs, and improve the capital intensity of the business (see Figure 1.1). A key driver for improving shareholder value is to ensure that the ROIC exceeds the company's cost of capital. Modern supply management can improve ROIC in many ways, including actions to improve margins and actions to improve asset utilization.

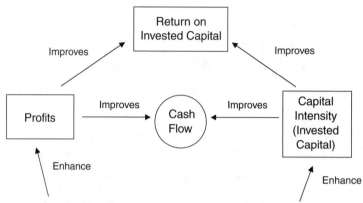

Figure 1.1. Modern supply management can improve ROIC in many ways. (Source: Greybeard Advisors LLC)

What's really cool is that software leviathans are awakening to the promise of these treasures and developing increasingly powerful IT solutions that leverage the Internet to multiply the savings potential and add speed. And the reason extremely few companies are doing this well? Poor executive leadership.

The reality in Western business is that only a few companies have both assigned a strategic role to purchasing and sustained that role over time. Other companies have assigned a strategic role to purchasing for a period of time, or until a new corporate priority (or fad) moves into the top slot. Most companies have not yet fully realized the enormous opportunity that purchasing offers.

For the most part, the tools for success (explained later in this book) are available to everyone. The processes, technology, and best practices are reasonably well known and available.

The big challenge seems to be internal to the organization itself. Key executive-office issues are a lack of understanding of the opportunity presented by improved supply-side performance; lack of active support for purchasing; poor choice of leader for the purchasing function; incorrect reporting relationship between the chief procurement officer and the executive suite; a lack of alignment between corporate, financial, and purchasing objectives; and most importantly, a weak or totally lacking mandate.

The purchasing issues include the following factors: the top person is not a true leader, skill sets are missing or deficient, purchasing objectives are not shared with other key stakeholder departments (such as operations or engineering), and best practices are not understood or embraced.

For the most part, corporate purchasing has competently done what it was told to do. For most of the past 50 years, purchasing was a discipline that processed purchase orders, negotiated contracts, and made sure that stuff arrived on a timely basis. That was about it. That's all purchasing was expected to do. In that same period of time, the world of business turned upside down. Western manufacturers were driven by Japanese competition, energy shocks, rapidly improving technology, and various competitive pressures, such as shortened product life cycles and reduced barriers to entry (see Table 1.1).

All played a role, but the most stunning driver of the past four years was the economic downturn combined with what many refer to as the "Wal-Mart effect" — the ability of large companies such as big-box retailers to demand strong year-on-year price reductions. Even major brand manufacturers such as Procter & Gamble could not count on price increases to cover rising costs. For most of the 20th century it was a given that if inflation rose 4%, you could hike your prices 5%.

Purchasing was expected to minimize cost pressures and "make something happen," with the "what" defined by someone else and without purchasing's involvement. In other words, the process by which a decision or strategy was made often did not involve purchasing and often was a process that was generally not inclusive of other disciplines. The result was declining competitiveness and profitability.

One of the first companies to get whacked was Xerox Corp. A Japanese partner, Fuji, could make copiers for up to 40% less, triggering a massive recreation of Xerox. CEO David Kearns felt Xerox was headed for total collapse in the 1990s and launched a turnaround that featured all classic aspects of the supply chain, including a bigger role of suppliers in design and manufacturing. Product development time was slashed by a year and manufacturing costs were cut 50%.[1]

Supply side was front and center because external costs represented 80% of total cost of goods sold. Commodity management was centralized on a global basis. The supply base was hatcheted, with emphasis on partners that could boost quality. Suppliers were invited to participate in development projects.

Table 1.1.   Competitive Pressures Force Change

Competitive Pressures

Globalization
- Low-cost countries emerge as manufacturing powers
- Low-cost countries emerge as major consumers
- Western companies reorganize globally

Super Buyers
- Big-box buyers force annual price reductions; limited opportunities for increases
- Demands for individualized products at low prices (i.e., "mass customization")
- All customer expectations toughen: speed, reliability, tech support, innovation

Shareholder Expectations
- Corporate ownership becomes more centralized and sophisticated
- No tolerance for earnings surprises
- No tolerance for anything but steady increases in profits

Rise of Technology
- Widespread use of computers completely changes velocity requirements
- Information technology focuses on supply and supply chain
- Optimization emerges as powerful weapon in spend analysis and market making

Rise of the Supply-Focused Chain

The Lightbulb Effect
- Leading CEOs recognize the role of costs in total profit performance — an additional dollar of sales equals 10 to 20 cents of profits, while a dollar reduction in costs of purchased goods and services equals a dollar in profits

Internal Reorganization
- Internal functions such as purchasing, manufacturing, engineering, and logistics begin working together toward common strategic goals established by the CEO

The New Resource
- Suppliers are treated like partners that introduce new technology and efficiencies into corporate organizations that increasingly function like long multilinked supply chains

The Technology Factor
- Technology is treated like a competitive weapon rather than a burdensome overhead

Most of the dramatic changes and the best learning come from companies like Xerox that went to the wall and had to reinvent themselves.

Chrysler Corp.: Lee Iacocca led a restructuring in the 1980s that included a major focus on suppliers, even for R&D. Purchasing executive Thomas

Stallkamp recalls: "We had no choice; we had very little funds for research."[2] For example, development of body panels for the Viper was turned over to supplier teams around 1990. Normally, suppliers never communicated with each other because all details were kept secret by purchasing. In the Viper project, companies that made products such as adhesives, fiberglass, and resins sat, talked, and made trade-offs that allowed for the most efficient development that was possible. The result was a powerful, lightweight car that could accelerate from 0 to 100 miles per hour and back to 0 within 15 seconds. Plus the project was completed with a very small R&D outlay. Chrysler went from the corporate scrap heap to star. Stallkamp was named president and later left when new German owners had a different approach. Soon Chrysler was once again mandating across-the-board cost reductions to its supply base. And Chrysler once again was a weak performer.

IBM: IBM's stock lost $6 billion in value in the early 1990s despite the company's technical and scientific brilliance. Losses from 1990 to 1993 were significant. It was a supply chain train wreck. Even IBM's own employees declined to use employee discounts to buy expensive personal computers.[3] CEO Lou Gerstner arrived in 1993, and two great hires followed: Jerry York as chief financial officer, who in turn hired R. Gene Richter as chief procurement officer.

In personal discussions, Richter told us his job "was easy" because he had complete support from his executive sponsor, Jerry York. He made one big change: he boosted the role of suppliers. IBM for the first time began sharing confidential information with its major external partners. He made another very important, but simple, change: he required written sourcing plans for all purchased products. Purchasing transactions became electronic overnight, and Richter predicted that all IBM purchases would move to the Internet — a task that proved almost impossible because of once-a-year transactions with small vendors with minimum Web capabilities. Richter made purchasing a revenue generator when he sold a purchasing services contract to United Technologies. Today, purchasing is a major component of IBM's Global Services business. At leading-edge companies today, such as Intel, purchasing contributes revenues in an even more significant way: patent royalties.

Harley-Davidson: Like Xerox, Harley in the 1980s was getting hammered by Japanese competitors on cost and quality. It was a classic engineering-driven American company. Engineers didn't consider the big commercial picture — like what the bike would cost. Engineers typically look internally for solutions and don't tap outside expertise. And that's a shame because suppliers know their technologies best and they know best practices for use of their products. In the mid-1990s, Harley management saw the light and launched a turn-around that included supply management. In 1995, Garry Berryman was hired from Honda of America, where he had learned to trust suppliers. He split the purchasing department into two groups, one focused on product development and the other to perform more traditional purchasing activities. He recruited top-level engineers from schools such as MIT to work with Harley design engineers and suppliers' design engineers to build great bikes.

Lucent Technologies: One of the most stunning examples comes from the former heart of the AT&T behemoth — the unit that emerged from Bell Labs, the inventor of the transistor. Lucent Technologies was clobbered by the telecommunications collapse in 2000–2001. It was buried in inventories of some $7 billion that were almost useless because they were customized, overspecified, and could not be resold easily. Lucent had also been very late to the outsourcing trend and still owned most of its own manufacturing plants. In a bid for survival, Lucent reorganized in early 2001 and created a group called Supply Chain Network that managed engineering, R&D, distribution, logistics, and supply chain management under operating officers in the company. Lucent outsourced manufacturing plants and created focus on strategic supplier partnerships that led to almost 20% in year-to-year price savings. Chief Operating Officer Bob Holder told co-author Doug Smock in a meeting in the summer of 2002 that one of the biggest improvements in the new system is in forecasting. Sales teams had done a poor job of forecasting margins because of their lack of visibility into product cost. That duty was given to Supply Chain Network, which developed an uncanny ability to accurately forecast profit margins six quarters out. That ability spelled survival for Lucent when confidence was sagging on Wall Street. Lucent's stock price went from $75 a share at the end of 1999 to 76 cents a share in the fall of 2002 and climbed back to $3.61 in November of 2004.

The most important message from these examples is that purchasing, or more broadly supply chain management, can play a significant role in boosting corporate profitability. Unfortunately, in most of these cases, companies had to be driven to the brink of disaster before seeing the light. There's no need for you to suffer the same fate.

Organizations that have achieved significant performance breakthroughs have first come to understand and believe that purchasing can have an enormous impact on a company's total performance (top line and bottom line). And then they fundamentally redefined the role of purchasing in their company.

That new role is characterized by the following:

◆   Purchasing is an ongoing corporate priority (rather than a project-of-the-month)

- Reports to a senior executive officer (typically chief executive officer, chief operating officer, or chief financial officer)
- Has a clear, strong mandate to effect transformation and change in the organization's supply chain and procurement practices and to impact return on investment directly
- Has a clear mandate to manage all supplier discussions, negotiations, and selections (strategic role) and to control all external spend (tactical, operational role)
- Has objectives that are part of the corporate priorities; these objectives and accomplishments typically go beyond cost reduction and can include improvements in return on assets (payment terms, inventories), asset recovery, risk management, compliance and governance, customer satisfaction, supply chain efficiencies and cycle times, and product development cycle times, as well as reduced variations in manufacturing and product deliveries
- Leads cross-functional teams which cross all internal "boundaries" and can itself contribute to culture improvement within an organization (i.e., help create an "inclusive" business culture)
- Can serve as the "eyes and ears" for the organization, due to purchasing's unique position of interacting with many suppliers from many industries; in this role, purchasing can play a key role in identifying competitive opportunities and competitive threats
- Leads the effort to tap the resources and competencies of current and prospective suppliers

The benefits of purchasing playing that new role — as demonstrated by leading organizations — are nothing short of competitive advantage and outstanding business performance improvement in the following areas:

- Cost structure (for many manufacturing and process industries, purchased goods and services, prior to embarking on a procurement transformation, typically amount to 40 to 60% of gross revenues, as shown in Table 1.2)
- Organizational discipline with regard to "speaking with one voice" to suppliers
- Return on assets (payment terms, inventories, etc.)
- Asset recovery (turning idle plant and equipment into value)
- Risk management
- Compliance and governance
- Customer satisfaction
- Supply chain efficiencies and cycle times
- Product development cycle times

Table 1.2. The Role of Costs

Corporate Sector	Costs as % of Revenues in 2005
Health care	40–60
Electronics	50–75
Automotive	50–70
Retail	30–50
Petroleum	40–70
Chemicals	40–70
Steel	55–70
Pulp and paper	50–65
Financial services	30–40

- ◆ Creating a supply chain that competitors find difficult to compete against
- ◆ Reduced variations in manufacturing and product deliveries
- ◆ Reduced capital investments
- ◆ Top-line revenue growth
- ◆ As a result of the above, increased stockholder value

In addition, purchasing's transformation into a proper role can contribute to a CEO's broader agenda of instituting organizational culture change and reinforcing a results- and action-oriented culture throughout the organization.

In the final analysis, each organization needs to assess its overall competitive and strategic situation and determine the role purchasing should play in support of corporate priorities. In many cases, it will make sense to embark on a path to transform purchasing into a competitive weapon (most of the comments above relate to this path).

Where are you on this journey?

2

Where Are You Now?

Ask me no questions, and I'll tell you no fibs.
—Oliver Goldsmith,
Irish playwright

If you still think of your process as purchasing, you are living in the 1960s. Competition today is no longer company to company, but rather supply chain to supply chain. Since many of us in the same industries use many of the same suppliers, a good procurement process must evolve into fully integrated supply management. The company that does the best job of integrating its supply network — in terms of objectives, strategies, processes, and data linkage — creates optimal competitive advantage for the entire supply network and optimal value for its shareholders and customers. Table 2.1 provides a snapshot of what organizations look like before and after transformation.

Take a quick pulse to determine if your supply organization is alive and well or a significant drag on your corporate competitiveness. Ask the following 10 questions. You should have a good sense of the answers yourself. Following the list, we present what we feel are the right and wrong answers.

1. Are supply chain goals integrated into the strategic plan of your business?
2. Do you know who your chief purchasing professional is?
3. What is the reporting relationship of the chief procurement officer to you? Does he or she have consistent access to you and other senior-level executives? Does he or she make presentations to the board of directors?

Table 2.1. Supply Management: Before and After Transformation

Before Transformation	After Transformation
No strategic sourcing	100% of spend covered by written sourcing plans
Fax communications	Web-based communications
Spreadsheet analysis of data	Algorithm-based optimization analysis
Prices rise 3 to 6% annually	Costs drop 5 to 7% annually
Defect rates of 40,000 parts per million or higher	Six Sigma quality
On-time delivery rates of 65 to 90%	Deliveries and inventory levels optimized through expressive bidding
Proliferation of specifications	Map to performance standards
Everyone has safety stock	Lean principles employed
Buyers "place and chase" orders	Buyers are strategic members of corporate teams
'Purchasing" is the corporate Siberia	Supply management is integrated into the larger organization, often through a supply chain concept
No data are shared with a huge supply base, not even forecasts	Suppliers are partners that lead in innovation
A tactical back-office function	A driver of shareholder value

4. Does your procurement team have top- and bottom-line objectives? How do you set stretch objectives? Are procurement's objectives shared by other functions in the company?
5. What percentage of the external spend at your company is supervised by purchasing and covered by a written strategic sourcing plan?
6. What percentage of spend is leveraged through internal spend pools?
7. Do you have the right leadership in your procurement function? Is your procurement head a leader, a follower, or roadkill?
8. What is the working relationship between purchasing professionals and those in other disciplines (manufacturing, engineering, R&D, finance, etc.)? Do they operate in silos?
9. What are the opportunities for training and improvement for the purchasing professionals in your company?
10. And most important, what is your level of personal commitment to achieving improved corporate performance through a best-in-class purchasing organization?

The answers:

1. Are supply chain goals integrated into the strategic plan of your business? We feel this is a critical indicator that separates failing organizations from those that at least have a fighting chance to succeed. A yes answer to this question indicates that you at the very least understand the potential promise of supply-side benefits. A best-in-class example is Procter & Gamble, which has worked in recent years to properly position purchasing within the company. Leaders of business units such as Baby and Family Care or Health Care increasingly recognize the importance of good sourcing work. The influence of purchasing at P&G has been rising and spreading. CEO A.G. Lafley includes purchasing breakthroughs as one of six core capability areas that are monitored on a regular basis and on a formal basis twice a year. "If we are going to improve margins, we are going to have to do it largely through cost control," comments Keith Harrison, P&G's global supply manager, who oversees purchasing, manufacturing, engineering, and other operational functions. Breakthroughs are significant improvements, such as capturing more spend in the services area or implementing technology, such as expressive bidding (explained in a later chapter), that dramatically improves cost performance.

If your strategic plan is to become more global, then purchasing needs to be included in that plan. If your strategy is to develop more proprietary products, then purchasing can play a role by tapping technology in the supply base. If your plan is to dramatically increase marketing, then make sure you have a sourcing plan for marketing. If you plan to grow through acquisitions, purchasing can play a crucial role not only in the due diligence phase, but also in leading the postacquisition achievement of synergies. Almost whatever you do, purchasing — working the right way with well-chosen suppliers — can help you do it better.

2. Do you know who your chief purchasing professional is? On the surface, this seems like a ridiculous question. But first-hand experience tells us it pertains. In some Fortune 500 companies, it is even hard to identify who the chief purchasing officer is because purchasing is so fragmented. Some business units may have a fairly strong purchasing leader, but there is no central leader. Amazingly, we have found some business unit presidents — of extremely large divisions — who have no clue who their head buyer is. Typically, those units were making money hand over fist and paid virtually no attention to costs. Even if you are making a ton of money, you are failing your fiduciary responsibility to your shareholders if you are not reaching your full potential. And if you know absolutely nothing about the supply side of your company, you are missing out on an opportunity to influence one of the most important drivers of top-line and bottom-line growth.

3. What is the reporting relationship of the chief procurement officer to you? Does he or she have consistent access to you and other senior-level executives? Does he or she make presentations to the board of directors? Some purchasing leaders feel that the chief procurement officer should report directly to the chief executive officer and even be considered for board status. We don't agree. The important issue is to make sure that the chief procurement officer is no more than one level removed from the CEO and has regular access to him or her. In a well-run company, you would expect the chief procurement officer also to make presentations to the board. You should have scheduled meetings with your chief procurement officer at least quarterly and on-demand access either way as needed.

4. Does your procurement team have top- and bottom-line objectives? How do you set stretch objectives? Are procurement's objectives shared by other functions in the company? The correct answer is that procurement has both top-line and bottom-line objectives (as noted in Chapter 1), and these objectives are shared with other functions in the company. You as CEO know what the objectives are and have input to those objectives, and there is an independent internal scorekeeper (e.g., finance). The opposite end of the spectrum is that procurement has limited "savings" objectives, nobody knows what the heck constitutes procurement's definition (and calculation) of "savings," and those limited objectives are procurement's alone.

5. What percentage of the external spend at your company is supervised by purchasing and covered by a written strategic sourcing plan? The correct answer: 100%. There is no excuse for anything less. Best-in-class companies have already achieved this. Most companies do a pretty good job on money spent for production products (called "direct" in purchasing talk), such as steel, electronic components, and plastics. Their impact on corporate performance is well known. Many organizations do a poor job on services, information technology, office products, temporary labor, and a host of other areas that are increasingly important. Best-in-class organizations are tackling costs for legal and consulting services. Best-in-class organizations are taking aim at health care and marketing costs. Buyers at P&G supervise the company's $5.4 billion marketing buy. Everything at P&G must be covered by a sourcing plan. It is a metric that is followed. Attacking marketing expenses, such as promotional items, is a way to show big results fast. For example, one major company took a fresh look at both "standard" off-the-shelf promotional items and "specials" (involving the creative juices of marketing personnel), pooled that total spend, and found one vendor that could orchestrate the whole category — for a considerable reduction in costs. Of course, you set your priorities here. If the real estate people are already doing a good job, make it your chief procurement officer's last project.

6. What percentage of spend is leveraged through internal spend pools? That is, is each plant or business unit buying its own office supplies or is that "spend" aggregated through a corporate "pool"? This is tougher to answer, but the percentage should be as high as is reasonable. Many companies have struggled with this issue. Certainly, noncritical products, such as office or repair and operating supplies, should be covered by an enterprise-wide spend pool. At the other end of the spectrum are highly engineered, big-ticket components that are critical to the future of a given business unit. Not a good candidate for aggregation. Packaging and freight are good candidates. This is an important area in which to set goals and demand answers that make sense.

Another issue: Most companies have highly fragmented product specifications that serve no useful purpose and are roadblocks to supply chain goals, especially aggregation for leverage, lean inventories, flexibility for reuse or resale, and even testing costs. For example, John Deere launched a major strategic sourcing program in 1999. One of the keystones was reducing the supply base and building partnerships with critical suppliers. Deere bought 46 grades of a plastic resin called polypropylene. As engineers designed products such as tractor steering wheels, they selected grades of resin without concern for supply chain goals, such as the ability to move inventory of materials across the enterprise if demand slowed for a given product. Engineers often choose specifications well above those required for the application. Deere had a proliferation of polypropylene grades. That meant tests were required for weathering and durability for multiple grades or colors. A cross-functional team, headed by a buyer and composed mostly of engineers, was launched with the goal of reducing the number of grades to around eight. Deere planned to reduce the supply base for polypropylene from 20 to less than 6.[1] Around the same time, Deere also tried to standardize industrial gloves used by factory workers; 424 different types of gloves were used. Annual expense: $1.4 million. There was strong worker resistance, and it took a senior management mandate to improve the glove buy.[2]

7. Do you have the right leadership in your procurement function? Is your procurement head a leader, a follower, or roadkill? Having the right procurement leader is critically important to ensuring the success of any supply chain strategy. This individual should understand your overall business objectives as well as have a superior grasp and understanding of the fundamentals of supply management. Having the full range of knowledge in supply chain from purchasing through logistics is a key enabler for the leader to perform this job efficiently. Also, a good working knowledge of the technology that is available is a must. Most good supply leaders are able to move between industries and apply the skills needed to get the job done. This leader should be a good judge of people and have great sales and communication skills. Ultimately, what this individual spends a great deal of time doing is selling the value of the organization. He or she also needs to be a visionary and one that is tuned in to the changing business climate. Great supply-side leaders are innovators and not afraid to take a risk. Being able to gain the respect of critical business leaders as well as having credibility with the supplier community will cause this leader to be effective.

8. What is the working relationship between purchasing professionals and those in other disciplines (manufacturing, engineering, R&D, finance, etc.)? Do they operate in silos? Traditionally, the role of most purchasing organizations supporting manufacturing businesses was to negotiate, develop contracts, and place orders for parts and materials. Engineers designed and decided sources at the quantities and schedules defined by the manufacturing organization. This separation of activities led to supply base proliferation and spend diffusion. Another problem: purchasing focused much of its energy on expediting parts deliveries and coordinating the short-term resolution of quality issues. In the 21st century corporation, purchasing must play a strategic — not tactical — role.

It is important that sourcing and technical professionals work in teams, starting with new product development. At Buell Motorcycles in East Troy, Wisconsin, founder Erik Buell would launch product development through a meeting with internal product development teams made up of engineering, sourcing, and other professionals. He would stipulate key performance goals for the new sports bike: acceleration speed, look and feel, durability — and price. It was the job of the buyers to make sure engineers kept the project within cost guidelines — a trait that had become an almost fatal characteristic of Buell's parent, Harley-Davidson. Sourcing engineers would also scout the supply base for new technologies, such as a dramatic new metal molding technology used in the Firebolt that reduced a 22-part structure to one piece. Then buyers brought in key supplier partners to help develop the bike. Giving technical personnel free rein is a prescription for corporate disaster.

Of course, the purchasing and finance departments must be closely engaged. Best-in-class companies today are also forming close alliances between sourcing and marketing.

9. What are the opportunities for training and improvement for the purchasing professionals in your company? Some companies have no opportunities for training for purchasing professionals. If yours does, is the focus on the right subjects? Topics covered should include strategic sourcing, supplier partnering, negotiating, innovation tools, and stewardship. Again, start with the process: strategic sourcing and the role of suppliers. Then make sure your people are getting trained in new technology (covered in Chapter 7). An important subject is stewardship, including social responsibility. You must make sure your suppliers are following, at a minimum, legal mandates on the environment and labor. Companies should also have goals to promote diversity among the supply base (covered in Chapter 15). A good resource is the Institute for Supply Management Web site (www.ism.ws). Sadly, training is often the first line item eliminated when times get tough. Improving your purchasing skills and effectiveness should be your first priority when times get tough.

Do you rotate your best high-potentials through the purchasing department? Some best-in-class companies make a point of doing so. Purchasing provides a unique opportunity to learn about supply markets, negotiations management, internal cost considerations, team leadership across multiple functions, and the incredibly enabling power of your supply base.

10. And most important, what is your level of personal commitment to achieving improved corporate performance through a best-in-class purchasing organization? Everything you do — and don't do — sends a powerful signal throughout the enterprise. For example, do you subject your purchasing department to an annual, tactical budget debate with every location in your company, where the opportunity to optimize the whole company's performance is lost in local "service charge" arguments? Or does the head of purchasing present his or her business case to the executive team, outlining purchasing's commitments for the coming year in exchange for a strategic decision regarding purchasing resources and budget?

Even if you just say supply side is important, that's a positive start. We are not advocating that you learn strategic sourcing or contract management. We are advocating that you at least know the concepts and ask the right questions. Incorporate sourcing into your strategic plan. Set at least one or two measurable goals related to sourcing, and then measure them. Quarterly is fine as long as the chief procurement officer has access to your office. It is also important that you show interest in your most powerful allies — your supply base. Make sure your business unit leaders have a personal relationship with the CEOs of your two or three most important suppliers. Participate personally in annually recognizing your very best suppliers. Let them know you value their role in your success. Organizations go through phases as they move toward outstanding supply management. Ask your chief procurement officer to indicate where you are as a first step.

R. Gene Richter, a famous American chief procurement officer, developed a maturity curve (see Figure 2.1) to show typical steps in the transformation process. His maturity curve concept has been widely adapted. See the discussion of Procter & Gamble in Chapter 11 for another view of this process. Phase I ("Getting Started") is characterized by: (a) a considerable amount of maverick buying (ordering materials and services without regard to the negotiated contracts), (b) minimum coordination between decentralized procurement organizations, (c) a few major breakthrough contracts

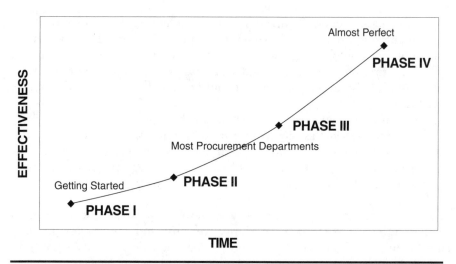

Figure 2.1. Procurement organization maturity curve. (Source: R. Gene Richter)

negotiated each year, (d) a need to ask suppliers how much was spent last year on various materials and services, and (e) the company doesn't think that acquiring legal services, employee benefits, or advertising is "buying."

Phase II is known as "Where You Want to Depict Being When Asking for More Resources." It is characterized by: (a) most major commodities are negotiated and leveraged, (b) maverick spending is minimized, (c) most transactions are automated, (d) buyer training is starting to pay off, (d) supplier pricing is under control and there is good coordination with accounts payable, and (e) people are starting to develop elaborate excuses for not involving procurement in the acquisition of legal services, employee benefits, and advertising.

Phase III is "Where You Want to Depict Being at Performance Review Time." It is generally characterized as follows: (a) most sourcing decisions are now based on multiple factors instead of just price, (b) the number of suppliers has been reduced to less than five in each global commodity category, (c) all categories are managed by a multifunction, multigeography team (led by a procurement member), (d) a written sourcing strategy exists for each spend category and is being implemented, (e) procurement is being asked to get involved early in the design or project development process, and (f) there is virtually no maverick buying.

Phase IV is the "Almost Perfect" phase. Here: (a) all procurement decisions are perfectly aligned with corporate goals and objectives; (b) within each category, each supplier's percentage of business correlates with its performance rating; (c) suppliers rank your company as their best customer (not their easiest); (d) other functions within your company give procurement an 80 to 90% approval rating; and (e) employee morale is at an all-time high. The end result of Phase IV is that the whole supply chain (including manufacturing, logistics, scheduling, distribution, and accounts payable) now reports to procurement, business friends want to come work for the head of procurement and headhunters keep calling, and — primarily because of the work done by procurement — your company stock options are worth millions (Richter's words).

In all seriousness, once you have committed to the concept that supply-side management is a critical component of corporate success, the most important steps are:

1. Establish clear and measurable goals.
2. Make sure that purchasing — or more broadly supply chain management — is appropriately aligned in the company.
3. Part and parcel, of course, is that you have the right corporate structure (centralized, decentralized, or hybrid).
4. Then you must make sure you have a leader in place who can implement the change you desire.
5. In today's environment, it is particularly important that you have the right tools and training in place.
6. And lastly, measure performance on a regular basis.

II

An Executive Roadmap to Successful Supply Management Transformation

3

Goals

The Right Place to Start

Our selling prices were going down 1% a year while our costs for purchased goods were still rising...If we didn't do something about the monster, it would eat us alive.

> —Legendary CEO and management visionary
> Jack Welch in his autobiography

Poor supply-side management often results from deficient — or even a complete lack of — high-level goal setting.

When purchasing executives meet, they often discuss banal metrics such as cost to process a purchase order or dollars spent per full-time equivalent employee. Many have measured cost performance based on actual costs versus producer price index data reported by the U.S. Government Bureau of Labor Statistics. Some report on "avoidance costs" based on "avoided" price increases.

It's no wonder that CEOs or presidents question the value of purchasing. The purchasing people themselves couldn't explain, or really understand, their potential value.

The truth today is that the business world is a battle of global supply chains. One is pitted against the other. Your entire supply chain must be aligned with appropriate goals and measurements.

To start, goals for supply management must meet the normal management accepted wisdom. They must be SMART: specific, measurable, attainable, relevant, and time sensitive. We would add an extra S for stretch — attainable, but with a very strong effort.

Second, you must assess where you stand relative to your competitors and best-in-class standards, regardless of the business you are in. The best-in-class companies achieve significant cost and quality advantages over their competitors. There is often a huge disconnect on this subject between purchasing executives and their CEOs.

Case in point: Former GE CEO Jack Welch sacked purchasing executives not long after they received a prestigious award for purchasing performance. GE's purchasing team was high on nifty systems and acronyms that had rooted during the quest for scientific management under the direction of Reginald Jones, who was chairman of GE before Welch took the helm in 1981. The erudite GE purchasing team, however, was weak on meeting what Welch — and most CEOs — considered its core mission: keeping the company competitive on costs. In a harbinger of things to come in corporate America, an analysis of costs in 1992 by new GE wunderkind Gary Reiner showed that selling prices were falling 1% annually while prices of purchased products were rising. Welch launched an in-depth review of sourcing in 1993. "Business leaders knew they had to send their very best people. If they didn't, we'd see new faces the next time," Welch related in his autobiography in 2001.[1]

Jack Welch was a visionary on many management subjects, including leading the way in developing new ways to improve white-collar productivity and costs (the famous GE "work-out process"), but he could be faulted for the company's shortcomings in supplier management. In the 1990s, GE even came to believe that supplier partnerships were part of the problem behind its purchase costs going up. GE began to create more competitive bidding, adopting something insiders referred to as "2 plus 1." This meant having two suppliers for every item, plus one waiting in the wings for the opportunity. It did generate short-term price gains, but by taking this approach, GE missed the enormous supply chain benefits associated with constructing the right types of long-term supplier relationships.

Welch was hardly alone in failing to recognize the enormous impact of effective supply management on corporate performance. He urged purchasing executives to emulate Ignacio Lopez de Arriortua, who had been appointed purchasing czar at General Motors and launched in 1992 and 1993 an across-the-board cost-cutting mandate that harmed supplier relations. To this day, Lopez remains the poster boy for inappropriate purchasing practice, even though in some ways he was ahead of his time. One of the most important contributions from Lopez and then GM CEO Jack Smith was a realization that supply-side management was a game-changer.

Detroit was the acknowledged leader in supply management in the 1980s and 1990s. The style employed by Lopez compared starkly with the turnaround philosophy at Chrysler Corp. at that time. For a comparison, see "A Tale of Two Spenders" in Chapter 10.

Quick to adopt best practices in many areas, GE was skeptical in the 1990s about the role of technology in purchasing. In one of Welch's interesting ironies, the concept of reverse auctions was conceived at GE by a young up-and-comer named Glen Meakem and his team, who formally proposed the concept to GE leaders, including Reiner, in 1994. The specific Meakem idea was rejected by GE because it was developing other capabilities in the areas of electronic catalogues and electronic data interchange to cut costs.[2] GE was basically skeptical about the impact of information technology on purchasing at this time. Meakem later made hundreds of millions through development of his reverse auction concept at a company he co-founded called FreeMarkets, which became part of Ariba. Eventually, GE made extensive use of Internet reverse auctions through an internally developed approach.

The point of the overall Welch story is that many purchasing and supply teams are out of sync with corporate goals. That's not really their fault. It's the CEO's.

The endgame, of course, is cost performance and predictable, sustainable returns that please your shareholders. But there are many ways to achieve those goals. Most chief purchasing officers receive annual cost targets, typically reductions of 3 to 4%. The IBM purchasing group is expected to report 5% better than best in class net of all price changes. That is an ambitious, unambiguous challenge. Make your purchasing people stretch.

We recommend a three- to five-year overall cost reduction target that is mutually owned by purchasing and other stakeholders, such as manufacturing, engineering, R&D, information technology, and finance. It goes without saying that achievement of that target requires significant investment in capital, brainpower, and personal commitment. In later chapters of this part, we outline what we feel needs to be in place to achieve your goals, and also outline the right way to measure results, and reveal what it is possible to achieve in cost reduction.

Make your expectations realistic, but tough. Setting stretch objectives involves an honest internal assessment of where you stand in comparison to what other companies in similar situations have achieved and then the establishment of a few measurable "wow" objectives. Those "wow" objectives excite the organization because people understand that achieving them will fundamentally determine your organization's ultimate success. In the parlance of the best-seller *Built to Last*, you want to define some Big Hairy Audacious Goals (BHAGs).

Pick three to five goals, or sets of expectations, starting with cost. All cost savings should be hard — and verified by a finance officer and the stakeholders in the business units. The standard approach is cost this year versus the previous year ("year-over-year").

Most departments also measure savings per full-time-equivalent employee, although that is a tired and not particularly meaningful metric. Do make sure you count savings created by your purchasing professionals through creative effort. If purchasing discovers a new supplier or manufacturing approach that cut costs, that counts. If purchasing spearheaded a team that created specification standards that measurably reduced inventory costs, that counts. Make sure your calculation is not strictly based on unit price; it's unit price times volume that matters. Also make sure your measurement is net, not gross. The net calculation is particularly important because it is what hits the bottom line after consideration of the impact of "headwinds" — price changes for steel, resins, copper, and other materials that bobble like a surfer on a swelling sea.

Big one-time buys, such as personal computers, need to be calculated as a value creation using industry benchmarks. Some chief procurement officers call that "cost avoidance," but that is a problematic term. In old purchasing talk, that term referred to buyers' successful efforts to reduce price hikes. If supplier X announced a 12% price increase for widgets and the buyer only accepted 8%, the buyer avoided that 4% times the volume involved. Of course, that's nonsense. What's really important is the price paid versus the market or the price paid this year compared to last year.

Another symptom of "old" purchasing is use of cost of a purchase order as a key metric. The dot-commers thought this was the Holy Grail. It wasn't really important. Reducing total transaction costs and purchasing cycle times was important. Freeing up staff to do professional, strategic work was important. Amazing numbers of departments still measure cost per purchase order. Its only benefit is that it is easily measurable. It's fine to track cost per purchase order, but if you think it is a strategically important metric, your organization is lagging.

Here are a few examples of top-line and bottom-line objectives, consistent with the framework presented in Chapter 1 (Figure 1.1), that procurement and other functions can and should share in order to achieve real benefits:

1. **New product development cycle time**: Would reducing the time from product concept to shipping that new product improve your competitive standing and win new sales? If you could reduce that cycle time by 50% and get to market before your competitors while also reducing total cost of sourcing and manufacturing, would that be meaningful in your business? Some companies make a point of involving all internal functions — plus prospective suppliers — in an aligned effort to create a competitive advantage in product development cycle time. The more aligned your internal and external resources, the more likely success will be achieved.

2. **Total cost of ownership**: This relates to reducing not just the purchasing acquisition costs but also the "cost in use" during the manufacturing and shipment process, including costs of returns or defects. Procurement cannot impact these costs in a vacuum; R&D, operations, quality assurance, and logistics can all participate in selecting the right supplier, the right material specification, the optimum inventory management process, etc. Everyone who is a stakeholder in the process must be a participant in the objectives as well, with something at stake (e.g., their annual bonus).

Those are good stretch objectives that make a real difference to the business and have a direct impact on improving return on invested capital.

Another basic metric we like is commitment to a sourcing strategy. How much of your external spend is covered by a written sourcing plan? In other words, how much of your external spend is being supervised by a professional buyer? It should be close to 100%. Enormous benefits are being derived by application of sourcing skills to purchase of legal services, consultants, travel, media and marketing expenditures, and other areas often not included in the sourcing domain.

Another important, but basic, metric is commitment to supplier relationship management. How well do you use your suppliers, and is the relationship a win-win for both parties? Best-in-class organizations actually do surveys of suppliers — and even internal clients — to measure performance. Do you adequately use the technical assets and supply chain capabilities of your supplier partners? Have you even made an effort to find out?

A simple metric will suffice here. First identify your most critical suppliers. Then find out how many receive annual executive reviews. A key executive review is a face-to-face meeting between a business unit leader, the lead buyer, and the supplier's executive team. Share goals and forecasts. What are your biggest problems? Review the supplier's performance scorecard on cost, delivery, quality, innovation, and other areas you measure. Suppliers really appreciate the communication. It's amazing how seldom it happens.

Require your supply management teams to measure progress toward goals monthly and report them quarterly and then conduct personal reviews. Include business unit leaders in formal reviews to make sure they know they will be held accountable toward progress, particularly if building spend leverage is an important goal.

Of course, many other metrics could be added here. In Table 3.1, we summarize examples of "weak" and "better" metrics for supply management. Your purchasing teams should be monitoring many other metrics for their own information. These can include such issues as supply base reduction, minority business participation, number of electronic auctions conducted,

Table 3.1. A Quick Guide to Supply Metrics

Weak	Better
◆ Operating cost per purchase order ◆ Operating cost per employee ◆ Purchasing cost performance versus the U.S. producer price index ◆ Cost avoidance or some unverifiable concept of "savings" ◆ Purchasing expense as a percentage of sales ◆ Purchasing employees as a percentage of company employees ◆ Purchasing spend per purchasing employee	◆ Percentage of spend covered by strategic sourcing ◆ Net purchasing cost reduction performance (excluding cost avoidance) versus best in the world (verified by finance) ◆ Cost targets shared by the entire internal supply chain organization ◆ New product development cycle time ◆ Quality of supplier relationships ◆ Number of true partnerships designed and implemented with suppliers ◆ Level of innovation ◆ Average annual improvement in competency level of supply management employees ◆ Supply base reduction ◆ Quality (parts per million)

extent of low-cost-country sourcing, and progress on projects such as product life cycle management or contract management implementation. Tech-savvy chief procurement officers use a "dashboard" to monitor key metrics daily. Dashboards usually refer to computer programs that electronically track key issues, but they don't have to be complicated and they don't require use of computer programs. They just need to track the right metrics. Hopefully, you will have a good sense for important goals after you finish this chapter. If it's important, measure it!

Meet with your business and purchasing leaders and mutually develop the metrics you want to drive your business. Then meet with your chief procurement officer at least quarterly to review the results and also learn how you can contribute to future results.

4

Supply Management's Role

Process Integration!

I was amazed (and a bit appalled) at the lack of functional integration in the companies I worked for. In particular, I just couldn't understand why there was so little real communication between the operational units of the companies — the design, engineering, manufacturing and procurement organizations.

> —Robert A. Lutz, former president of Chrysler and
> current chairman of General Motors North America

Historically, the role of most purchasing organizations supporting manufacturing businesses focused on negotiation and implementation of contracts for the parts and materials that engineers designed. They then placed orders at the quantities and schedules defined by the manufacturing organization. Since this serial "over-the-wall" process led to supply base proliferation and spend diffusion, purchasing also focused much of its energy on expediting parts deliveries and coordinating the short-term resolution of quality issues.

There was a growing realization in the 1980s — and to a much broader degree in the 1990s — that competition was not really company to company but rather supply chain to supply chain. In the Western world, some pundits referred to these new relationships as the "American keiretsu." This evolution shattered the conventional wisdom that treasured a broad supply base as a means to foster competition — and lower prices. As companies optimized their supply chains, it became clear that shareholder value is driven through the combination of processes that are focused on creating value for the end customer. *Simply put, businesses came to the realization that a loosely coordinated group of companies focused on the optimization of their individual objectives could not possibly compete with a supply chain operating as a team.*

Supply chain management — one of the most misused business terms of recent years — is the integration of each element of supply, design, production, and distribution from extraction of raw material to the end customer. The key word is integration. There is no room for engineering, purchasing, or logistics to operate as a stand-alone function. And make no mistake: purchasing is where the rubber hits the road on supply chain management. The term was widely applied in the 1990s by professionals in logistics and distribution, particularly with reference to massive big-box retail distribution centers. But neither of those functions acting alone has anywhere near the potential supply chain impact of a coordinated team-based supply-side management. Consultants and software companies further muddied the waters on supply chain management with a proliferation of jargon and acronyms that poorly explained the concept. The introduction of the term supply chain management was important, however, because Western businesses were rapidly changing, and supply chain management captured the essence of process integration and teamwork.

In this book, we use the term supply management to refer to the concept of purchasing as a strategic, supplier-facing function. We define supply chain management as the management of materials, services, and products all the way from extraction of ore to the delivery of products to the final customer. Our focus is on supply management, but we recognize that supply managers operate as a key functional group in the supply chain and sometimes even run the supply chain. The terms supply management and supply chain management are often used incorrectly as synonyms.

Integration of the supply chain processes begins within a company's own walls. More and more in the 1980s and 1990s, corporations discovered that their business objectives must be tied to those of the end customer(s) of the supply chain(s) in which they participate. The process objectives of the business must be hard-wired to the business objectives. They rarely are, particularly when it comes to purchasing. And the objectives of individuals within the processes and their compensation schemes must be directly linked to those of both the process and the overall enterprise in a line-of-sight fashion.

Experience has taught that we need to begin supply chain process transformation by looking at the work — the process, and then the people, and then the organizational structure. As we change the way the work gets done and how the people in the process think, focus, and behave, it may be necessary to change the organization if it gets in the way. Otherwise, leave it alone. Changing organization structures often creates a lot of (often unnecessary) interpersonal nervousness, defensiveness, resistance, and conflict that otherwise would not be there. (We deal with corporate structure in detail in Chapter 6.) First, you must focus on the process — and teaching and enabling people.

Purchasing is a process within a business. It has inputs and outputs. For every input, there is a human source. For every output, there is a customer. These are the stakeholders in the process, and for optimal performance, these stakeholders must be integrated into the process, not merely passive observers of it.

The integration of stakeholders in the supply chain process is accomplished in two ways:

◆ Definition of those stakeholders and what each needs, how they need to behave relative to their potential supply chain impact, how they are behaving today in that arena, and what the impact of that behavior is and could be on results (quality, cost, delivery, service)
◆ Study of an influence matrix that defines what motivates the behavior of the stakeholders and how to influence it (see Table 4.1)

As with any negotiation, we need to package and sell the behavior we need to achieve. Senior management needs to see how the support and involvement needed will positively impact the bottom line, to what degree, when, and what the support will cost. Marketing wants to understand how its support and engagement will improve the on-time delivery of the product with shorter lead times at a lower cost with better field performance, so it can grow market share. Engineering is interested in how the support will help produce a better design and get it to market in a shorter time without adding risk, while letting it focus more of its energies on R&D and new product development instead of production support. Manufacturing wants to see how the needed support will improve its parts flow consistency with less inventory, thus improving its efficiency, utilization, and on-time performance.

You get the point — stakeholders must recognize the needed behavior for improved supply chain performance in their own domain.

Many businesses have multiple supply chains, but fail to recognize this fact and apply the same processes and strategies to each. For example, most manufacturing businesses have an original equipment manufacturing (OEM)/ OEM supply chain making new products/components. In an automotive supply chain, a Tier Four supplier is a tool-and-die maker that provides molds to a Tier Three supplier, the injection molder. The molder makes parts for the Tier Two supplier, the seat maker. The seats go to the Tier One supplier,

Table 4.1. The Influence Matrix

Primary Goal	CEO, President	Sales & Marketing	R&D, Engineering	Operations Mgmt	Supply Mgmt	Finance	Product Support
			Functional Responsibility				
Long-term goals	X						
Short-term earnings	X						
Return on assets	X					X	
Governance/controls	X					X	
Sales		X					
Marketing planning		X					
New product development			X		X		
Product functioning			X				
Outbound delivery performance				X			
Manufacturing cost				X			
Make versus buy			X	X	X		
Finished product quality				X			
Materials cost					X		
Globalization			X	X	X		
Inventory strategy				X	X		
Inbound delivery performance					X		
Incoming product quality					X		
Warranty cost							X
Spare parts delivery and availability							X
Working capital				X	X	X	

Source: Adapted from various sources

which produces modules shipped to the auto producer. Companies such as auto producers also have significant aftermarket businesses, which are often far more profitable than OEM.

Customer experiences with the aftermarket often are crucial to driving a consumer's next purchase decision. Service is generally the key aspect in the aftermarket for most businesses, whereas cost is often a stronger driver in commodity OEM businesses. For differentiated OEM businesses, cost may be a much less important factor to the end customers than perceived quality and reliability. Rising market share for brands such as Honda and Toyota would seem to prove the point. And the strategies in the supply chain that support these differing business success factors are often not robust — including structural design and process.

General Motors is a case in point. As Bo I. Andersson was replacing Harold Kutner as GM's chief procurement officer in 2001, he said in an interview that managing quality issues through GM's complicated, multi-tiered supply chain was his single biggest challenge. The problem often was a lack of basic communication. Implementation of a simple process change improved measured quality metrics by 50% very quickly. Andersson initiated weekly conference calls with plant purchasing personnel to discuss quality issues. He also posted supplier quality data on a GM Web site for suppliers. Andersson had immediate success because he sent a strong message through the command chain that quality was an important issue. In fact, GM's supply chains had been failing to function in a coordinated way. Some suppliers endured significant financial problems which they attributed in part to GM purchasing practices. Andersson discovered that some suppliers had experienced delays of six months to receive payment.[1] Other suppliers, such as the toolmakers, felt there was too little communication on critical manufacturing issues, forcing them to make guesses on tool design.[2]

If you are trying to optimize the supply chain performance for a corporation that has 23 different autonomously operating businesses with widely divergent supply chain processes, the structural approach is clearly different than if you are dealing with a single large, well-integrated business entity. Further, business process structure often evolves as process maturity advances (more and more synergy develops as people and processes mature), synergy that initially had to be facilitated with formal structure.

If you are at the early stage of a supply-side transformation process at your company, an appropriate area to examine is vertical reporting design. Best-in-class companies are creating supply chain organizations in which purchasing, manufacturing, design, and logistics are functionally integrated under one supply chain czar. That model ensures closely coordinated teamwork between the departments on cost, cycle time, quality, and other critical issues that will determine competitiveness and ultimately shareholder value.

If you still operate under a rather traditional business process model (and most companies certainly do), at least make purchasing part of the CEO's cabinet.

There is more than one successful model relative to where the chief procurement officer of a business reports. A strong case could be made that the chief procurement officer should report to the CEO. However, other structures can be extremely effective if the chief supply manager is positioned properly and has regular access to the CEO. Supply management needs to be addressed strategically and as an ongoing part of the business's strategic plan. That includes regular meetings between the CEO and chief procurement officer and significant executive support for supply chain transformation.

Oddly, that is one of the hardest bridges for many companies to cross. Like the late great comic Rodney Dangerfield, purchasing can't get any respect.

In an interview, Kent Brittan, vice president of supply management at United Technologies Corp., put it this way: "I think there is a social issue. Purchasing has not been high on the social ladder no matter what you do. So many companies have trouble taking the big step of making the CPO a direct report to the CEO and I view that as a social step."[3]

Brittan does not have a social problem at UTC. He is a direct report to CEO George David and is rewriting the book on how a supply chain transformation can affect profitability. (Note: Brittan assumed a different role at UTC in early 2005.) Brittan became vice president of supply at UTC in 1997 after serving as chief financial officer for the company's Otis Elevator division. A detailed account of that transformation can be found in Chapter 12. In brief, Brittan looked for opportunities first to build enterprise leverage in money spent on production materials.

"When we started strategic sourcing in aerospace, I was with one of our division officers and started talking about suppliers. I realized he was making his own deals and T&Cs [terms and conditions]. I really blew my stack. I said this is ridiculous because your suppliers are Sikorsky's suppliers and Pratt & Whitney's suppliers. This is crazy. Information moves in organizations. So we put together a chart showing overlap. It didn't show just the commodities. It showed the companies. So I went to the boss and said we have to change. He said, 'Do you think you can sell it?' Well, I put this plan in front of people and they just laughed. They said, 'How soon can we start?'"

The process doesn't always go so smoothly, of course. In fact, strong purchasing executives are at times inserted in organizations that are not culturally ready to change. That's when special efforts are required. One approach is to make the business leaders champions of the process.

Brittan's supply team launched a program called UT500 in 2001 that established a $500 million savings goal just in general procurement, that is, the noncritical materials and services that keep a company functioning, but aren't used to make production products. Every direct report to CEO George David was assigned to chair a team that supervised the spend for a specific category, such as information technology, outsourced engineering services, real estate, office supplies, and so on. Brittan provided staff support that understood sourcing techniques and processes, including electronic reverse auctions. The division presidents and staff executives dove into the process and achieved spectacular results. The $500 million savings goal was achieved in just two years and the program was broadened.

UTC became a darling on Wall Street — and the supply strategy played an important role. In fact, UTC's total return to shareholders grew sixfold from 1994 to 2004, compared to about fourfold for General Electric.[4]

One of the most critical areas of teaming involves technical organizations within highly hierarchal companies. Companies that give design engineers carte blanche lock in very high costs and build inventory assets that can be close to useless when demand crashes, as the Lucent example illustrated. Rigid engineering structures were a major factor creating financial distress at another great American business icon, Harley-Davidson, as pointed out in Chapter 1.

One company in the forefront of purchasing and technical collaboration is Procter & Gamble, viewed by outsiders as a conservative American company. When it comes to purchasing, P&G has conservative values but innovative processes.

"We work in close partnership with research & development on innovation and product technology development," says Richard A. Hughes, vice president of corporate purchases, Procter & Gamble Co., Cincinnati, Ohio. "We have substantially increased our focus on developing and delivering innovation through a strong partnership with our research & development colleagues via an effort entitled Connect and Develop."

There are more "gee-whiz" examples of purchasing coordination with engineering in the high-tech industry, but the P&G experience is interesting because it comes at a traditionally organized American business with very strong business units that champion brands such as Tide, Pampers, and Crest.

In 2001, P&G changed internal structure so that R&D was organized globally, matching organization of the business units and the central purchasing department. Each business unit has a Material Leadership Team with co-directors, one in research and one in purchasing. "This is a tremendous contrast to what we did when we operated regionally," comments Ghobad Rahrooh, R&D director for P&G's Global Baby Care Business Unit. "Purchasing and R&D people had different agendas. In that case, we were getting a worse deal because suppliers played R&D and purchasing people off against one another."

Purchasing and research personnel now meet jointly with suppliers with a common agenda — and P&G speaks with one voice to the supply base. The teams share material platform goals with suppliers and work in a collaborative way to develop low-cost, high-quality next-generation products. Developing a product migration program with technical and commercial goals allows maximum possible use of processing equipment and yields big savings for end customers — the ultimate goal of an effective supply chain. There is also a trend toward greater use of new technology developed by the supply base rather than by P&G scientists. P&G is covered in more detail in Chapter 11.

Best-in-class supply chains understand that the collective effort of suppliers can produce significantly more technical innovation than any one company, even one on the scale of a Procter & Gamble. The other big payoffs include a more rapid implementation of new technology and development

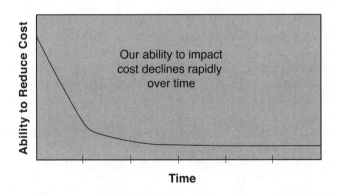

Figure 4.1. Get upstream in the design cycle. (Source: R. Gene Richter)

of new products that meet budget targets. A diagram (Figure 4.1) was used by R. Gene Richter to demonstrate the point that high costs can be locked in during the initial development phase of a project. Involvement of purchasing professionals later through processes such as value analysis offers limited opportunity to dramatically affect a product's cost structure.

The overall point of this discussion can be very simply put: integration of business processes at the very earliest opportunity through closely aligned teams and improved communication with suppliers creates major benefits for companies.

Having said that and given all the technical and electronic wizardry available to modern Western businesses, it's amazing how often supply chains can still go awry because of poor understanding of demand factors.

Marshall L. Fisher, professor of operations management at the Wharton School at the University of Pennsylvania, comments: "One recent study of the U.S. food industry estimated that poor coordination among supply chain partners was wasting $30 billion annually. Supply chains in many other industries suffer from an excess of some products and a shortage of others owing to an inability to predict demand."

One potential solution is to move sales forecasting into the supply chain organization. That's what Lucent did to improve its ability to forecast margins. Another is to study the types of products your company makes to better assess their volatility. Fisher says supply chain processes need to be different if a product is classified as "functional," which are staples needed for daily life, or "innovative," which have short life cycles and high stock-out rates. He says that functional products need an efficient process and innovative products need a responsive process.[5]

Such problems are magnified even more in today's world when big-box retailers can offer promotions that enormously spike demand. A promotion for cell phones two days before Mother's Day can keep supply chain executives sleepless for weeks, at first for trying to meet demand and later for explaining to CEOs why sales opportunities may have been lost.

The ultimate answer may be a Dell-type system in which orders are placed for products with specific features and then the supply chain responds to that demand. But for most, the practical answer is development of processes that enable collaboration and teamwork across the enterprise and with suppliers as if they are an integral part of your enterprise.

5

Pick the Right Leader

Look for Great "People" Skills

Management is doing things right;
leadership is doing the right things.
—Peter F. Drucker,
management guru

Many CEOs talk the talk on purchasing, but don't really walk the walk. This is most evident in whom they choose as their chief procurement officer (CPO). In 2002, after the economy crashed, many CEOs were told they were behind the curve on purchasing. But since they didn't really understand purchasing, they had no clue where to start. Some resorted to the good old-fashioned solution — fire the messenger. As we said earlier, purchasing typically pursued a solid professional approach in Western companies. That is, purchasing officers did what they were expected to do. And they did it well. The typical CEO knew that his or her profit performance lagged in 2002–2003 and knew best-in-class competitors were boosting net income without boosting sales. So the CEO blamed the buyers.

A few CEOs felt for sure in 2002 that reverse auctions (absent a fully crafted sourcing strategy) were the Holy Grail of good procurement. What a mistake. One major American manufacturing company even imported an outside CPO with little purchasing experience whose only claim to fame was electronic reverse auctions. His strategy worked well when markets were weak — and there was no significant interest in long-term supplier development. But this particular CPO did not fit in well with the corporate culture of the hiring company. Nor did he have many ideas for success beyond reverse auctions, which have a place, but in the appropriate sourcing context. We will deal with reverse auctions in more detail in the technology report in Chapter 7.

The point here is that you need to be very careful in the appointment of your next chief procurement officer. It's true that there has been an increasing trend to import CPOs from the outside. A 2003 study by the Center for Advanced Purchasing Studies (CAPS, www.capsresearch.org) found that about one in three CPOs was hired from another company. That is a dramatic increase from even 10 years earlier and a strong indication that many CEOs did not have much faith in their existing approach to purchasing. But that was more an indictment of the role given to purchasing and senior management's approach than the purchasing staff. The CAPS study showed that companies suffering the most pain, such as chemical manufacturers, did the most outside recruiting.

This phenomenon created a tier of purchasing superstars. People such as Dave Nelson, now at Delphi Automotive, were being actively recruited, offered major compensation packages, and moved from challenge to challenge. One of the first was R. Gene Richter, who moved from a purchasing management job at Ford to a CPO job at Black & Decker, then Hewlett-Packard, and then finally IBM, where he created a model of the modern purchasing approach.

It is important to first look internally to see if you have the right candidate. This approach worked to perfection at companies such as Procter & Gamble that have a long tradition of promoting from within. It's the right signal and, more importantly, it's an acknowledgment that the real issue is overall corporate strategy and emphasis.

There are many factors to consider when making this selection, but the most important is the candidate's ability to work with and lead people. Your new CPO will not be a czar; he or she will be a team leader. And first and foremost, he or she must be able to attract and retain a cast of extremely talented and highly motivated people. No particular skill set is critical because the required skill sets will constantly change. Furthermore, given the nature of advanced purchasing and the enormous opportunity that is at stake, the ideal leader will also:

◆ Have cross-functional work experience and be a well-rounded businessperson
◆ Be credible with key internal constituents such as operations and finance*
◆ Be comfortable interacting with the CEO's office and the board of directors*

- ◆ Have high energy and a strong work ethic
- ◆ Have the highest level of integrity
- ◆ Be a strategic thinker
- ◆ Be a high-potential executive capable of moving beyond the CPO role
- ◆ Be results oriented
- ◆ Be congenial, team oriented, collegial, and not arrogant*
- ◆ Be intensely focused on the success of the company, as opposed to personal and political gain
- ◆ Have the personal courage to make tough, unpopular decisions that are correct for the business*
- ◆ Be willing to establish, and personally sign up for, aggressive business objectives*

Some of these characteristics (for example those marked with an asterisk above) take on even greater importance in a decentralized or a weak hybrid purchasing structure. In those environments, the CPO or chief supply chain officer must be a persuasive advocate for doing the right thing, convincing people to set aside local priorities and local perspectives and adopt a big-picture, whole-company view.

Other attributes may also be important in specific circumstances. For example, in a traditionally decentralized manufacturing company with powerful business unit leaders, the CPO candidate needs to be familiar with critical manufacturing processes and engineering issues. Otherwise, the individual will lack necessary credibility as he or she attempts to lead significant change. In a field with a strong research and development orientation, such as cosmetics, the candidate should have some technical pedigree.

We also feel it is important that the CPO candidate understand purchasing or have the ability to learn it quickly. The CAPS research study indicated that 36% of new CPO hires have come from outside purchasing. Finance and manufacturing executives are often chosen. Table 5.1, from another CAPS research project, shows a trend toward CPOs with finance and information technology backgrounds. A leader from finance can work well in purchasing. One great example is Kent Brittan, who moved from finance at Otis Elevator to vice president supply management at United Technologies Corp. and achieved very positive results. A leader from manufacturing can work — but often that move is done more to protect turf in the business units.

Remember first and foremost that leadership skills are far more important than a specific career background. Either you have the right stuff or you don't.

A typical scenario resembles what happened not too long ago at a Fortune 500 company. A new CEO was appointed. One of his first tasks was to replace the outgoing head of procurement (who had accepted a new career assignment within the company). The CEO proceeded to select a guy who

Table 5.1. CPOs' Backgrounds Broaden

Functional Area	CPO Average Number Years of Experience in Functional Areas	
	2003	1987
Purchasing/supply	12.74	17.05
Operations/production	4.25	4.20
Finance	2.55	0.78
Management information systems	1.32	0.54
Other	0.93	0.71
Engineering	0.88	1.34
Marketing	0.85	1.60
Accounting	0.71	0.65
Transportation/distribution/logistics	0.52	1.03
Total (years of experience per respondent)	**24.71**	**27.87**

Data source: CAPS Research, 2004. Study conducted among Fortune 1000 U.S. companies and Financial Post 100 Canadian companies by P. Fraser Johnson, associate professor of operations management at the Richard Ivey School of Business at the University for Western Ontario and Michiel R. Leenders, professor emeritus of the Ivey School.

talked a great story, in spite of past concerns about this person's leadership skills. No professional assessment, such as 360-degree Leadership Practices Inventory, was conducted to confirm this candidate's strengths or weaknesses. The CEO just "went with his feel" based on his personal rapport with this candidate that he would "do fine."

One of the first acts by the new head of procurement was to meet with each of the new employees that had been recruited on college campuses during the past CPO's tenure. The message was simple, direct, and puzzling at first: you needed to spend at least four years in your entry-level buying job "to master the details" before you could be considered for a new assignment. Every one of the new hires immediately began to look outside the company for a new job. Half of them actually departed the company within six months, and word eventually spread throughout the procurement organization that the new CPO was working to reduce head count — cheaply — by encouraging employees to depart. Trust in the new CPO was not enhanced by this approach to employees, and his effectiveness was further diminished by other actions which raised doubts about his understanding of procurement's role.

Finally, in an effort to stem the loss of results from the increasingly ineffective procurement organization, the CPO suggested to the CEO that procurement in this hybrid, center-led environment be formally centralized. The CEO agreed, in spite of the company's organization structure which favored strong business units. The result was a further disconnect between procurement and its internal clients and a belief by some of the business unit heads that this CPO had a personal agenda that was inconsistent with their business objectives.

In less than two years, a well-functioning procurement organization had been reduced to a tactical mess that was no longer contributing to the success of the company. The message: selecting the right leader cannot be done casually. It must be done with an understanding of the skills needed and a fact-based approach to identify which candidate might in fact possess those critical leadership abilities. Technical expertise, personal selling skills, and other skills might be nice, but the most important skill needed to achieve greatness in procurement and supply management is the ability to lead and transform, not the ability to manage details (see Table 5.2). And someone either demonstrates leadership skills or doesn't.

A further point: with the wrong person in a leadership job, it won't make any difference what your organization structure looks like. On the other hand, the right leader can achieve great things even if the organization design is not optimal.

Unless you have incredible intuitive skills, it is best to use a fact-gathering, anonymous survey to assess the leadership capabilities of the candidates for key positions. Those who are surveyed include people "all around" the candidate, including subordinates, peers, and boss(es). This process is referred to by the mavens as a 360-degree process. They often tie it into what is called a Leadership Practices Inventory, which is a comprehensive, fact-based profile of a candidate's skills and capabilities to be a genuine leader. This assessment, plus on-the-job performance, results, and demonstrated leadership/transformation skills, make for good decisions on succession planning.

The alternative is to pick leaders the old-fashioned way — by the seat of the pants or the buddy network. Sometimes it works (by sheer luck), but often the organization suffers.

Table 5.2. Attributes of Leaders Versus Managers

Management	*Leadership*
◆ Control complexity	◆ Create change
◆ Develop plans	◆ Set direction
◆ Allocate resources	◆ Create strategy
◆ Organize and staff	◆ Align people
◆ Prevent negative outcomes	◆ Promote positive outcomes
◆ Control people and processes	◆ Empower people and processes

Source: Based on information from a leadership program by Carol and Jack Weber of the University of Virginia's Darden School and also information from the book *What Leaders Really Do* by John Kotter.

Any great leader conceivably could be a great CPO. *It is the leadership skills and the values that are important.* First people. And then understanding the tremendous empowerment that can be achieved through the supply base. Initial focus should not be strictly on cost targets. Cost reductions are the benefits that come from an outstanding purchasing approach that is well led.

6

Corporate Structure
Lead from the Center

We trained hard...but it seemed that every time we were beginning to form up into teams, we would be reorganized. I was to learn later in life that we tend to meet any new situation by reorganizing; and a wonderful method it can be for creating the illusion of progress while producing confusion, inefficiency and demoralization.

—Petronius Arbiter, Roman satirist

One of the most contentious debates around purchasing concerns corporate structure. Centralization versus decentralization. Of course, no corporate structure is built with the primary goal of improving supply-side management. Purchasing has always been the tail of the dog.

Modern corporate structure did not even begin to evolve until the last century and was highly decentralized. The trend toward conglomerates and diversification in the 1970s contributed to decentralized behavior. Companies were patched together by financiers who evaluated each purchase on its profit and loss and not for its synergy in the whole. LTV was a classic example, as was Textron. Such companies typically had tiny corporate staffs and were proud of it. At the same time, manufacturing behemoths such as John Deere were strongly driven by decentralized manufacturing units and also paid inadequate attention to purchasing topics such as performance-based specifications or cross-division leverage for strategic materials. America was the dominant economic power in the post–World War II era and benefited from an abundance of inexpensive raw materials and high domestic consumption rates. Profits were rolling in as stock prices rose.

As global competition emerged, the equation shifted. Then, as Western companies adopted global structures to sell worldwide — and then to source globally — debates raged over corporate structure. Some companies drifted back and forth between global and regional structure and then to business unit dominance. Lack of commitment to a clear plan made many great companies look downright silly. The key issues usually were allocation of sales, marketing, research, and later information technology resources, not purchasing. Table 6.1 shows procurement organization structures for best-in-class organizations since 1984. Centralization has been a fairly consistent favorite over this period.

In the 21st century, it has become clearer that purchasing is a game-changer and needs to become a serious part of the structure conversation. One of the most prominent proponents of a strong central structure was R. Gene Richter. In a series of purchasing conferences he led in 2002, Richter said: "Companies often correctly select decentralization as the appropriate way to manage geographically diverse business operations. Heads of divisions or general managers are given profit-and-loss responsibility. This in fact is a very effective way of managing sales, design engineering and manufacturing teams. But purchasing is an exception because of the numerous advantages that accrue from combining spend categories and speaking to suppliers with one voice."[1] The centralized purchasing team at IBM developed 100% control of external spend and delivered significant savings to the revitalized company.

A centralized system can only work if it has complete support from the CEO of the company. Any wavering and the system crumbles like a house of cards. In the book *Who Says Elephants Can't Dance?* Lou Gerstner, the former CEO of IBM, commented: "Shared activities usually fall into three categories: The first and easiest category involves leveraging the size of the enterprise. Included here would be unifying functions like data processing, data and voice networks, purchasing, basic HR systems and real estate management."[2]

At Gerstner's IBM, chief purchasing officers for business units reported on a solid line basis to Richter, the corporate chief procurement officer (CPO). In this setup, business unit leaders still had the head count responsibility, but did not control purchasing strategy.

Richter was such a strong supporter of this concept that he even advocated development of a board of directors resolution that the CPO be given all authority to buy external materials, facilities, and services. In Richter's scheme, the CPO could then redelegate some categories to more specialized individuals. These categories could include banking and legal services, employee benefits, advertising, and real estate. That would put muscle into efforts to stop "maverick" buying, or buying not covered by professional sourcing agreements. It was also a way of assuring continuity even when there were personnel changes at the chief financial officer or chief executive officer level.

Table 6.1. An Analysis of Organizational Approach of Past Winners of *Purchasing Magazine's* Medal of Professional Excellence

Organization	Year Award Won	Centralized	Hybrid	Decentralized	Observations
General Electric	1984		X		Utilized purchasing councils and advisory boards to coordinate internally. CEO Jack Welch, not satisfied with department's cost performance, later replaced several purchasing officials.
Xerox	1985	X			Early example of centralized commodity management. Revamped approach to supply management after study of Japanese rivals.
Alcoa	1986			X	Subsequent to award, moved to center led, with central and business unit groups working together. In 2005, adopted a strong centralized approach under CPO Christie Breves.
Chrysler	1987	X			Classic example of achieving the benefits of centralization. Procurement executive Tom Stallkamp later became president of Chrysler for his work on SCORE, which shared cost savings with suppliers and pumped innovation into the flagging carmaker.
Black & Decker	1988		X		Evolved to centralized procurement in 1990 (U.S.) and centralized on global basis in 1995.
NCR	1989			X	Central group had advisory role. Subsequently evolved to centralized model.
Ford	1990	X			Centralized procurement with minor exceptions (plant maintenance items).
Motorola	1991		X		Small central office negotiates company-wide contracts for major commodities and maintenance, repair, and operating supplies. During 2003, Motorola centralized procurement.

Table 6.1. An Analysis of Organizational Approach of Past Winners of *Purchasing* Magazine's Medal of Professional Excellence (continued)

Organization	Year Award Won	Centralized	Hybrid	Decentralized	Observations
Hewlett-Packard	1992			X	A decentralized corporate environment, but purchasing (under R. Gene Richter) began to leverage buys for key commodities, aided by procurement strategy boards.
Intel	1993	X			Effective use of multidisciplinary teams and long-range purchasing plans.
Tennant	1994	X			Made dramatic progress in reducing supplier base and moving toward single sources.
Honda	1995	X			Procurement reported directly to the president of Honda America. Led by legendary buyer Dave Nelson, who later went to Deere and Delphi Automotive. Protégé Garry Berryman later led transformation at Harley-Davidson.
Sun Microsystems	1996	X			Effective use of supplier councils. Made significant reduction in supply base.
Allied-Signal	1997	X			Strong example of team-based commodity management approach.
AMR (American Airlines)	1998	X			Transformed itself from a reactive, tactical purchasing group into a strategic function attuned to the business units.
IBM	1999	X			Effective use of commodity councils, plus purchasing as a "service" for sale outside IBM. Also a leader in technical purchasing. The trifecta for R. Gene Richter (HP and Black & Decker).
Harley-Davidson	2000	X			On the edge of extinction, Harley built a powerful central purchasing department whose primary role was to tap the innovation power of its suppliers.

Company	Year			Description
Deere & Co.	2001		X	Deere built a centralized team four years prior to the award, but much real purchasing power resided in powerful divisions. Deere had a long tradition of supplier partnering on design.
Lucent Technologies	2002	X		Lucent created an extremely innovative Supply Networks organization that even forecasts corporate profit margins. Made a major move to outsourcing.
Cessna Aircraft	2003		X	Cessna is a division of Textron, which uses cross-division teams to build synergy. Textbook case of how to achieve economies of scale in a highly decentralized organization. Cessna procurement was led by co-author Mike Katzorke, who also had a hand in the Allied-Signal program.
Hewlett-Packard	2004	X		One of the main drivers of the merger of HP and Compaq was to achieve economy of scale in purchasing. HP had been decentralized, but the tilt of the new organization is definitely toward centralization. HP is one of the great leaders in social responsibility in the supply base.

Adapted by the authors from original analysis by Joann Borgo

For most of the Western world, Richter's approach is not completely realistic. Decentralized organizations have enormous inertia. More than one powerhouse CPO (not Richter) has moved into a challenging situation, implemented centralized strategic sourcing, and then was replaced in two or three years with a division manager who "understands" the corporate culture.

All organizations go through the constant challenge of structural change. The key to how supply management should fit depends on many factors: size, geographical dispersion, and business focus of the company (manufacturing, services, research, or something else). The type of end products produced is important for manufacturing companies. Company culture is a significantly important aspect of how companies are organized. The choices stem from where the organization is today from a maturity standpoint. Specifically, who is leading the organization? What changes has it been through? What is the state of the economy?

There are three common types of procurement organization structures (with key pros and cons outlined in Figure 6.1):

Centralized: The Richter IBM model would be the ultimate. The leader normally has a title of CPO or senior vice president of supply or purchasing and has formal profit-and-loss responsibility. Plant-based purchasers "place and chase"; they execute purchase orders based on contracts negotiated centrally and make sure the products arrive on time. In the age of electronic systems and enabled suppliers, "place and chase" eases into the sunset. Engineering, finance, and operations people are also centralized and key to the success of a fully leveraged enterprise. Sometimes related functions are rolled into a vice president of supply chain or supply networks, as in the case of Lucent Technologies. Lucent has a vice president of supplier management under the president of Supply Networks.

Decentralized: This can be led at either the plant or the business unit level. In centralized systems, purchasing often reports through finance; in decentralized systems, purchasing often reports through manufacturing or operations. This approach is more plant focused and tactical. It doesn't capture the benefits of supply management in today's world. Usually in this scenario, finance, engineering, and operations are vertically integrated in the business unit.

Hybrid: Often called "center led," this approach can capture close to full benefits of a centralized system and avoid serious disruption of corporate culture. If you can't get Gene Richter's board of directors' mandate, this approach may be the most sustainable. Normally led by a CPO or senior vice president of supply, the hybrid structure includes a small corporate purchasing staff which establishes policy, coordinates cross-enterprise strategic sourcing teams, provides training, and establishes standards in ethics and stewardship. Actual sourcing is done by business unit purchasing professionals. A good example is Procter & Gamble, described in Chapter 11. At the very

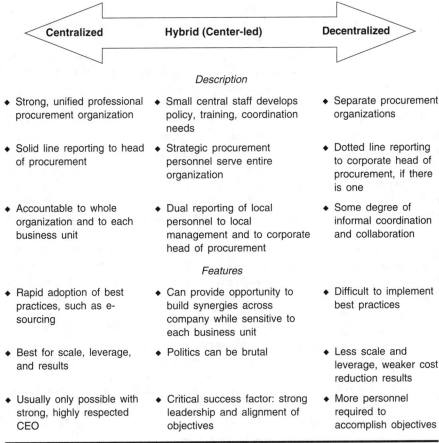

Figure 6.1. Characteristics of the three most common organizational approaches.

least, "indirect" product categories such as office supplies are sourced under corporate contracts. Best-in-class organizations capture as much enterprise leverage as is practical. Achieving that goal is where the art is. For more information, see the discussion on strategic sourcing in Chapter 13.

Functional organizations such as engineering, operations, and finance have influencing attitudes that support the supply management direction. Fundamentally, most companies operate within a center-led concept. This allows for the most flexibility. It provides significant "local" autonomy. It also allows individual business units the ability to pursue their specific business agendas. It is a relatively nonthreatening approach from an organizational perspective, but it must be top driven and requires a true leader to be successful. Many agendas can be pursued simultaneously. Senior leaders at both corporate and divisional levels must be more than supportive; they must demand a certain level of effort at compliance. The weakness of the center-led approach is that organizational structures can be duplicated many times over. This can be overcome, however, if managed properly. The advantage comes if senior leadership sets clear cross-enterprise goals and objectives, then measures progress toward these objectives and rewards achievements.

The Center for Advanced Purchasing Studies, in Scottsdale, Arizona, reports that 51% of companies use a hybrid system, while 32% are centralized and just 16% remain totally decentralized. The numbers are even more skewed away from centralized structure among manufacturing companies. Service-oriented companies are more likely to be centralized. Larger companies are more likely to be decentralized. And this is interesting: between 1995 and 2003, 42% of the study group changed corporate structure, reflecting one of the biggest problems concerning structure — lack of commitment to an approach.[3]

As CPOs often commiserate when meeting among themselves, the only thing more damaging to performance than having the wrong structure is a company's propensity to regularly experiment with changes in corporate organization. That periodic "pendulum swing" wreaks havoc on generating new and sustainable results in procurement.

Organizational models, particularly in supply chain, need to be flexible. It is important to be able to perform more with less when times are tough. The more flexible the workforce, the more nimble the company. Stronger commodity management is needed to deal with price increases.

But don't get hung up on mandating a very specific structure. Make sure that strategic central direction is in place. The specifics must be determined by your corporate culture and business requirements. As Peter F. Drucker pointed out in *Management Challenges for the 21st Century*:

> And from the very beginning more than a century ago, the study of organization has rested on one assumption:
>
> *There is — or there must be — one right organization.*
>
> What is presented as the "one right organization" has changed more than once. But the search for the one right organization has continued and continues today.[4]

What's important is your commitment, strategy, approach, and your entire company's alignment around a few key objectives. Organization can be an enabler — but there is no definite right or wrong.

7

Innovation and Technology

From Auctions to Optimization

*Because whether you're two friends tinkering in a garage, or you work inside one of the most venerable enterprises on earth, the rise of a global connected world offers a truly rare opportunity: **the chance to start something totally new.***

—IBM's 1998 Annual Report

One of our definitions of a best-in-class purchasing organization is willingness to innovate. Successful early use of a winning supply chain technology tool can lead to significant competitive advantage. We define technology here primarily as automation and application of computer software to purchasing disciplines. There are generally two classes: e-sourcing and e-procurement. E-procurement tends to be tactical, the processing of purchase orders — the whole "req-to-check" process. Significant strides have been made here with the primary focus on reduction of cost per purchase order. Early leaders included Ariba and IBM Global Services. Many systems also attack the compliance or "leakage" issue, that is, the issuance of purchase orders outside of the purchasing department. In the last two years, more focus has been placed on higher level electronic sourcing, such as the application of computer analysis to strategic processes through high-level optimization, artificial intelligence, and other information technology. Somewhere in between are such

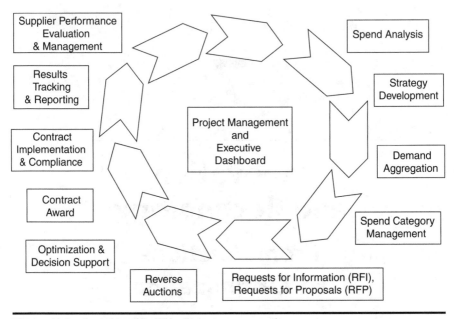

Figure 7.1. Integrated supply management tools.

processes as electronic requisitions and reverse auctions. All of these strategic tools offer the potential for enormous and quick paybacks. Figure 7.1 illustrates how technology tools fit into a continuum of good supply practice.

Innovation is a must-consider adoption for a well-run company. Having said that, however, there are seven caveats:

1. The state of the technology is in constant flux. The quality of the systems has improved dramatically in the past two years and undoubtedly will improve dramatically again in the next two years. Processes and services that were offered four to five years ago are by and large nonexistent today. So are many of the vendors. Reverse auctions were the buying fad du jour in 2000. Today they are applied more carefully.

2. Integration into legacy software systems can be expensive, time consuming, and may not always give you all of the cross-enterprise functionality you seek. The traditional paradigm for enterprise software is heavy programming, inflexibility, and high total cost of ownership. Most corporate information technology architectures are made up of stand-alone enterprise applications for human resources, manufacturing, finance, and other departments that have their own data repositories and systems. IT infrastructure has become the single biggest bottleneck in improving cross-enterprise data sharing. Efforts are under

way to change the model, such as SAP's Enterprise Services Architecture, a standards-based, open system that allows addition of composite applications, even from other suppliers. Another example is the Teamcenter platform from UGS which allows open integration of other systems, such as the burgeoning programs described in this chapter.

3. There are more than 80 vendors selling software products to the purchasing community. See Appendix A for profiles of leading suppliers. Most are specialist companies attacking a specific problem. As a result, there are only a few vendors that can handle all of your sourcing needs. In addition, some companies are weak in real hands-on purchasing knowledge, the fatal flaw of the dot-commers, and they invariably underestimate the conservative nature of how companies buy. A handful of vendors are making progress toward implementation of a full suite of integrated products that meets the needs of a typical Global 1000 or Fortune 500 corporation and which can connect to legacy systems. This development offers huge potential benefits to the user, at moderate cost. Scalability is a very important issue for you to consider when making a technology investment in the supply chain.

4. Much of the current savings focus today is on indirect materials and services, that is, those products not consumed directly in the manufacturing process. There are several reasons. The most important is opportunity. Many companies have historically done a superior job sourcing direct materials such as electronics or chemicals because of their obvious impact on profitability. And there tend to be sourcing professionals in place for those products. New center-led sourcing approaches start with low-hanging fruit such as office supplies and travel. Leading organizations are even tackling very tough spend categories such as consultants and law firms. Savings of 5 to 10% are not uncommon when technology tools are first applied to direct goods. Savings are based on the difference between the amount spent either year to year or sourcing event to sourcing event. Savings in excess of 20% are not unusual for indirect and can rise much higher. One area of huge reported savings has been the spend on marketing.

5. Sometimes technology is in conflict with good sourcing practice and common sense. It is best to partner with key suppliers for critical components. Technology companies and supply chain consultants advocate lots of suppliers to hype the action in bidding events. A basic rule applies here: Always go with sound purchasing practice first and technology second.

6. IT companies and supply chain consultants are trying to define the business, fostering confusion. Systems may be called anything from "spend management" to "supplier relationship management," with a plethora of newly minted jargon in between. The experts on sourcing

are still your own people. Trust their instincts about what works and what doesn't.

7. Make sure your spend data are in good shape before implementing an automated sourcing system. Many customers realized poor return on investment on initial e-procurement installations because they could only process 15 to 20% of their spend through their systems.

Yes, there are many cautionary statements to be made about technology investments. But having said that, corporations have been too slow to implement electronic sourcing approaches. A study by the Center for Advanced Purchasing Studies in 2004 shows that most North American companies make only "slight" to "moderate" use of IT for the supply chain (see Table 7.1).

Here's a quick look at the sourcing functions where technology can play a role.

Spend Analysis: This is the starting point and a very critical area. How much does your company spend across the enterprise, regardless of geography and

Table 7.1. The CEO Imperative for Electronic Sourcing

1 = None, 2 = Slight, 3 = Moderate, 4 = Substantial, 5 = Extensive

E-Commerce Usage	Average Rating
Electronic/online purchase order system	3.18
Electronic data interchange	3.05
Electronic online supplier catalogue	2.84
Real-time electronic linkage with suppliers	2.57
Online reverse/e-auction	2.49
Online bidding/tendering	2.31
Private B2B exchange/extranet operated by your company for your suppliers	1.87
Private B2B exchange/extranet operated by your company for your customer(s)	1.79
Industry-sponsored e-marketplaces (e.g., Covisint)	1.60
Private B2B exchange/extranet operated by your suppliers	1.54
Private e-marketplaces (e.g., Global Healthcare Exchange)	1.47
Private B2B exchange/extranet operated by your customers	1.42
Other electronic procurement methods	1.30

Data source: CAPS Research, 2004. Study conducted among Fortune 1000 U.S. companies and Financial Post 100 Canadian companies by P. Fraser Johnson, associate professor of operations management at the Richard Ivey School of Business at the University for Western Ontario and Michiel R. Leenders, professor emeritus of the Ivey School.

business units? Until recently, only a handful of Fortune 1000 companies could even venture an answer to that question. Obviously, it is important to know. This concept is sometimes also called data warehousing.

You can build significant leverage by identifying your total spend on computers or anything else and then offer a consolidated bid. You can also generate considerable savings in areas such as testing costs if you combine evaluations across business units and geographies. Many purchasing executives have had to go to suppliers and ask for a report on how much of their products they buy — and where. That kind of performance is no longer acceptable in today's business world. The rapid move toward consolidation of even very large companies increases the imperative to understand the spend. Even for very sophisticated companies, however, this is not an easy job because products are defined and specified so differently. Procter & Gamble had 20 different specifications just for water before it began the transformation process during the past three years. General Mills had a multitude of definitions just for boxes. Many companies now try to standardize on uniform product codes, such as the Universal Standard Product and Services Classification (UNSPSC) or standard supplier classifications, such as DUNS. The technology companies use knowledge engines, sometimes called artificial intelligence, to parse through your codes and automatically put products in appropriate classifications. Make sure your purchasing department has at least tackled the low-hanging fruit through analysis of whatever feeds are available: vendor reports, accounts payable, procurement systems, enterprise resource planning systems, procurement cards, or bank feeds.

Market Making: This is where most of the action is, and there are four categories here: reverse auctions, electronic market making, decision support analytics, and sourcing services.

Reverse auctions were a sensation in 1999 and 2000 and then really took off when weak industrial markets combined with a major push to reduce supply-side costs after September 11. In a few cases, this was an overnight panacea, and the rush to implement them pell-mell undid many years of hard work by purchasing pros and created anger and panic in the supply community. A reverse auction is an online bidding event in which a group of companies are invited to bid on a large piece of business, divided into preset bundles and lots. Incumbent suppliers are invited, as are several other vendors qualified by either the purchasing department or the reverse auction vendor. A "reserve" price is established, which is in effect the starting point of the auction. The reserve price is x% below the previous contract and reflects the cost of switching business, even though many reverse auction winners were the incumbent suppliers.

Vendors participating in the event watch competitive bids pop up on a computer screen. In the last three or four minutes of the event, there is often a frenzy of lower bids as companies, especially incumbents, rush to keep the business. Initial savings results were spectacular — often well above 20% (see Figure 7.2). Suppliers and some best-in-class purchasing organizations hated the events because they ignored the importance of the supplier relationship and put excessive focus on price alone. Use of reverse auctions has quieted as markets firmed. They still have a place in selected situations, particularly markets that are highly liquid, or competitive, and where supplier relationships are not a key criterion. They are used successfully for plain vanilla electronic components, commodity-grade polyethylenes, and similar products. Reverse auctions were pioneered by FreeMarkets, now part of Ariba, and are now widely available from vendors such as Procuri, Emptoris, and Verticalnet, among others.

Electronic market making is also an electronic bid-gathering process, but not done on a real-time, event basis. It is often referred to by the shorthand form eRFx ("electronic Request For something"). One of the early adopters was GlaxoSmithKline, which reported that savings equal those of reverse auctions, but without the mad scramble.

Decision-support analytics are tools that give suppliers opportunities to play a bigger role in shaping their bids based on their knowledge of the products involved and their own internal economics. It is an area of tremendous potential. Traditionally, suppliers were not allowed to influence bid lotting or bundling or other dimensions. In fact, suppliers were given even worse treatment than that. In the words of R. Gene Richter, the late chief procurement officer at IBM: "There was a feeling that everybody in the industry was trying to steal our ideas. Everything at IBM was a secret."[1] Suppliers weren't told how their products would be used. Planned volumes weren't shared. Parts were shipped to central locations to disguise manufacturing plans. IBM dramatically changed its approach after Richter became the top buyer in 1994. More recently, IBM even deployed buyer-engineers to work at supplier partners to help steer their technical development in directions that mesh with IBM's own plans.

Today, technology takes that process to a totally different level. Called expressive, or combinatorial, bidding, the process lays out user requirements and gives suppliers a broad swath to suggest how products should be bundled or lotted and shipped. It's a big winner in logistics where suppliers can selectively bid on shipping lanes that maximize their efficiencies. If trucks come back full, the buyer shares the savings. Suppliers may even identify specification alternatives when no performance is compromised. Many engineers, for example, specify a particular melt flow for an engineering resin, when polymer reactors actually make the resin within a wide certification range. Only the supplier knows that. With expressive bidding, the buyer can benefit. Two pioneers in this optimization technology are Emptoris, which teamed with scientists from the Massachusetts Institute of Technology, and

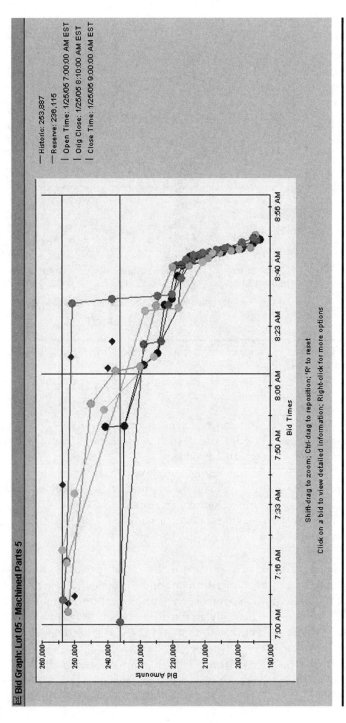

Figure 7.2. Reverse auction bidding results. (Source: Ariba/FreeMarkets)

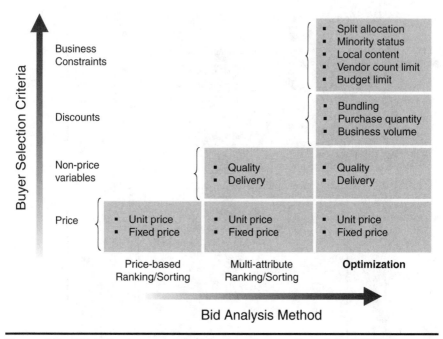

Figure 7.3. Optimization analyzes all factors. (Source: Copyright ©2005 Emptoris, Inc. All rights reserved.)

CombineNet, which was founded by scientists from Carnegie-Mellon University in Pittsburgh. Leading-edge users, such as Procter & Gamble, have put 10% of their spend through this process.

Figure 7.3 illustrates the increasing complexity that can be handled as you move from price-based ranking or sorting to multiattribute ranking or sorting, to optimization. With optimization, many nonprice factors can be explicitly considered. This decision-making sophistication is a far cry from the old days of "three bids and a cloud of dust purchasing."

Sourcing Services: This is an important niche category. Some companies are outsourcing purchasing on noncritical products, particularly in the indirect area. This is a source of huge controversy within the purchasing community. In some cases, the controversy is generated by pure motives just to maintain employment. Others make the case that all purchasing is a core competency and a source of competitive advantage. For that reason, it should be maintained internally. The fact is, though, that companies in today's economy need to focus their attention on those activities where the payoff may be greatest. When Lucent Technologies went through a near-death experience after the high-tech and communications collapse of 2001, it outsourced most of its indirect buy. It freed up resources and achieved significant savings. Outsourcing of some piece of procurement may be the right strategy for you. It deserves a look, and this topic is covered in greater detail in Chapter 23.

Contract Management: Another important area of technology focus is contract management. The central problem attacked here is poor organization of contracts. Few companies have maintained central repositories of contracts so that buyers in other divisions or locations can use them. In the 20th century of purchasing, it wasn't so important. Companies were highly integrated, and their supply base was local. Today, suppliers play a much bigger role and supply chains are extremely complex. A significant larger percentage of suppliers are foreign and often in countries with poorly developed legal systems.

Some ahead-of-the-curve supply organizations have developed their own contract management systems, which at the very least create a central repository and allow creation of basic templates with cut-and-paste boilerplate statements already approved by the legal department. A buyer negotiating a contract for services in Europe can find out if similar contracts exist and quickly update terms, dramatically shortening the time involved in contract development. This process is also important because it ensures that companies speak with one voice to their global supply base.

Even companies with good sourcing and negotiating systems often fail to make sure that contract terms are communicated and implemented. "Many buyers spend a lot of time with suppliers to get the right terms. Those contracts get put on the shelf and somehow those terms are not getting transferred to the purchase order level," comments Craig Brown, vice president of the Technology Manufacturing Group at Intel. "We did an audit and found that over half of negotiated discount payment terms were not being taken because the contract did not populate the purchase order and accounts payable did not get the signal. What we want is a closed loop so that when a contract is negotiated, there is an auto feed of those kinds of terms."[2]

Software companies are offering packages that make this entire process even simpler. Terms can be integrated with other software used by other departments such as accounts payable, ensuring follow-through. Compliance to contracts in general is also an important issue reinforced by a good software program. Are users actually buying through the contract using the stipulated terms? This is obviously of particular importance when minimum volume requirements trigger savings.

Software can also create alerts when contracts need to be renegotiated. Vendor performance can be tracked against contracted obligations. Organizations moving contract management to the Web are saving significant sums through better contract enforcement, particularly in the area of maverick spending and supplier overcharging. Good contract maintenance is growing in importance because of federal legislation, in particular Sarbanes-Oxley, which was passed in the wake of accounting and other corporate misdeeds at companies such as Enron. Sarbanes-Oxley requires corporations to provide more public visibility of obligations and to maintain auditable trails of communications.

Product Life Cycle Management: Another area is product life cycle management, where suppliers can collaborate with buyers and design engineers during the development phase of a product. The best systems connect all relevant departments, including planning, manufacturing, marketing, sales, and maintenance. Someone in marketing may propose a product idea. Internal design engineers can offer opinions while buyers begin to develop initial costing data. Buyers also invite partner-suppliers, which can suggest whole new design ideas or manufacturing approaches that can result in tremendous savings. As designs are modified, suppliers can quickly comment if a change suddenly changes the economics. These approaches are particularly important as manufacturers move toward outsourcing and highly complex, global supply chains. The software can also easily manage environmental, health, and safety issues. Vendors include Agile, PTC, IBM, MatrixOne, and SAP.

Exchanges: Another area is the category-oriented vendors that offer exchanges or specific buying expertise in particular areas such as retail, life sciences, print, or construction. One example is ChemConnect, a survivor of the dot-com bubble of 2000–2001, which offers an online market where companies can buy and sell chemicals. It works well because many chemicals and plastics are historically sold as wide spec when producers have excess inventory or want to maintain pricing levels for prime spec materials.

As a CEO or other senior corporate executive, it is most important to make sure your supply chain team is aware of the latest innovations in software and how they can improve purchasing performance. Make innovation in supply chain one of six or so key areas that you monitor with your chief procurement officer on a quarterly basis and that you personally support.

Application of technology to purchasing, starting in the dot-com area, has been hampered by the complexity of internal IT processes, which traditionally were built like a Maine farmhouse — one room at a time without thought toward final goals. Projects in general have been IT driven, not process driven. Making sense of this maze, and the capital implications, remains the single biggest problem when applying technology to the supply chain. Take a look at the big picture and all of the options available and proceed from there.

The fact is that most supply chain executives have historically not been happy with their IT implementations. These expensive investments fail to meet expectations for a multitude of reasons, but by far the most important is inability of companies to change people's behavior and reform internal business processes. That is why we say that strong executive support is the most important factor in achieving success in any aspect of supply chain change. Oddly, the reverse is also true: CEOs order a supply chain IT implementation without making sure that appropriate business processes are in place.

Don't jump whole hog into technology. Walk and then run if it works. Establish meaningful metrics to measure its performance. Make sure each piece fits into a long-term puzzle. And remember that your basic purchasing approach must be in good shape before you can order a technology implementation. Ask the questions in Chapter 2, make sure you get the right answers, and then invest in the technology that best fits your company.

8

Measurement and Expectations

Show Me the Money!

If you're not keeping score, you're just practicing.
—Vince Lombardi,
football philosopher

Measurement

CEOs, COOs, or CFOs, when asked "how is your purchasing department performing?" will often respond:

> The purchasing department reports great results, year after year, but I can't find the savings figures on the bottom line of my income statement.

Purchasing executives, when reporting their cost reduction results, often hear the following questions from their internal clients:

- ◆ Are these savings real?
- ◆ Are these numbers net of inflation?
- ◆ How were these figures calculated?
- ◆ What are these compared against? What is the baseline?
- ◆ Who (in finance or other areas) agrees with the calculation?
- ◆ Where are the savings? I can't find them on my bottom line.

Cost reduction is one of many potential areas of performance contribution, and its correct and relevant measurement is very important (detailed comments about measuring cost reduction appear later in this chapter). Other areas of strategic importance to measure include:

- Improvements in working capital (better payment terms, better inventory programs with suppliers)
- Improvements in the "monetization" of underutilized corporate assets (e.g., plant, equipment) through "asset recovery" initiatives in which you identify the idle or underutilized assets at each company location, make them available to other company locations to avoid spending cash on new equipment, or sell them on the used equipment market for cash
- Risk management and pricing volatility (hedging)
- Overall effectiveness and efficiency of the supply chain in meeting key operational needs (e.g., customer satisfaction, product development cycle times, supplier nonconformance, supplier delivery performance, variations in manufacturing and product deliveries, etc.)
- Organizational compliance with contracts, sometimes best measured in terms of "dollars of lost opportunity" (see Table 8.1)
- Percent of total corporate spend managed by purchasing
- Percent of total spend that is "spot buys" (relates to price risk exposure)

Percent noncompliance with sourcing contracts is a good measure, but it becomes even more relevant to talk about dollars of lost opportunity resulting from the noncompliance. In the hypothetical example shown in Table 8.1, the percent noncompliance is multiplied by the total potential benefit from the contract (i.e., the annual spend multiplied by the contract benefit) to arrive at a figure for dollars of lost opportunity.

Table 8.1. Lost Opportunity Calculator

Contract	% Noncompliance	% Annual Spend	Contract Benefit	Lost $ Opportunity
Office supplies	30%	$5,000,000	30%	$450,000
PCs	15%	$3,000,000	15%	$67,500
Services X	40%	$7,000,000	10%	$280,000
Raw materials Y	10%	$10,000,000	5%	$50,000
Average noncompliance				
Simple average	26.25%			
$ weighted average		23.00%		
Lost $ opportunity per year				$847,500

All of these metrics focus on the strategic role and value that purchasing can deliver. Other tactical metrics provide indications of the operational efficiency that purchasing's processes and systems (and those of interrelated departments) have. These metrics typically are managed "in-house" by purchasing (i.e., not a corporate objective). For example, some purchasing departments pay careful attention to the average cost (and time) to process a purchase order and the average cost (and time) to process invoices for payment. Other tactical metrics include the percent of total payments processed via electronic tools (such as electronic data interchange, electronic funds transfer, or procurement cards) and the percent of purchase spend processed through e-procurement systems.

Other operational metrics (also managed in-house by purchasing) provide an indication of the relative intensity of purchasing's activities. For example, it is not uncommon to wonder about purchasing's operating expense as a percent of company sales and the purchase spend per purchasing employee.

All of these tactical and operational measures serve a purpose, but should not be confused with the strategic objectives that directly relate to the top line and bottom line of the company. The strategic should be drawing the greatest attention. If that is not the case, change is needed.

Benchmarks for many tactical and operational metrics exist, such as those developed by the Center for Advanced Purchasing Studies. However, care must be taken in using those benchmarks due to two realities. *First, it is dangerous to look at tactical or operational efficiency benchmarks in the absence of considering what purchasing accomplishes in its key objectives.* For example, it is possible for a company to have a relatively high purchasing spend per employee or a relatively low cost to process a purchase order, putting it in the top quartile of those benchmarks, but that same company might not be delivering top-tier results in cost reductions.

Second, a company that has been focused for many years on purchasing transformation and excellence might naturally show different "metrics" than a brand new transformation effort at another company. For example, a mature purchasing company might be generating new cost reductions equal to 1% of total spend per year, whereas a company that just embarked on strategic sourcing might achieve 3 or 4% in its first full year of efforts (lots of low-hanging fruit). Thus, benchmarks that are the arithmetic result of "apples and oranges" can be dangerous if not carefully understood.

Remember: you get what you measure. Therefore, measure only what you want people to focus on and to achieve. The right performance measures drive appropriate focus, behavior, and results. Too many metrics can dilute focus and cause the important strategic objectives to not receive the necessary time and attention. The most successful companies focus on the strategic objectives, make them corporate priorities of not just purchasing but also those functions that interact with purchasing, and link executive and management incentive compensation meaningfully to achievement of those shared objectives.

One of the common mistakes in reporting purchasing "cost savings" is to measure and report only the results from the projects/initiatives that purchasing leads. This is a natural mistake, triggered by the view that purchasing should only report what it controls (i.e., its "savings projects"). However, the key to having a credible measurement of cost reductions in purchasing spend is to realize that *three* factors must be measured and reported in order to have a net figure that is relevant to the income statement that senior executives and division presidents look at.

P&L Impact From

- Initiatives (purchasing projects)
- Volume fluctuations
- Marketplace factors (e.g., natural gas price fluctuations)

- **Total profit-and-loss impact**

The total (net) of these three changes will fairly closely align with the results coming out of a company's accounting system. When this is the case, it greatly enhances purchasing's credibility. It is also important not to mix in "cost avoidance" figures. If it is of interest to track cost avoidance, do so, but track it separately. Only cost reduction really counts toward improving year-over-year corporate performance. It is also important to include cost reductions that result from cross-functional team efforts. After all, that is what we want to encourage — and oftentimes teams can generate the biggest impact results. For example, a value analysis review of a product's design results in a more cost-effective approach can yield measurable savings. Lucent Technologies has shaved as much as 50% from product cost through use of workshops with suppliers that include design engineers and purchasing professionals. Suppliers are asked to submit cost reduction ideas which are then reviewed by internal teams. Such practices should be encouraged and savings should be measured and verified.

Overall cost reduction measurement needs to be compared to a meaningful benchmark, such as the prior year, the current year budget, or a baseline year. Jack Welch measured GE cost performance against GE's own changes in sales prices. That's obviously important in determining corporate performance, but not necessarily meaningful. Remember that American corporations traditionally neglected purchasing savings because they could easily raise their own prices. Corporations need to improve their cost performance regardless of what's happening with their own pricing. Otherwise, they are not fulfilling their fiduciary responsibility to their shareholders.

Measurement against outside sources is an important way to monitor performance. One of the single biggest issues is competitiveness on prices paid. Buyers at large chemical firms often buy subscriptions to expensive consulting reports that monitor prices. Some check pricing reports issued by trade media. Still others compare performance to the U.S. Bureau of Labor Statistics producer price index (PPI). Use all of these sources at your own risk.

For example, the PPI is what it says it is: a producer price. So right from the start, this benchmark may be a con if it is used by your purchasing department. No purchasing department in the world should be paying a producer's list price without a very careful understanding of what it is. List pricing is a strange fiction. Possibly companies list prices just in the hope that someone might actually pay at that level. Maybe they persist because their salespeople can walk into a buyer, show the list prices coupled with proposed price hikes, and then discuss the wonderful opportunity they have available. And some buyers might even count that fiction as a cost avoidance! The problem with the PPIs gets even worse. They historically were solicited from just three sources, even for very complex, disparate types of machinery that could not in fact be grouped together as apples and apples. Another failure is that the PPI is based only on U.S. sources of supply. As whole industries have migrated offshore, there are often few if any reliable U.S. sources. Consider electronics, for example, where many important parts are only made in Asia. Some high-tech manufacturers buy over half of their "direct" product — mostly electronic and related parts — from China.

So if your chief procurement officer (CPO) starts the measurement review with a big smile because of his or her team's progress versus the PPI, suggest he or she consider a different barometer. Having said that, there are purchasing executives whom we respect who do historical validation of PPIs and swear they are effective for some items. A few PPIs may match up with reality, but why take the risk?

So what do you benchmark cost performance against? Certainly prior year and budget. Your own numbers shouldn't lie. Also push your CPO to identify as many reliable external sources as possible. IBM's purchasing department benchmarks against the "best in class" globally. It hires consultants and other experts to determine best-in-class cost performance. Some CPOs are informally benchmarking cost data with peers. "They won't tell us what they paid for a specific airline ticket," says one CPO, "but we can group together like tickets in baskets and do comparisons." Electronic auctions give visibility into current pricing, but should not be used strictly for that purpose. Participation in consortia also provides visibility into industry pricing.

But cost performance is not strictly measured by prices paid. That's just one component, as already pointed out here. When you pay the prices, of course, is also critical. Many companies have derived significant competitive advantage through contracts that only allow quarterly price changes. That was a common practice in the plastics industry, but terrifically resisted by the resin suppliers when margins eroded after September 11, 2001.

One other critical issue in cost measurement is involvement of the finance department. Credibility is significantly enhanced by involving finance, or the plant or division controllers, in "signing off" on the calculated benefits of individual projects or initiatives. If this is impractical, a good backup plan is to have a nonpurchasing stakeholder who has a vested interest in the project (e.g., an operating superintendent, engineering manager) provide the sign-off, with periodic auditing of randomly selected projects by finance or internal audit.

Finally, to drive the benefits all the way to the bottom line, it is necessary to ensure that favorable variances created by projects/initiatives cannot be spent by well-intentioned cost center managers (unless there is a formal review). The simplest way to accomplish this is to adjust budgets during the year, at the division or cost center level, by the expected results of each non-budgeted success. Then, if someone wants to propose a way to spend the favorable variance created by a purchasing initiative, the proposal is explicitly reviewed based on its own merits.

Note that it is important, in the three-component approach described above, not to mix in the results from capital project initiatives. The successes from capital initiatives should be measured and reported separately from the "operating" results noted above. That way, the operating scorecard can align with the profit-and-loss statement.

Finally, tie your measurement protocol into compensation for all sourcing team members, regardless of whether or not they are "purchasing depart-ment" employees. Also, most purchasing management receives some type of bonus compensation. Instead of tying that compensation into just overall financial performance, tie it into how well people met their cost and other goals. Table 8.2 provides a list of measurement principles.

Reasonable Expectations

> *High expectations are the key to everything.*
> —Sam Walton,
> founder of Wal-Mart

Here are a few real-life illustrations of the impact that advanced purchasing can have:

- ♦ At a Fortune 500 manufacturer, the top executives "knew" that the purchasing department "did a good job." Strictly for career develop-

Table 8.2. Measurement Principles for Procurement Team Members

- Measure results, not effort or image.
- Use same criteria as used to measure suppliers.
- Give all members of the team the same rating.
- Force rank teams.
- Get total buy-in on industry benchmark by those being measured.
- Encourage maximum achievement.
- Measurements must cascade upward to include all procurement management.
- Directly relate all variable compensation to measurement results.

Source: R. Gene Richter

ment purposes, a young executive out of the finance department was put in charge of purchasing. With a newly formed procurement council, he decided to take a "fresh look at everything." One year later, more than $50 million of quantifiable, true cost reductions had been generated. Four years after that, the cost structure of the company had been permanently improved by almost $300 million.

- The purchasing department of a Fortune 100 manufacturer decided to experiment with a new tool known as "reverse auctions." Some people thought this was actually a passing fad, but this purchasing department wanted to see for itself. Twelve months later, over $75 million of new cost reductions had been facilitated using reverse auctions. In many cases, cost reductions of 25 to 35% were achieved on individual projects.

- At another firm, the purchasing department decided to change its targeted payment terms with suppliers. Implemented in an ethical, planned fashion over 18 months, the firm achieved a 50% lengthening of its average terms of payment with most of its suppliers, while increasing the discount it would receive (if it chose to pay earlier) from 0.5% to as much as 2%.

- At another company, the purchasing department decided to explore the willingness of suppliers to store inventory, on-site or nearby its plant operations, until the company actually needed the material for production runs. The initiative proved highly successful and had the effect of reducing the company's investment in inventory because the suppliers took that responsibility.

With a serious corporate commitment to advanced sourcing, it has not been unusual for a purchasing department — working closely with its internal client departments and plants — to achieve sustainable improvements in corporate cost structure of 8 to 10% of total spend. Often, this is achieved progressively over five to seven years in several "waves" of sourcing efforts and leadership initiatives, each building upon the prior wave (see Chapter 13).

The percent cost reduction can vary considerably among different major categories of spend (e.g., raw materials versus logistics services versus technical goods). Even within major categories of spend (e.g., within the broad category of raw materials), results can differ widely based on the competitive dynamics of individual supply markets and the creativity of the purchasing department in designing sourcing and negotiation strategies.

For the CEO looking for an order of magnitude, here are some results (all expressed as cost reduction as a percent of spend) that are possible *if you are willing to make a meaningful and sustained corporate commitment to advanced purchasing:*

Raw materials	2 to 5%
Packaging	10 to 20%
Indirect materials and services	10 to 20%
Information technology	15 to 30%
Professional services (including consulting, legal, human resources)	8 to 15%
Logistics (rail, truck, barge, ocean, air)	7 to 15%
Media/marketing/promotional items	10 to 20%
Other indirects (nonproduction costs)	5 to 15%
Capital projects	7 to 15%

Any opportunity assessment at a specific company must then take into account the dollars of spend in each major category, to arrive at the potential total opportunity across all areas of spend. To the extent that prior efforts involved strategic sourcing, the opportunity assessment should deduct the results of those prior efforts to arrive at the assessment of the future opportunity.

This raises an interesting point about the natural focus of senior executives on direct spend (raw materials and packaging). One of the authors was interviewing an internal client shortly after being recruited into a major company. The client, a business unit president, offered an opinion that "purchasing needed to spend more time and attention on raw materials." The new CPO asked why the executive felt that way. The answer was straightforward: "Raw materials are my biggest area of spend. If we could achieve just another 1 or 2% reduction in raw materials costs, that would be meaningful to my bottom line."

The CPO's response was twofold: "With your support and involvement, we'll do better than 1 or 2% on raw materials, and we need to increase our focus on the 'indirects,' since that is where even greater opportunity awaits." The business unit president took issue with the second point, because he knew that the annual spend for indirects was dwarfed by the annual spend

• Hypothetical manufacturer:

Raw Materials Purchases:	$1 billion
assume 5% cost reduction:	$50 million step change in cost structure
Indirect Materials & Services:	$0.5 billion
assume 15% cost reduction:	$75 million step change in cost structure

Figure 8.1. The math may surprise you.

for raw materials. The CPO showed him the illustration in Figure 8.1. The reaction was immediate: "When can we get started?"

The business case for adopting an advanced purchasing perspective is compelling. One question to ask yourself is: How much am I willing to invest, in order to put that potential onto my bottom line, year after year?

There is a clear correlation between resources devoted to strategic purchasing and the results achieved. One of the authors compiled six years of data from his experiences with one company (annual new cost reductions, total full-time-equivalent resources available to purchasing) and plotted that data. He found that the relationship was fairly linear and that for *each* new strategic full-time equivalent available, approximately $1 million of new cost reductions could be hitting the bottom line one year later.

What should you expect? Very significant improvements in profitability, cash flow, product quality, and reduced cycle time for new product development. And your shareholders and other stakeholders should expect you to deliver these results.

9

Transformation

Making Sure the Changes Stick

*It's only when the tide goes out
that you learn who's been swimming naked.*
—Warren Buffet,
legendary investor

Years ago, co-author Mike Katzorke was riding up the New Jersey Turnpike with his boss one beautiful spring afternoon after a meeting at the University of Pennsylvania's Wharton School, which invested considerable effort in the study of supply chain management.

He found himself thinking about the discussions and what he had observed over his career relative to what a few good companies had achieved in transforming three-bids-and-a-cloud-of-dust purchasing into strategic supply management and then toward supply chain management. He came to the realization that they had all made progress, and then the structure that operated the process dissolved. They went backward for quite a while before catching themselves in free fall and began correcting the situation. Some never made it back.

Katzorke's boss at the time had designed and led the charge at one of these companies and was now working on doing it again as the corporate vice president of purchasing at another company. "Why do you think this happens so frequently?" Katzorke asked him. After thinking about it for several minutes, the boss gave a profound answer: "You know, I don't know."

75

Three of the co-authors have personally led the transformation charge eight times, and we think we do know the answer: *It is because too many companies build the change on the strength of one individual, and when that person is pulled out, the process collapses.* Why? Because the company drove for quick savings, and there was no process or supporting framework to sustain the progress after the initial step-change was achieved. Often, companies go for a quick win instead of continuous improvement through fundamental change. *We must build sustainable process change into the business such that it becomes just the way we do things, with a clear recognition that we are designing a process for the long term, not just a one-time initiative.*

Let's assume for the moment that you, as senior executive, have done a great job selecting your initial procurement transformation leader and that your chosen leader is following the recommendations and best practices outlined throughout this book. What else needs to be in place so that progress can continue once that leader moves on to his or her next career assignment?

Before we tackle that question, let's not take for granted the recommendations and best practices outlined in this book. Figure 9.1 illustrates the key recommendations from Parts I through III, and also includes the best practices described in Part IV, organized into a graphical framework that can serve as a roadmap. In the experience of the authors, having all of these elements in place creates a critical mass of momentum that can endure the inevitable ebbs and flows of corporate politics and organizational pendulum swings.

In short, you start with an executive commitment to the strategic integration of supply management into the highest levels of corporate thinking, strategy, and operations. You establish a few of the right objectives, which are shared across the organization and which drive incentives and consequences. You pick the right leader: an individual who has the right skills and is an enabler of bright people to implement 21st century processes, particularly strategic sourcing and supplier partnering. That leader in turn creates a leadership culture at all levels of his or her organization. You select a structure that works in your culture and also make sure the role of supply management includes cross-functional teaming with finance, technical functions, manufacturing, logistics, and other disciplines to create a process that speaks with one voice to suppliers. You invest in the technology that captures the power of the digital age. And you embrace and embed best practices.

With these key elements in place, what else do you need to have in place so that progress can continue once your initial leader moves on?

Ideally, of course, you would fill the shoes of your initial leader with another true leader. But if that is not immediately possible, it becomes even more critical that most of the elements of advanced sourcing be in place. In

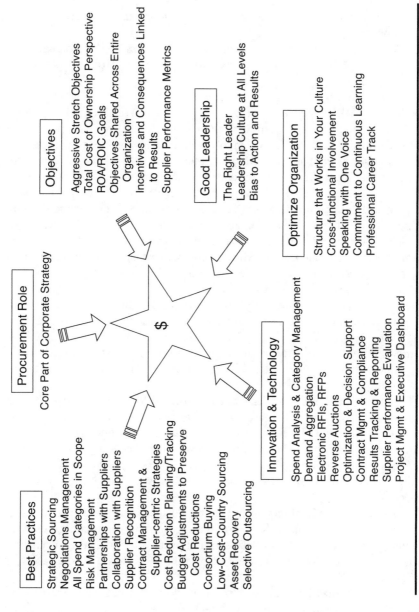

Figure 9.1. Key elements of taking it straight to the bottom line.

addition, to enhance the probability of successful and sustainable transformation, the authors stress the need for two particular areas of focus:

1. A solid and ongoing change management or business transformation process
2. A financially linked "skin-in-the-game" process that recognizes the realities of the influence matrix presented in the "role" discussion in Chapter 4.

In his book *What Leaders Really Do,* Harvard University Professor John Kotter notes that there is a multistep process to initiate and maintain a successful transformation.[1] It first involves convincing people that there is a need or a crisis, as well as a benefit associated with change. Next, it involves developing an inspiring vision of change and communicating that vision regularly. Making sure all actions are consistent with that vision is a necessary further ingredient. Eliminating barriers is also crucial; you need to make sure that people are involved and are able to contribute to the change effort. Successes can help reinforce the change effort, particularly if they are well communicated and celebrated. And finally, you must maintain a constant focus and attention on the change effort. In other words, it cannot be just another "program of the month."

Kotter's framework is not only useful in constructing the initial plan for transformation; it is a helpful reminder of how to keep a transformation on track. In the experiences of the authors, too many transformation efforts become derailed because the basics of business transformation are dropped in the transition from one leader to a successor, just like a dropped baton in an Olympic relay race.

The change model is not rocket science, but it does require being honest with yourself about where you are on the change continuum. Have you really created a *shared* need? Is there really a clear vision of where you are trying to take this process, where it is now, and why it is necessary for the enterprise? And once you have done the first two above, how do you really mobilize commitment? It takes a process, not just speeches and promises (or threats).

For example, if our objective is to attack the cost of what we procure, and we define supply chain as from ore in the ground to product obsolescence and everything that happens in between, it's pretty clear that the purchasing person isn't the only one who needs to be involved and be accountable for delivery of benefits.

One way this has been done is to go back to the influence matrix and involve the managers who are most likely to effect its success or block its success. Did you ever meet someone from manufacturing who wanted to outsource in a major way, especially to low-cost economies? How many engineering heads do you know who have value analysis or value engineering as their primary interest? But we can devise a process to overcome the obvious obstacles if we use the influence matrix and pragmatically apply it.

The best way to do this is through creation of executive-led teams that include the appropriate functional leaders. Each team should have cost targets established by the CEO and the chief procurement officer and should be sponsored by a direct report to the CEO. The executive sponsor creates the mandate for collaboration across divisions and functional groups and leads development of new business rules that pave the way for success of the teams. An excellent example is the UT500 program at United Technologies outlined in Chapter 12. Tyco is also using executive-led teams to create change in its global strategic sourcing initiative.

Such a system makes it clear, for example, that engineering must significantly participate in delivering savings from value analysis, which is the process of breaking down a product and determining how it can be made better and for less money. Manufacturing would play a key role in finding lower cost sources in China, India, or another low-cost country. That may seem odd — but it's the manufacturing person who will buck the change the hardest. That's why we make it partly his or her responsibility to deliver the savings. Procurement will actually identify the sources and provide the framework and tools. Manufacturing officers or managers will be involved in approving those sources and using them to achieve the targeted benefits. Deliverables should be measured monthly against specific projects, with specific deliverables and specific schedules with specific accountabilities and associated consequences. This model is a real-world one and has been very successful not only in delivering the money, but influencing future decisions in the stakeholder groups providing additional future long-term benefit.

And finally, you must get "skin in the game." The expression refers to personal commitment and was coined by celebrated investor Warren Buffett to explain situations in which high-ranking insiders put their own money on the line to support companies. Executives and operations managers can talk all they want, but they have the most credibility when they have a vested stake in the outcome.

After co-author Katzorke began a supply chain transformation process at Cessna Aircraft in 1998, the company developed a business process model that focused on core processes, each championed by senior leadership members (of which Katzorke was one), with the overall transformation process led by the CEO of the business. The model proved to be an effective mechanism for incorporating supply chain values into corporate culture and get "skin in the game." Katzorke established a Supply Chain Transformation Center where linkages from the customer and shareholder to the key business objectives to the process objectives were linked right down to the individual buyer, engineer, manufacturing, quality, and finance contributors. It made evident the current state, needed change, and relative priorities of those changes and clarified not just what needed addressing but how it would be addressed *in an integrated fashion as an enterprise.* It also displayed current state in metrics and tracked progress of improvement.

The Transformation Center was first used to pursue alignment of the senior leadership by taking the CEO of the business and the COO of the business through the room. The senior leadership team was taken through the room as a staff. Next, each senior leadership team member held his or her staff meeting in the room and staff members were taken through it. This drill down and training continued all the way down to the professional individual contributors in the trenches, such as design engineers.[2] The integrative "aha" that came to COO Charlie Johnson through this process resulted in his leadership becoming the key enabling factor for the supply chain transformation that resulted in Cessna winning the *Purchasing* Magazine Medal of Professional Excellence.

The co-authors have found that "skin in the game" can be enhanced by something as simple as engaging senior business and functional leaders in a "steering committee" that meets periodically to review sourcing results, provides "air cover" for new teams, and helps to remove obstacles. A further enhancement involves having senior executives act as the sponsor for one or more sourcing teams and even play a scripted role in supplier negotiations.

To summarize, in the authors' collective experiences across eight transformations, a successful and sustainable transformation requires:

- ◆ A shared need that everyone understands and a perceived benefit of adopting change to address that need
- ◆ An exciting vision of change and what that change can mean to the organization
- ◆ Clear communication about the vision and agreement on the approach, deployment, and measurement process
- ◆ Elimination of obstacles
- ◆ Executive actions consistent with the vision
- ◆ Reinforcement of the changes being adopted, typically by celebrating successes
- ◆ A clear and structured method to get leadership "skin in the game," which can include many of the items listed above plus personal executive involvement in the process and also financial "skin in the game"
- ◆ An integrated rigorous leadership discipline to "stay the course" with both the plan and the change management process

III

Post-transformation

Best-in-Class Examples from Supply Management Transformation

10

Automotive Purchasing

A Tale of Two Spenders

Alliances require a complete corporate focus, starting with senior management, to break the paradigm of individual companies building walls around themselves.

> —Thomas T. Stallkamp,
> creator of the Extended Enterprise
> in Chrysler procurement

Suppliers are corporations' most important allies in the competition of global supply chains. Curiously, it is only a very recent development that Western companies attempted to share even very basic information with them. When R. Gene Richter assumed the top procurement post at IBM in the 1990s, he discovered that all IBM corporate information was kept secret. Suppliers were told to make a specific part, but were never told how or where it would be used.[1] "In procurement we were the guardians of confidential information, the guard at the door who didn't let any suppliers know anything. You couldn't have effective collaboration with suppliers...What happened is we woke up. We realized that we couldn't be expert in everything."[2]

Richter's core point was that American businesses operated on a system of distrust in regard to just about everything — and especially suppliers. The new business model must be built on a foundation of long-term relationships, focused on core business functions — those that are most critical to the future of your company. Identify noncore areas and apply a different model: outsourcing, outtasking, or application of electronic reverse auctions focused on price. In purchasing, supplier development is the Holy Grail. Another principal tenet of Richter's approach was to recruit very talented professionals and then empower them to work with suppliers and make decisions within a carefully designed framework.

One of the visionaries on the role of suppliers was Thomas T. Stallkamp, a procurement executive at Chrysler Corp. in the early 1990s, who invited suppliers to participate in cost reduction programs and to participate in new platform design. Over at General Motors Corp., a very different approach was implemented under the reign of Chairman Jack Smith and purchasing executive Jose Ignacio Lopez, who ordered all suppliers to reduce prices across the board or face rebidding of their business, regardless of existing contractual or partnering relationships. Lopez seemed to embody what quarterly-numbers-focused chief executives wanted in supply management — a brutal, take-no-prisoners approach. What were the actual results of the different approaches?

After earning a paltry $4.2 billion in 1989 on sales of close to $127 billion, GM's losses grew steadily in magnitude the next three years, reaching $23.5 billion in 1992 (see Figure 10.1). Jack Smith was ushered in as CEO, replacing Robert Stempel, and Smith pulled with him his chief purchasing officer in GM Europe — Lopez. They had led a turnaround at GM Europe by diversifying the supply base and improving distribution. As a result, the old paradigm of relying on suppliers within a radius of 100 miles or so of a manufacturing plant was smashed long before the creation of the European Union, which dramatically accelerated that trend.

Lopez was named vice president for worldwide purchasing in 1992 and launched PICOS (Purchased Input Concept Optimization with Suppliers). Buyers were told to rebid all contracts and come back with at least 10 bids, including a minimum of one from a nondomestic source. Lopez made it clear that internal GM divisions, such as Delco-Remy, would no longer be given

	GM Net Income	Chrysler Net Income
1987	$3,551	$3,713
1988	$4,856	–$2,551
1989	$4,224	$723
1990	–$1,986	–$795
1991	–$4,453	$68
1992	–$23,498	$359
1993	$2,466	$1,050
1994	$4,901	$1,290
1995	$6,881	$2,025
1996	$4,963	$3,529

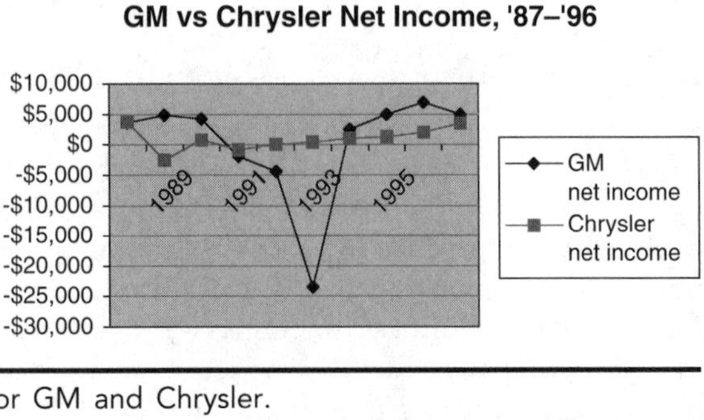

GM vs Chrysler Net Income, '87–'96

Figure 10.1. Net income for GM and Chrysler.

preferential treatment. He decreed "productivity" gains of 50% within three years and wanted cost reductions of 10% and higher. Short-term results were dramatic and impressive. According to one financial analyst's report, Lopez racked up savings of some $300 million in the last three months of 1992. He had to displace a significant amount of supply base, however, to achieve those savings. About one-quarter of the parts bought by GM were being made by different suppliers by spring of 1993 — possibly the most enormous supply base transformation ever made. It was no surprise that GM had significant quality problems in the 1990s. It was not unusual to hear high-quality, technically oriented (and bitter) manufacturers say, "I will no longer sell to Detroit" after the Lopez experience.

"Lopez, at least in these early stages, focused on price, resulting in confrontational relationships with suppliers," commented Professors Michael H. Moffett and William E. Youngdahl of Thunderbird, The Garvin School of International Management, in a paper written to spur classroom discussion. "A common criticism of this focus on price alone is that it cultivates no significant interaction between buyer and supplier and, in many cases, destroys any semblance of cooperation or joint production."[3]

The GM policy triggered a firestorm in the automotive supply community. Many materials and components developers had focused on automotive as an entry market for new technology. It was a time when high-end plastics producers, for example, made huge progress in lightweighting cars through development of composite body panels, synthetic intake manifolds, multi-layer polymer gas tanks, and highly integrated instrument panels. Engineering resin producers such as GE and DuPont invested small fortunes in program development with the hope of locking into a new platform, usually many years out, and building a foundation for expanding applications for a given high-tech material. GE Plastics' Xenoy polycarbonate/polybutylene terephthalate blend, for example, was born in a pioneering effort to use polycarbonate, and later alloys, for car bumpers in Europe.

If General Motors — the 600-pound gorilla of the car business — was now rebidding existing business strictly on price, it meant that years of development effort had to be written off at a loss. Adding insult to injury, some suppliers alleged that Lopez took proprietary process technology and shifted it to other suppliers, including competitors. The model that drove materials technology development in the United States was under attack, as well as the profitability of long-time incumbent suppliers of basic parts.

To say the least, there was definite reluctance by suppliers to participate in new development programs with General Motors. As a result, Lopez's short-term "price wins" were substantially offset by the damage done to the overall product development programs.

The topper came less than a year later when Lopez disclosed that he planned to take a post with Volkswagen in Germany. GM filed a criminal complaint against Lopez claiming that he had stolen confidential GM documents, including detailed pricing data and future product development plans for European models. GM and VW later settled out of court.

Chrysler faced similar financial distress at the end of the 1980s, peaking when the carmaker reported a record loss in 1988. Chrysler suffered from a plethora of problems, including adversarial relationships with an excessively large supply base, but Chrysler's biggest problem may have been poor internal work processes.

In his autobiography, *Guts*, Robert A. Lutz, who became president of Chrysler in 1988, commented:

> I was amazed (and a bit appalled) at the lack of functional integration in the companies I worked for. In particular, I just couldn't understand why there was so little real communication between the operational units of the companies — the design, engineering, manufacturing and procurement organizations.[4]

Chrysler experimented with new management techniques, from brand management to quality circles, but remained an extremely bureaucratic inward-focused organization. As long as Detroit was just competing against itself, the balkanized internal work processes and failure to seek supplier input simply resulted in higher prices, poor quality, and slow product development for American consumers. Introduction of Japanese competition employing a new, and much better, business model exposed poor supply chain practices in Detroit. Chrysler had benchmarked supplier development models used by the fast-rising Honda, but rejected them as too foreign for an American business.

Lutz joined Chrysler in 1986 as executive vice president and moved to president two years later, leading Chrysler's automotive activities in sales, marketing, product development, manufacturing, and procurement — in effect, the whole supply chain plus marketing.

Lutz's "Aha!" moment came with the acquisition of American Motors Corp., which rolled out impressive new Jeep models with a fraction of the engineering staff employed by Chrysler, which was constantly under internal pressure to hire even more engineers. AMC's Chief Engineer Francois Castaing became Chrysler's chief engineer, and he quickly reorganized the department from vertical groups (chassis, body, power train, etc.) to cross-functional teams that approached work on the basis of platforms that developed a whole vehicle.

The "engineering company" began to metamorphose into the "supply chain" company, just as the struggling Harley-Davidson was about to do in Milwaukee (see the discussion in Chapter 1). At both Chrysler and Harley-Davidson, it was chief engineers who realized that engineering-driven development approaches were creating very high-cost products that required enormous technical overhead.

Lutz and Castaing called together new development teams and laid down clear development parameters: target cost, maximum investment timing, and the marketing "sweet spot."

Involvement of procurement was particularly critical at Chrysler, which relied heavily on suppliers. Close to 70% of total vehicle cost derived from purchased components, well ahead of Ford (50%) and GM (30+%) at the time. The role of procurement also grew as Chrysler began to focus more on absolute cost rather than variable cost, that is, studying a platform cost from the ground up rather than component to component, year to year.[5]

Enter Stallkamp, a seminal figure in modern Western procurement. He had joined Chrysler as a purchasing officer in 1980, after serving in various purchasing posts at Ford along with Gene Richter. Always self-effacing, Richter — usually with a broad smile — often called Stallkamp the real rising star of Ford procurement in the 1970s. Stallkamp became vice president of procurement and supply at Chrysler in 1990. He later also assumed general manager positions for car programs, an interesting dual approach that Chrysler continued into the 21st century.

One of Stallkamp's key moves was development of a program called SCORE, for Supplier Cost Reduction Effort. The genesis, of course, was Chrysler's financial distress. The program was announced in 1990 to a group of the company's 150 largest suppliers. Suppliers were asked to submit written proposals that would cut costs. Suppliers had previously submitted such ideas, but found engineering unwilling to take the time or the risk to evaluate them. The carrot was significant: suppliers would receive half the payout from verified savings.

Lutz recalled that the most important aspect of SCORE was the symbiotic relationship between suppliers and Chrysler: "[We] were really both links in the same value-added chain — and that we could demand price cuts from suppliers till the cows came home, but if we didn't work together to get total costs out of our common chain, we'd just be fooling ourselves in the end."[6]

Stallkamp, Castaing, and other high-level executives met monthly and gave all SCORE submissions a thorough review. Engineers resisted, but management insisted that ideas be given a try. Chrysler trod carefully with the supply base, by putting initial focus on its own shortcomings. Then suppliers were asked to suggest how lower tier suppliers could improve their performance. Finally, focus was directed on the products and processes of the prime supplier.[7]

Suppliers were initially skeptical of the new program, recalls P. Jeffrey Trimmer, who was general manager of the Jeep/Truck platform at the time. "You don't wipe away years of confrontation with a new program," he said.

"But as time went on, more and more suppliers signed on as they learned SCORE was a tool not only for meeting the needs of their customers at Chrysler, but it also helped to improve their own bottom line. SCORE in many ways was like a giant locomotive — slow in starting, but gradually building speed and momentum."[8]

Stallkamp said in an industry speech in 1993 that he was "flabbergasted" when an aluminum casting supplier said that Chrysler could save huge amounts — and also enable lightweight cars — by switching from cast metal to injection-molded nylon intake manifolds. Chrysler would have found out in time about the revolutionary materials development undertaken by BASF Corp. in Ludwigshafen, Germany, that resulted in a major switch to synthetics for manifolds over a ten-year period. But because of SCORE, Chrysler was in the game early, using the nylon part on its new Neon subcompact. The savings per car just on that part were $4. "It would have been an almost impossible achievement to realize a $4-per-car savings on this type of item under the old adversarial system of auctioning the business to the lowest bidder," Stallkamp said in a presentation sponsored by trade publication *Automotive News.* Some of the suggestions were unbelievably simple. One supplier noted that a single fastener had two numbers in the Chrysler system. Switching to one number saved $40,000 in administrative costs. Untangling that kind of maddening, unnecessary complexity in supply chains would become a major focal point of supply chain transformation in 2004–2005. It was not a small problem.

Chrysler made SCORE part of its formal supplier rating process, recording total number of ideas and dollars of savings generated. Future business awards were based in part on performance ratings. Suppliers could boost their rating if they kept less than half the award. One major supplier, Magna, gave 100% of its SCORE savings back to Chrysler and more than doubled its sales to the carmaker in the early 1990s.

Another perspective on SCORE comes from Trimmer of the Jeep/Truck platform: "We had been assigned massive cost reduction tasks on our various new product programs, which we had no idea how to accomplish. Normally on automotive programs, what you do is line up a bunch of cars and look for things you can strip off the cars — a process we all hated. I remember talking to Francois Castaing about this, and he assured me that Stallkamp's SCORE program would enable us to achieve our tasks. He was absolutely right, and the fact that virtually all of Chrysler's new product programs of the 1990s came in under budget was a major tribute to the SCORE program success."

Cost reductions achieved through SCORE were expected to reach 5% of total business. The original target of 3% had been reached easily. "It wasn't clear if we could reach those levels of cost reductions, but economic conditions and global competition demanded that we try," Stallkamp recalled.[9] The program was later extended to lightweighting, warranty issues, and supply chain complexity.[10]

Lutz, who later assumed an executive position at GM, commented: "All told, Tom Stallkamp's SCORE program saved Chrysler more than $5 billion between 1989 and 1998 — which, I suspect, is one of the big reasons why, in 1997, he ended up succeeding me as president of the company!"[11]

Asked why SCORE became such an overnight sensation, Stallkamp much later recalled: "It was a combination of things. One was that it made Chrysler different from everybody else and suppliers liked the different approach. But primarily because it was a win-win for the supplier and the OEM and it made suppliers feel like they were not only a partner but that they were gaining something — recognition and business. It improved supplier relations while it reduced our cost at the same time."[12]

The real importance, however, of the new approach at Chrysler, Stallkamp emphasized, was not cutting costs on existing programs. It was about creating a different approach to suppliers in new product development. "Basically, SCORE is a collaboration technique," Stallkamp said more than four years after he left Chrysler.

Chrysler dramatically winnowed its supply base and reached out to certain companies to participate in new car design. It was an application of the same principle that Richter had advocated: suppliers know much more about their technologies than any customers possibly could. And in a trend that was still developing in the 21st century at premier companies such as Procter & Gamble, no company could possibly retain enough engineering and research staff to introduce all of the new technology required to be globally competitive.

Chrysler trademarked its process the "Extended Enterprise." P&G later called its somewhat different approach "Connect & Develop" (see further details in Chapter 11). There were six major elements of the Extended Enterprise approach at Chrysler. First was a centralized, fully integrated procurement organization. Second was a focus on long-term relationships with suppliers. Third was development of strategies through use of cross-functional teams. Fourth was a comprehensive (not price-focused) approach to costs that included management of material economics as well as SCORE. Fifth was supplier development, a concept not well developed by American companies (John Deere was an exception). Sixth was the leveraging of supplier technology.

Borrowing from the Honda approach, Chrysler invited supplier engineers to become residents in Chrysler's own technical facilities. Suppliers, given the choice between the GM and Chrysler approaches, anxiously participated, eager to promote the collaboration model.

One of the most spectacular applications of the idea — then and to this day — was in the Viper development. The Viper was one of the hottest and most fun cars ever developed.

Like most American sports car enthusiasts, Bob Lutz was a great fan of the Cobra developed by Carroll Shelby in cooperation with Ford Motor Co. in the 1960s. It was beautiful and it was fast. And it was different from the stale kind of cars that Chrysler had been losing money on. Shelby was already on board as a consultant at Chrysler, so Lutz asked his engineering and design chiefs to sketch out a cool car for Chrysler. It certainly wasn't an idea hatched by the money guys; American carmakers love to promenade beautiful concept cars at their annual beauty contest, the Detroit Auto Show. To Lutz, the Viper was a personal kick and an opportunity to put a different shade of makeup on the old gray lady.

Lutz initially didn't like the design concept for the Viper because it didn't look like the Cobra. That quickly faded, however, because the Viper was a beautiful car.

And then, he recalls: "Much to the chagrin of the guardians of Chrysler's purse, we proceeded to explore the possibility of actually manufacturing the car."[13] Dodge's blue-collar clientele, long treated to the likes of the very functional but uninspiring Dart, were about to get blown away.

The "guardians of the purse" fought the project, but executive management finally relented, giving Lutz's development team just $80 million — chump change for a whole new development program in Detroit. As a result, Stallkamp's buyers had to go to the supply base and ask them to perform core engineering for the project — a novel concept for Chrysler, but not so new for its recently acquired Jeep division. Most suppliers were eager to participate, but a few declined, citing the low volume potential for a high-priced sporty car.

One of the first major design decisions was to go with composite body panels, which had debuted in another stunning American sports car, the Chevrolet Corvette, in 1955. Composites technology was still very much in the developmental stage at that time. And here came the Viper team, with virtually no development budget.

Teams of suppliers were asked to collaborate to solve problems that crossed corporate and technology barriers. For example, companies that provided adhesives met for the first time with companies that provided complementary products such as fiberglass to discuss how their products could be modified to achieve better end results. In some senses, the companies were competitive and previously had never collaborated on mutual technical problems. The result was breakthrough technology on the Viper that improved production efficiency and quality. In one other innovative approach on the Viper, Chrysler put tool development in the hands of the suppliers.

Detroit always had owned the molds and put them "on wheels" whenever it wanted a lower price from another molder.

A momentous advantage resulting from the new approach at Chrysler was a colossal cutback in new product development time.

Meanwhile, GM was trying to dig out from the Lopez debacle. In a 1997 article titled "Ghost of Lopez Still Haunts Auto Suppliers," the *Business Journal-Milwaukee* detailed problems that lingered in supplier relations. And Bo I. Andersson was still trying to solve the quality problem when he replaced Harold Kutner as GM's vice president of worldwide purchasing, production control and logistics on December 1, 2001. He said his single biggest issue was resolving quality problems between supply chain partners in Detroit's complicated multitier sourcing system.[14]

One of this book's authors encountered an example of the lingering Lopez legacy in the late 1990s. At an otherwise relaxing get-to-know-you dinner meeting with the CEO of a major supplier, the subject of different "procurement styles" came up. When Lopez's name was mentioned, the supplier CEO became very still, turned red, and about 30 seconds later made a one-sentence statement that seemed to summarize the long-term damage done by Lopez: "I am still looking for ways to get even with GM." This was after Lopez had left GM. To every CEO who is tempted to try a short-term, confrontational style with suppliers, we ask you to think about this example. Do you really want suppliers to be lying in the grass, waiting for an opportunity to "get even"?

Most purchasing professionals certainly disdained the tactics used by Lopez, in terms of both results and business ethics. In a few ways, however, his impact could be framed in a positive light:

1. He forcefully put the spotlight on the importance of supply management just as this was becoming apparent in boardrooms across the Western world.
2. The door opened for nondomestic suppliers under Lopez, another trend in its infancy in 1992, particularly at highly integrated General Motors. Lopez had developed his worldwide purchasing plan in Europe and then implemented the same idea in North America.
3. The GM supply base — out of control at more than 20,000 — was trimmed.
4. He promoted further internal integration at GM, which had also moved to platform teams, but he had little chance to reap much success in a nine-month time frame.

Lopez has had supporters. GE's Jack Welch was previously mentioned. In the book *Supply Chain Redesign* published in 2002, Professors Robert B.

Handfield of North Carolina State University and Ernest L. Nichols, Jr. of the University of Memphis wrote: "By creating an internal culture focused on driving improved internal integration among purchasing, engineering, logistics and operations, Lopez helped turn around a company on the verge of collapse."[15]

Certainly if Lopez had had more time and not subsequently been charged with racketeering by GM, he probably would be remembered in a better light. Stallkamp's legacy was short-lived. His successor, Tom Sidlik, who had been a finance officer in the 1990s, replaced SCORE in 2001 with a program called Material Cost Management (MCM). "Phase One was a mandatory 5% supplier cost reduction, which single-handedly destroyed Chrysler's supplier relations," recalls Trimmer, who had become director, operations and strategy for the Chrysler Group procurement and supply organization. The 5% across-the-board price reduction mandate was a page Sidlik had taken from a Ford action in 1990 that Stallkamp and Lutz had refused to follow. The new MCM program also included an aggressive cross-functional program that was hampered because supplier relations were so badly damaged by Phase One.

The MCM is an example of significant mistakes in supply management that major companies continue to make.

"I think they try to overcontrol and they use the leverage that they have in an old-fashioned, arbitrary way rather than attempt to build relationships," says Stallkamp. "You can still have a lot of leverage, but you can use that leverage with collaboration. Right now, most companies are not trying to build true relationships. Most big manufacturers are not seeing their suppliers as part of the team. They're treating them like servants or subordinates."[16]

In this context of supplier distrust of Detroit purchasing practices, the Big Three (now more appropriately called the Detroit Three) launched an industry procurement exchange in 2000 called Covisint. Championed in particular by GM's Kutner, Covisint was viewed by GM, Ford, and Chrysler as an opportunity to standardize on electronic sourcing initiatives and corral the combined purchasing power of the automotive original equipment manufacturers. GM's Andersson expected in 2001 to move $25 billion of GM's total spend of $90 billion to Covisint.

From the beginning, Stallkamp, who had become CEO of MSX International, was critical of the exchange. He said it wouldn't work because of supplier mistrust. That was surely the biggest problem. It was viewed as three 600-pound gorillas morphed into a *Tyrannosaurus rex*.

Reverse auctions became the focal point of seething supplier unhappiness. Jim DiGiacinto, who headed Bethlehem Steel's sales to the automotive market at the time, comments: "Covisint started with the promise and the hope that the world of high technology was finally coming to the smokestack industry, and what it turned out to be was nothing more than a point of leverage that absolutely destroyed value. I can't say that strongly enough."[17] DiGiacinto makes a forceful case that Covisint's application of reverse auctions destroyed meaningful differentiations between suppliers that had been carefully cultivated by skilled purchasing professionals and suppliers aiming for long-term relationships.

Suppliers also suspected that price confidentiality with specific customers would be compromised. And then Kutner upset several Tier Ones and Twos when he announced initiatives to extend communication portals to their customers. Many had already made substantial investments in their own systems. Besides, they wanted to maintain control of their own communication pipelines with their supply base. They realized that those relationships were their most important competitive weapon. Covisint also had to battle the massive internal bureaucracies of its founding members, who were protecting turf and jobs. Setting common electronic standards and protocol was an important mission, but even that effort flagged. Covisint burned through four CEOs in 25 months before key assets were sold.

The American automotive giants could have improved efficiencies and quality through a successful electronic supplier-facing platform. But Covisint never had a chance because of the underlying confrontational posture toward suppliers.

The essential difference between Stallkamp and Lopez was treatment of suppliers. Are they fungible commodities that can be treated like interchangeable parts on an assembly line? Is there any inherent value in long-term relationships? Can suppliers and their customers mutually develop technology and reap the benefits in a fair and structured way? Are there enormous benefits that accrue from that type of approach?

We feel that the Stallkamp-Richter approach of cultivating supplier partnerships yields the best long-term results and may in fact be a company's strongest competitive weapon in the global war of supply chains.

Addendum

Jeff Trimmer became chairman of a trade group called The National Initiative for Supply Chain Integration that espoused the value of collaboration but failed to gain traction and disbanded. He is now retired and teaches the SCORE approach as a Batten Fellow at the University of Virginia's Darden School.

Tom Stallkamp fell out with the new German ownership of Chrysler and became CEO of MSX International, a Detroit-based company that focuses on outsourcing of engineering and other services. He left MSXI in 2004 and wrote a book with Wharton School Publishing called *SCORE!: A Better Way to Do Busine$$: Moving from Conflict to Collaboration.*

Jose Ignacio Lopez became a textbook figure in the study of industrial espionage. He was forced to resign from VW and attempted unsuccessfully to launch an auto company in the Basque region of Spain. German and American authorities filed charges again Lopez in connection with the GM/VW debacle. Lopez fought extradition to the United States on grounds that he had suffered brain damage in an auto accident in early 1999.

11

Consumer Products

Procter & Gamble

We're driving a cost-reduction and cash-improvement mindset deeper into the Company with clearer reporting structures, clearer account- ability and the disciplined use of Total Shareholder return at the business unit level.

—A.G. Lafley, Chairman of the Board,
President, and Chief Executive,
in the 2004 P&G Annual Report

Entering 2005, two of America's giant consumer products companies — Procter & Gamble and Colgate-Palmolive — confronted similar pressures but recorded significantly different results. Both companies were squeezed by a rapid run-up in raw material costs in the face of growing inability to control their own pricing as the purchasing clout of big-box retailers grew. Both companies also faced global battles to build market share for their marquee brands.

The investors' channel on Colgate-Palmolive's corporate Web site at the end of 2004 proudly showed the company's 20-year record of outstanding stock performance through December 31, 2003: a 2995% return versus 2270% for its peer group and 1048% for the S&P 500. But 2004 was a different story. Its stock price peaked at around $59 a share in midyear and then plunged to under $44 in mid-October — a 25% decline. Most of the drop came immediately after Colgate-Palmolive issued an earnings warning on Septem- ber 20: per-share earnings would be in the range of 57 to 59 cents for both the third and fourth quarters of 2004. Analysts had been forecasting per-share earnings of 64 to 69 cents in the third quarter and 66 to 71 cents in the fourth quarter. Analysts hate surprises. The sharp plunge in Colgate-Palmolive's stock price that ensued may have been somewhat of an overreaction. After all, Colgate-Palmolive still had an excellent chance to match record gross profits reached in 2003 even after the combined effect of increased spending for marketing and higher costs for plastics, chemicals, metals, and other products.

On December 7, the other shoe dropped. Chairman and CEO Reuben Mark announced a dramatic cost improvement program:

◆ Approximately one-third of Colgate-Palmolive's factories across the world would be closed over a four-year period. "Finished products for the 223 countries in which Colgate does business would be sourced from fewer, more sophisticated global and regional state-of-the-art manufacturing centers," according to a press release announcing the closures.

◆ All purchasing, from office supplies to media, would be centralized on a global basis, completing a transformation already made for major materials.

◆ Business support functions located in the subsidiaries, and not dependent on local expertise, would be centralized.

◆ Emphasis on innovation would be increased.

◆ Sales and marketing would be consolidated and beefed up.

◆ Effectiveness of global advertising would be improved through new global systems that capitalize on newly developed sales and marketing tools utilizing SAP software. "These mechanisms, which enable an integration of the supply and demand chains, are now in test overseas and will be expanded more broadly beginning in 2005," said Mark in the press release.

◆ The workforce would be reduced by approximately 12% from the level of 37,000.

Other consumer products giants had their own woes. Highly decentralized Unilever reported revenues similar to P&G, but only half the net income in the 2003–2004 time frame. Unilever had more than twice as many employees as P&G. Global initiatives were fought by powerful national product management. Coke and Kraft also struggled to innovate.

Meanwhile, Procter & Gamble was riding a wave of investor support based on a transformation and reorganization that had begun just before A.G. Lafley became chief executive in 2000. P&G's stock price at the end of 2004 was double what it had been when Lafley took over. Cumulative sales growth from 2001 to 2004 was more than 30% — the equivalent of adding a Nike or a Sun Microsystems to its top line. Its brands had a track record of growing market share in recent years. Its position was particularly strong in the huge developing countries — the giant prize eyed by all the consumer products companies. Entering 2005, P&G was number one in consumer packaged goods in Russia and China.

P&G had become the quiet giant that could — and did. The reasons for its success were, of course, broad-based. An important component was a surprising and low-key story of supply chain creativity that not only delivered lower costs but, more importantly, dramatically increased access to external technology. The P&G story is important because it did not involve razzle-dazzle or enormous investments in purchasing. It was based on solid implementation of fundamentals that we espouse in this book. The P&G transformation is also important because the company is built around strong divisions and has a conservative culture.

P&G created a Global Product Supply organization in the late 1980s and built a supply chain organization that included purchasing, manufacturing, engineering, and logistics. Purchases was organized on a global basis in 1992, even before P&G's giant business units (such as Baby Care and Beauty Care) were organized globally. Purchases staff members were embedded in the global business units, allowing a close alignment with business goals.

Supply management is a corporate priority at P&G because it impacts about 55% of the company's total revenue stream. In some business units, purchasing accounts for close to 70% of total delivered product costs. A 5% improvement in costs translates into a 20+% improvement in profits. Accordingly, virtually 100% of external spend, including advertising, legal expenses, and consulting, is supervised by Purchases professionals. Purchasing is one of the strategies listed in the P&G OGSM (Objectives-Goals-Strategies-Measures). Specific goals in areas such as innovation are set for purchasing, and subsequently they are measured and reviewed in regular meetings. As a result, Richard A. Hughes, vice president of Global Purchases, has regular access to Lafley. Purchasing leaders at P&G also participate in the Global Business Services Organization that manages accounts payable, employee services, information technology support, and other business services used within the company. When parts of those services are outsourced, purchasing people are in charge.

Purchasing at P&G has evolved in the stages indicated in Table 11.1. P&G did it the old-fashioned way, building a foundation framed in principles, skill development, and supplier relationships. Then, as businesses went through reorganizations and went global in the 1990s to build market share in developing countries, purchasing strategies were a match, including sourcing in low-income markets.

Supply management at P&G is effective because all of the fundamentals, including those established in phase one in the early 1980s, are excellent: organization, education, stewardship, and supplier relationships. Purchases

Table 11.1. Evolution of P&G Purchasing

Phase One: Foundation 1964-1984	Phase Two: Transforming the Enterprise 1984-1991	Phase Three: Globalization 1991-1999	Phase Four: E-business 1999-2001	Phase Five: Link and Leverage 2002-
♦ Organization ♦ Skill development ♦ Leverage ♦ Supplier relationships ♦ Spend identification ♦ Business growth	♦ Product supply ♦ Decentralization ♦ Common work processes ♦ Governance ♦ Measurements and tracking	♦ Linkage across regions ♦ Efficiency ♦ Effectiveness ♦ Integrated organizations ♦ Global scale ♦ Low-income-market sourcing	♦ E-linkages ♦ Reverse auctions ♦ Web-based anything ♦ Online collaboration ♦ Monetization of intellectual property ♦ Trading exchanges	♦ Enterprise-wide spend pool management ♦ Visible commitment/involvement of high-level executives in supplier base ♦ Single coordinated and integrated face and voice to suppliers ♦ Work and results are business (and market) oriented ♦ Manage suppliers' innovation resources across business units ♦ Integrated supply chain and value chain approach

Source: P&G

evolved as P&G's business units evolved and then went global. In the dot-com boom, P&G moved cautiously to implement electronic technologies. Today, it is a leader in optimization and, most importantly, innovation.

Lafley wants half of the innovation at P&G to come from outside the company. That's up from about 20% in 2000. Chief Technology Officer G. Gilbert Cloyd launched a program called Connect & Develop to boost access to innovation from outside sources. One of his captains, Nabil Sakkab, senior vice president of research and development in the Fabric and Home Care division, explains: "P&G's R&D department used to be like the Kremlin. Now we're more like the Acropolis — all ideas are welcome and get a fair hearing...The cost of R&D grows faster than sales and this is unsustainable. Big ideas are no longer the exclusive domain of big R&D departments — up to 30% of patents are now filed by small companies and entrepreneurs. Today's ideas are widely dispersed — and the Internet makes them easier to share or find. The future of R&D is C&D — collaborative networks that are in touch with 90% of research that we don't do ourselves."[1]

P&G's reach to outside sources is particularly interesting because it has been an R&D powerhouse of long standing. At the time of Sakkab's comments in 2002, P&G was investing close to $2 billion annually on R&D. Lafley assured that there would be no cutbacks in P&G R&D as Connect & Develop blossomed; it was a sincere effort to develop new ideas.

One of P&G's first steps was to make sure that technology ideas were being shared internally. The company created more than 20 "communities of practice" to bring scientists with similar experiences together in areas such as polymers to encourage transfer of knowledge from one business area to another. One of the devices to attract outside ideas was the creation of a Web site where technical problems were posed, such as how to make a molecule that can do X.

The most important linkage, however, was through business partners with the only supplier-facing function in the company: purchasing. P&G scientists and commercial professionals now work together as co-equals on product development teams. They speak with one voice to the external community.

"We have a totally seamless R&D and purchasing organization with one agenda: the best value to the company, to our customers," says Ghobad Rahrooh, director of R&D for the Global Baby Care unit at P&G. Material Leadership Teams are organized by platform; each is co-led by a technical and purchasing staff member. "They have joint responsibility for the material globally across the board. The Material Leadership Team is a single point of accountability across the globe. This is a tremendous contrast to what we did when each region had a contact person. We were getting a worse deal then because suppliers were playing purchasing and R&D people against each other. Whatever material we are developing now is better, faster, and less expensive than it was before."

David Zint, who supervises purchasing for resins in North America and is also associate director of packaging in the Global Fabric and Home Care business unit, adds: "Typically, a buyer will talk to an R&D person several times a week if not several times a day." Purchasing professionals become involved in new product development at the earliest possible stage. Suppliers' technical staff often work at P&G sites, and some P&G staff work at supplier sites. Terms of how each party benefits are spelled out in detail in advance in master agreements. Suppliers can use the technology in noncompetitive products, an approach that allows them to build scale and lower costs for P&G.

One key collaborator is BASF Chemicals in Ludwigshafen, Germany, which developed a critical foam ingredient that allowed P&G to develop Mr. Clean Magic Eraser, which takes marks off walls. A supplier also developed a highly absorbent acrylic acid derivative powder that can be embedded in baby diapers. Other recent-vintage P&G products that relied heavily on outside technology contributions include Olay Regenerist, an anti-aging cream; Spinbrush, a battery-powered toothbrush; and Swiffer Duster, a microfiber picker-upper.

Innovation ideas are featured in poster sessions that are open to all employees and must-attends for business leaders. Six corporate cost innovation awards are given annually for the best projects.

Technical and commercial professionals at P&G also collaborate on development of more universal performance specifications. "We have about 300,000 to 400,000 specifications at Procter & Gamble," says Dennis Begg, an IT guy who is associate director for innovation in corporate purchases. "We have begun to think about how we can rationalize our spend pools through specifications." A team was named to determine the essential steps and work processes, with the first look at packaging, paper, and plastic. "The idea here is how can we move from proprietary P&G specs to broader industry standard performance-based specs. This is a collaborative effort with our suppliers," Begg explained. Previously, P&G had 20 specifications for water and more than 15 global specifications for low-density polyethylene shrink-wrap. Now it has one and three, respectively.

Best-in-class organizations are striving to reduce supply chain complexity through specifications management. It is one of the toughest jobs in a supply transformation because engineers jealously guard the technical turf. For some companies, it's the last bastion of silo operations. The benefits are enormous: (1) spend pool leverage is greatly expanded; (2) it is easier to find backup suppliers if a source falls through; (3) inventories can be significantly reduced, freeing capital and space; (4) unused product can be transferred more easily internally or sold for a higher value if markets crash; and (5) testing costs can be cut dramatically. Flexible specifications also greatly enhance the potential value of electronic sourcing tools. Introduction of electronic catalogues was a logistical nightmare because companies, on the buy and sell side, were bogged down in swamps of proprietary specifications.

P&G was slow to move into electronic sourcing tools, in part because of its generally conservative nature and partly because of its "not-invented-here" cultural bias at that time. But Lafley also wanted innovation within the purchasing department. Given all of the fits and starts in the dot-com bust, P&G's initial conservatism may have been wise, but it may have been more a case of being lucky than being smart. Pushed by goals to develop innovation, P&G's purchasing department developed some capability in electronic market making through automated bids. "At that time, we were throwing things against the wall and seeing what stuck," comments Begg, who became the architect of supply management innovation through a master plan to accelerate innovation and drive cost savings that flow all the way through payment and replenishment. In purchasing, it's all about linking to the supply base.

At the heart of P&G's Purchases e-systems plan is Navigator, a tool to view and manage all of the interactions. Most companies call this a dashboard or a cockpit, but the former is getting to be a cliché and the latter didn't translate well to third-world nations. P&G puts its electronic Purchases systems into four buckets: quotes and proposals, specifications, transactions, and planning. The fact that specifications is in a bucket shows the sophistication of the P&G approach. Navigator links together contracts with strategic sourcing with leverage goals and so on. The tools fit into the overall plan. And the tools are a big part of the story at P&G.

The company uses online reverse auctions as part of its electronic sourcing portfolio, but relies more heavily on a much more advanced electronic sourcing tool: combinatorial expressive bidding, which is part of a class called optimization technology or decision-support tools. It is a dramatic example of how advanced math and computer modeling can revolutionize supply management.

The tool used by P&G was developed by CombineNet, a company founded in 2000 in Pittsburgh, Pennsylvania, by Dr. Tuomas Sandholm, an associate professor of computer science at Carnegie Mellon University with more than 12 years of experience in building e-commerce systems. Called the REV Profit Accelerator, the CombineNet tool uses advanced mathematical algorithms to very quickly analyze unlimited business constraints and what-if scenarios. P&G uses the tool to allow suppliers to creatively develop bids that make most efficient use of their production capabilities. Normally, purchasing departments would organize bids into predetermined lot sizes. The problem is that buyers often force suppliers into unnecessary constraints. Specified bundling probably does not recognize how suppliers make and palletize their products. With the expressive bidding tool, suppliers might, for instance, say (or "express" themselves), "Give me at least 75% of lot X and at least 35% of lot Y and I can offer you savings of 20%." The Internet makes the process lightning fast. The tool is most effective on logistics because it allows haulers to combine loads or arrange backhauls based on other business. Buying teams can then study the offers and determine where they can give a little and save a lot. P&G saved more than $300 million with expressive bidding in 2003–2004.

The expressive bidding tool is forcing a lot of discussion about what is really important. It was a given for the last 10 to 15 years that just-in-time (JIT) delivery was a great virtue. Expressive bidding is showing that the cost to the supplier to achieve JIT may at times be greater than the benefit to the customer. When suppliers have the option to transport based on their supply chain efficiencies, they may deliver savings that far outweigh an extra inventory and logistics cost at the customer. "When business leaders understand what the costs are of some of their requirements, they will often go back and change some of their parameters," Begg comments. Until expressive bidding, there was no systematic way of understanding those costs or studying the options.

Returning to one of the central themes of this book, professionals who strictly view the world from a purchasing point of view tend to be piece-part cost focused. Individuals who wear "supply chain" hats are focused on inventory costs; logistics professionals are focused on delivery costs. *The point of advanced supply management is to view costs in terms of their total impact on the enterprise in a strategic manner. Technology tools are important not only because of their analytical capabilities but because they force new ways of thinking.*

The downside of expressive bids is that analysis can be time consuming. Suppliers have come back with as many as 200 types of expressive offers in the P&G experience. It takes a while to convert apples to apples, narrow the list of the options, and then review alternative scenarios with business and technical stakeholders. But everyone knows that Lafley cares and will be reviewing progress toward goals with Rick Hughes and his boss Keith Harrison, Global Product Supply officer. Switching suppliers can be costly and time consuming. The lag time between project savings and actually realized savings can run six to nine months. One of the current goals at P&G is to reduce that lag time. The other issue is that expressive bidding is a very sharp knife. If used expertly, it is extremely effective. Used poorly, as Begg says, "it can also cut off your arm."

For bid events that do not require algorithms, P&G often goes to market with reverse auctions through software provider Procuri. In the 2004 fiscal year, P&G went to market through reverse auctions for an amount approaching 10% of its total spend.

The technology tools, particularly those involving expressive bidding, help leverage across business units. Building spend leverage across divisions and business units is a critical component of a supply transformation. Some of the company's best work has come in building leverage for indirect categories. One of the biggest scores has come in management of the media and marketing spends, areas traditionally outside the realm of strategic sourcing and professional purchasing overview.

P&G's global marketing officer asked purchasing to analyze compensation structures for advertising agencies. P&G is one of the top marketing spenders in the world, with an outlay of more than $5 billion annually. Traditional rate structures used by agencies disadvantage the biggest spenders because they charge a commission based on dollars spent. Generally, very big spenders should be able to highly leverage their clout.

Also, the incentives were wrong. The agencies have an incentive to do as much television advertising as possible, possibly ignoring opportunities to conduct other marketing that do not pay as well. "We needed to incentivize them to do better marketing, not necessarily to just do more TV," comments Gerry Preece, director of marketing purchases in North America for P&G. Preece began an analysis from scratch, using a strategic sourcing framework. "We needed to be very clear about the basis, such as: what kind of a relationship did we want to have with the agencies? Some people would say they want a very competitive relationship and others would say we've been dealing with these agencies for 80 years. Our approach was very inconsistent."

The first step was development of a relationship and then an appropriate alignment (or role), then definition of specific deliverables and measurement of those deliverables, and then finally, appropriate compensation structure. "We want behaviors to become predictable," says Preece. "That's the right way to manage a supplier." This approach moved beyond the advertising agencies to 16 other marketing categories, such as the media companies and design agencies. Hughes is studying where the strategic sourcing approach can next be applied. Consulting services is already under way.

Leverage is significant and growing in cross-unit strategic products. Companies such as P&G tend not to force compliance on strategic products, but rather create conditions so advantageous that business leaders are anxious to participate. About two years after launching the expressive bidding tool, Begg's team had trouble keeping up with the demand for its use.

When considering a supply transformation, it is essential that all of the fundamentals are in place. Just tacking strategic sourcing or expressive bidding on top of a poorly structured supply approach is a good way to waste money and create extreme frustration.

P&G's Corporate Purchases department maintains a solid approach in education and stewardship to make sure all the pieces fit together throughout the $51 billion global enterprise. Purchasing at P&G is based on five core principles. They revolve around issues such as valuing competition, honest and ethical treatment of suppliers, incumbency, and total value. These and other fundamentals are taught at P&G's Purchases University, which all purchasing employees are required to attend. One significant component is the Sourcing College, which includes courses on stewardship, strategy development, relationship management, execution, and systems and has one course on specific e-tool training. Lisa Cooley, associate director, Skills Mastery, runs the university and makes sure all regions participate.

Training, stewardship, and measurement are coordinated through the Corporate Purchases department, made up of just 28 people. The 1400-plus line purchasing people work in the business units and have a reporting relationship to Rick Hughes. It is a vivid demonstration that the hybrid decentralized model can be extremely effective. One reason it works so well at P&G is because A.G. Lafley understands the role of sourcing, sets goals, and measures performance across the entire organization.

Opportunities to create cost synergies were one of the big drivers behind P&G's proposed acquisition of Gillette, announced in early 2005. The deal was projected to generate $14 billion to $16 billion in incremental shareholder value, with $10 billion to $11 billion coming from the cost side. "We see opportunities in purchasing, manufacturing, and logistics through increased scale, improved asset utilization, and coordination of procurement," commented Clayt Daley, P&G's chief financial officer, in a presentation to investment analysts. The fact that both companies had already made major steps to improve the cost side of their businesses meant that savings could be achieved more quickly.

Bottom line: Supply transformation translates into significant shareholder value.

12

Aerospace
and Industrial
United Technologies Corp.

---

*With each GM division held responsible for its own performance,
common sense dictated that its officers must have full authority over
the tools and materials required to discharge that responsibility.*

—U.S. Navy Rear Admiral William Adger Moffet,
defending the concept of
decentralized procurement in 1925

In 1925, the Pratt & Whitney Aircraft Co. was registered in Delaware. From
the very beginning, it was a company dedicated to the proposition of decentralized procurement. There was a good reason: its very existence depended
upon it.

In the mid-1920s, the U.S. Navy was eager to develop an air-cooled
aircraft engine that would enable lighter, more maneuverable planes than the
water-cooled engines widely in use. Rear Admiral William Adger Moffet, the
founder and first chief of the Navy Bureau of Aeronautics, gave a conditional
thumbs-up to development of the pioneering engine to two aviation entrepreneurs: Frederick Rentschler and George Jackson Mead, an MIT grad who
already had experience with air cooling. Rentschler and Mead approached the
owners of Pratt & Whitney, a machine tool company in Hartford, Connecticut, co-founded in 1860 by a cousin of Eli Whitney. Pratt & Whitney had
boomed during World War I, but was anxious for a new revenue source in

1925. It had what Rentschler and Mead needed: capital, experienced tool workers, and idle capacity.

The rub was that Brig. Gen. William Mitchell, assistant chief, U.S. Army Air Service, attacked naval aviation and supported unified procurement of equipment through a U.S. air ministry, which he hoped to control. The Army had no size constraints for its aircraft and was fine with continued development of the water-cooled engine. Naval aviation was in its infancy in 1925 — and much of its immediate technical future was in the imagination of Rentschler and Mead.

Admiral Moffet told government oversight boards that competition between the services was healthy, and exhibit A was the proposed development of the air-cooled engine at Pratt & Whitney. After all, he contended, even General Motors did not pursue unified procurement in 1925. The reason: enhanced competition between the brands. "With each GM division held responsible for its own performance, common sense dictated that its officers must have full authority over the tools and materials required to discharge that responsibility," Admiral Moffet told a group of New York aviation writers at a dinner party at the Waldorf Hotel.[1]

Moffet won the day: Congress passed the Air Corps Act of 1926, which paved the way for separate aircraft development programs by the Army, the Navy, and the U.S. Postal Service. Pratt & Whitney got the green light to develop its engine. Soon a 425-horsepower-rated *air-cooled* engine was tested in a Wright Aeronautical Apache plane. The fully equipped new plane weighed 300 pounds less than its water-cooled-engine equivalent. "This weight saving meant swifter rate of climb, higher ceiling, shorter turning radius and slower landing speed — all with equal top speed," recalled Cary Hoge Mead in a book about her husband's work on the engine.[2] Congress approved a naval procurement budget that allowed Moffett to order 200 Pratt & Whitney air-cooled engines, called Wasps.

More than 75 years later, unified procurement became a topic of discussion at United Technologies Corp., the company that acquired Pratt & Whitney as well as other strong technology-driven manufacturers, including Otis elevators, Sikorsky helicopters, Hamilton-Sundstrand aerospace and industrial systems, Carrier air conditioning, and Chubb fire protection systems. It had sales of $37 billion in 2004, putting it among the top 25 American manufacturers.

Management disciple George David assumed the CEO post of UTC in 1994 and emphasized improved process as opposed to technology development as the surer path to productivity improvement. Unlike other modern CEOs who disdained the industrial conglomerate format, he embraced it and plumbed for strengths in their manufacturing commonalities. One of his favorite programs was a Japanese-inspired quality approach called ACE, for

Achieving Competitive Excellence. ACE is a systematic analysis of production systems that focuses on line workers.

David was well aware of the power of the cost-driven automotive purchasing giants. He sought to sell UTC's automotive business (and did so in 1999) and was eager to achieve efficiencies in purchasing. The first step was appointment of Kent L. Brittan as vice president of supply management in 1996. Brittan had been chief financial officer at Otis Elevator and had a clear mandate from the CEO to seek efficiencies on the supply side.

One of Brittan's first impulses was to eschew the concept of "purchasing." "The word purchasing or procurement does not really describe what we do," he said. "It's one element. But quite frankly my job is to think about the future and give direction to the company. I interface with a lot of people in this company including engineering, manufacturing and quality. And because of UT500 [an initiative focusing on general procurement], I interface with division presidents on a regular basis. The word purchasing itself is an important element of what we do. Obviously the words supply management and supply chain management much better describe the function."

For the first four years that Brittan served as UTC's chief procurement officer, his focus was very much on cost reduction. He had an open mind and looked for innovative solutions to old problems. One of his first moves was appointment of Shelley Stewart, Jr. as director of worldwide sourcing. Stewart, one of the co-authors of this book, had been vice president of purchasing at Hamilton Standard (now Hamilton Sundstrand). Brittan made major commitments to two new ideas that put UTC in the forefront of the just-emerging world of online procurement. One was Internet reverse auctions and the second was outtasking of tactical functions of general procurement.

Brittan was one of the first customers of FreeMarkets, which was founded in 1995 by Glen Meakem and Sam Kinney to launch a bidding technology over a private network. That was even before Netscape went public. The FreeMarkets technology moved to the Internet quickly. Brittan saw the opportunity and received immediate executive support. UTC even invested in FreeMarkets.

"My management loves FreeMarkets," said Brittan. "Online auctions became a tremendous marketing tool (for supply management) to line management. I haven't fully analyzed all of the psychological reasons for that, but I think it's because of the speed with which results are obtained. There is a feeling that they finally got the purchasing department to do what they wanted them to do. Line management loves the clarity with which savings are produced. And the savings are significant."

From 1996 through 2001, UTC sourced more than $2.5 billion in goods and services through FreeMarkets and achieved annual savings of more than 18%. "United Technologies has revolutionized the way sourcing is done through the use of innovative technologies," said FreeMarkets CEO Meakem in a 2001 press release. UTC was FreeMarkets' biggest customer, accounting for 34% of revenue in 1999. General Motors was second at 10%. The rest of American manufacturing moved dramatically into reverse auctions in 2000–2002 as costs to administer the auctions dropped and industrial markets, weakened by the events of September 11, were ripe for competitive bidding technology.

When a company begins a supply management transformation process, one of the first steps is establishment of strategic sourcing with a focus on leverage and cross-division commodity teams. UTC presented a particular challenge because of the strength of its divisions and its history of decentralization. Brittan established councils to tackle the low-hanging fruit: office supplies, production (maintenance, repair, and operating) supplies, information technology, energy, and travel. Compliance to corporate contracts, however, was a major problem.

The biggest issue was lack of a corporate system to monitor spending. Brittan began a benchmarking process and quickly hooked up with Gene Richter, who started to engineer corporate data systems when he became IBM's chief procurement officer in 1994. Anxious to jump-start his implementation, Brittan asked Richter if he could buy IBM's system. Richter said no, but discussed the idea with other IBM officials when he returned to Somers, New York. A few weeks later, the answer came back yes. IBM was morphing into a services company, and procurement services offered a growing opportunity.

IBM proposed an agreement that encompassed strategic sourcing consulting, purchasing services, and IT systems support. Purchasing was about to become an important component of IBM's Global Services business, and UTC was about to get a Class A program delivered from the premier procurement organization of the day.

Experienced IBM buyers became consultants to the UTC supply teams, helping them build data warehouses, identify suppliers, study markets, and develop processes for continual improvement — in short, the quality processes CEO George David loved on the plant floor at Otis.

The next step was implementation of a completely automated purchasing system, "req-to-check." New York–based IBM personnel took on the tasks of processing requisitions and invoices, fielding questions from UTC requisitioners, and training new users. Requisitioners ordered desktop computers electronically on their own. Approval rules were based on level of authority. Purchase orders went through the IBM system and were dispatched electronically to suppliers, which then issued electronic invoices when they shipped the order, often within hours. The UTC finance department matched orders with invoices and issued electronic payments. Scores of tactical buyers disappeared as the new age of supply management actually dawned. Initial focus was on the Carrier group, whose management strongly supported the concept. Carrier also presented an interesting challenge for future learning; it was extremely decentralized itself, with buying conducted at the branch and plant level. It was a "if you can do it here, you can do it anywhere" kind of situation. As with many big projects, the devil was in the details: creating unified accounting codes, product codes, supplier codes, and common authority levels, to say nothing of new common sources of supply.

The new system soon was generating detailed spending reports by group and individual requisitioner. Maverick buying was stopped in its tracks. Inventory levels were reduced as users gained confidence in the process. Piece-part costs dropped as unified contracts were developed and enforced. Savings targets were achieved, but the program had stirred the waters. Any such major culture change generates criticism. After *Purchasing* magazine wrote a favorable story on the implementation in June 2000, Chief Editor Doug Smock received several anonymous e-mails attacking the program. Imbedded line managers hated to be told what overnight delivery service to use or where to buy ballpoint pens. And while the emphasis in such systems often is on retraining purchasing personnel to assume more strategic functions, there is inevitably turnover. There was some resistance, Stewart remembers, from UTC staffers who considered the new program an electronic form of turf invasion. Stewart, who helped drive the implementation, said challenges dissipated as the advantages of the system became apparent in the pilot incubator at Carrier. Compliance created savings, and the speed of transactions improved cycle time.

IBM and UTC did not build leverage by co-mingling their purchases. IBM viewed the process as a service, not an exchange model. Five years later, IBM was still one of the big players in the procurement outsourcing arena.

In Brittan's first two major implementations at UTC, the emphasis was squarely on cost savings "We will always for the foreseeable future be given an assignment to deliver savings," he said in an interview in late 2004. "However, the world has changed, particularly for the aerospace industry, in the last few years. Aerospace is converting to lean manufacturing, and that in turn is creating the need for a lean supply chain." Lean is defined as the maximum output of saleable products at the lowest possible operational expense, while maintaining extremely low inventories. It is a spin on just-in-time that puts more focus on manufacturing efficiency. According to the Production System Design Laboratory at the Massachusetts Institute of Technology, "Lean production is aimed at the elimination of waste in every area of production including customer relations, product design, supplier networks and factory management. Its goal is to incorporate less human effort, less inventory, less time to develop products, and less space to become highly responsive to customer demand while producing top quality products in the most efficient and economical manner possible."

Principles of lean enterprise, according to the MIT Lab, include:

◆ Zero waiting time
◆ Zero inventory
◆ Scheduling (internal customer pull instead of push system)
◆ Batch to flow (cut batch sizes)
◆ Line balancing
◆ Reduction of actual process times

For aerospace, lean is a response to the decline in business and profitability caused by the events of September 11, 2001. Lean will improve return on invested capital through increased velocity. Major aircraft manufacturers, such as Boeing and Airbus, have moved to flow manufacturing. Flow means tack time, which is the daily production number required to meet orders on hand divided into the number of working hours in the day.

For the supply chain at UTC, lean requires delivery of complete, on-time, zero-defect products to manufacturing flow lines. "We thought for about half an hour we could get away with lean ourselves without having our suppliers lean," says Brittan. "But when you get down to it, that's impossible. Plus our suppliers' suppliers need to be lean. This is a huge task."

Implications for the supply base are significant. There will be a strong push toward consolidation. "Physical considerations are very important," comments Brittan. "When you move to a lean environment, you cannot have more than, let's say, 25 suppliers delivering product to your floor. You don't have enough space. What you want is to have modules delivered. The modularization is what's really going to drive the supply base reduction. At least first-tier reduction. You can see in the aerospace world that there is a very rapid consolidation of first-tier companies."

Second-tier companies certainly also will be significantly affected. For example, there will be more pressure on injection molders to develop better process capability through use of newer equipment with provable repeatability and closed-loop controls that produce much higher quality products. There will also be pressure on companies such as molders to develop more secondary capabilities, particularly in assembly and through additional processing capability. That will allow delivery of modularized components and reduce opportunity for errors caused by proliferation in the supply chain.

Cynics may say that such requirements are in conflict with use of online reverse auctions. But the higher requirements can be built into the prebid specification process, easily the most critical element of any bidding event.

In another development, UTC is deriving millions of dollars in savings from Phase Two of its approach to general procurement: the strategic approach. Phase One focused on automating transactions for indirect items such as office supplies, travel, and information technology. Phase Two focuses on rethinking the business rules that apply to procurement of all general spend that crosses divisional lines. The program called UT500 is a textbook study

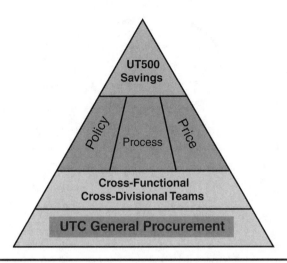

Figure 12.1. UTC's savings pyramid. (Source: UTC)

of alignment of supply chain goals and business goals, as well as appropriate involvement of senior executives to drive and lead change (see Figures 12.1 and 12.2).

UT500 was launched in April 2001 and was the result of finance and supply management collaborating on ways to reduce general procurement costs. UT500 is a combination of executive management rule setting and professional sourcing practice that orchestrates cross-functional groups to cut inventories, standardize, and save money through a very large collection of big and small ideas.

UTC reached a $500 million savings goal in the program in just two years — one year ahead of schedule. UTC's supply team aimed to save another $500 million by the end of 2005. If achieved, that would total a savings of $1 billion in four years.

UT500's spectacular success is due in part to executive sponsorship of the 13 teams that manage spend centrally. Spend pools covered include office supplies and equipment; real estate; maintenance, repair, and operating supplies; legal expenses; engineering services; travel; logistics; fleet; information technology; telecom; and temporary labor.

"I think the real success factor is high-level engagement by top executives across the business," comments Scott L. Singer, director of global general procurement at UTC. Each team is chaired by an executive sponsor. The sponsor of the real estate team, for example, is Louis Chenevert, president of Pratt & Whitney.

"Appointment of the executive sponsors serves two important purposes," says Singer. "First it sends a very strong signal of the program's importance

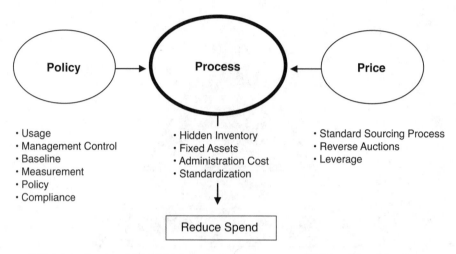

UT500 is "Lots of $1000 ideas rather than one $500 million idea"

Figure 12.2.   How the process works. (Source: UTC)

at UTC from a cost-management standpoint. And the second thing is that it allowed the executive sponsors to get educated in supply management techniques and what they mean specifically for indirect [spend]."

UTC began mapping the indirect plan in 2000 and launched the program in 2001. "Clearly the events of 2001 created an impetus and a sense of urgency," adds Singer. "We set up a three-year plan with very aggressive targets and then quickly blew through those original targets. We realized that we had locked on to something that was really important to the company." That was even more apparent when aerospace sales sagged after September 11, 2001.

Brittan uses the wholly owned UTC real estate company as an example of how the process works. UTC has more than 4000 physical locations that constitute close to 100 million square feet. Three-quarters of the locations are outside of North America. The great majority of the space is leased. The total annual real estate spend was about $1 billion in 2001. Real estate is clearly not a core function at UTC, which manufactures highly technical aerospace equipment, air-conditioning equipment, elevators, and other products, but it is a major cost.

Before UT500, the business units handled all of their real estate management internally; there was no effort to leverage the corporation's buying power. Many real estate transactions, as at most companies, were handled by individuals who were not trained in real estate. They primarily focused on other areas, such as running plants or offices or corporate finance. Not only was UTC failing to capture all potential savings, but it was creating busy work for people who had other responsibilities.

Ron Zappile, president of United Technologies Realty (UTR), says that money was saved while still providing the right space in the right location for the operating units. He established a marketing and communications program to explain the advantages to affected employees. He also incorporated UTR's role into the corporate financial manual so that UTR's approval was required on any corporate real estate deal anywhere in the world. As a result, finance managers across the world helped monitor compliance with the new policy. The actual footwork of finding property and negotiating leases was assigned to three systems integrators who specialize in real estate. Zappile has a staff of just six people.

At the outset of UT500, the furniture team was a subset of office services and equipment. Its executive sponsor was Tes Aklilu, UTC's director of quality. One of his first actions was to stop all new furniture purchases. "I was alarmed to see so much money spent on acquiring furniture at a time when we were restructuring," he recalls. "So we put the moratorium in place and said we would only acquire new furniture on a special exception basis until we could put together a new process for any future acquisition of furniture." The team's financial executive sponsor, Kris Krishman, then had a brainstorm. "Wouldn't it be nice if we had an inventory of all furniture throughout the business units and established a process whereby if you need furniture and someone else in the company had excess furniture, you can get what you need from them and save money." So a procedure was implemented that required requisitioners to first fill their needs through a newly developed catalogue of used furniture within UTC. (See the discussion of asset recovery in Chapter 21 for more information about this best practice.)

In one example of the impact of the new policy, two Carrier units saved $200,000 through use of preowned furniture when moving to a new office in Manhattan. When UT500 began, UTC spent $23.4 million annually for new furniture. By the end of 2003, the annual spend was just $1.7 million. In 2004, the furniture team became a part of the real estate team in an effort to maximize savings.

One of the most impressive implementations in the UT500 program came in a functional group often not affected by strategic sourcing programs: engineering. "A lot of people would look at UTC and say we are fundamentally an engineering and manufacturing company," comments Singer. "So this became a real classic example of how the UT500 program works." Engineering was an important component of the program because of the size of the spend, more than $200 million annually for engineering services. The engineering group was given a mandate to participate in the program by the project's executive sponsor, John Cassidy, the chief technology officer at UTC. The effort has been headed by Mark Miller, vice president of research and engineering at Sikorsky Aircraft. The engineers pick the focus of the project, and the sourcing professionals provide the tools, such as supplier analysis and electronic auctions.

"This project is about the value proposition for engineering and the fact that we optimize globally across all of the business units," comments Miller. One of the starting points was a look at outsourced engineering services, an increasingly important issue at many American original equipment manufacturers. UTC employs some 15,000 engineers but wants to focus their work on higher level, more strategic work. UTC had been outsourcing engineering services to more than 100 vendors. A sourcing team that included graduate engineer Steven Liu did a census of the suppliers as the first part of a process which became so successful that it is now called "the Big Bang" by some buyers at UTC. "It was pretty much the basic blocking and tackling of a classic sourcing event," says Singer.

The next big step was involvement of human resources professionals in development of basic engineering job descriptions that could be built into a request for proposal. Engineers led the process and developed five broad descriptions where $90 million of outsource spend was to be put up for auction in December 2001. Next, Miller's team studied the bid pool: everything from infrastructure and ISO certifications to professional engineering capabilities and historical performance. "Once the engineers got involved with this, they were very committed to developing a top-shelf bidding event," comments Singer. "They weren't about to let us monkey around with it." An electronic auction was conducted, and significant savings were achieved. Miller's team then began to train the new contract engineers in specific work methods at divisions such as Sikorsky and Pratt & Whitney. Supply management helped develop a system to monitor the suppliers' performance. "Using this approach, we've achieved savings of nearly $140 million for outsourced engineering services since 2001."

As an extension of the process, Sikorsky led a drive to establish two low-cost domestic design centers in 2004, one in Indiana and one in Kentucky. The Indiana center, operated by Butler International, has linked with the engineering department at Purdue University, and the Kentucky center, operated by Belcan Corp., is paired with the University of Kentucky. The educational institutions form a recruiting base and help provide training for the contract engineers.

Was there resistance in the technical community to involvement by supply management professionals? "Not at all," comments Miller. "They were very welcome because we had a collection of efforts going on and the supply management staff was instrumental in bringing the business units together.

They helped put a preferred supplier model together and helped to monitor the quality of the services."

Another important initiative in the engineering group has been a drive toward enterprise commonality, not only in parts but in the design and analysis tools that engineers use. UTC began working in earnest on standard work methods and tools in about 2001, led by Pratt & Whitney. At Sikorsky, a commonality retention board was established for the current model of the S-92 helicopter to maintain as much commonality as possible at both the design and part levels.

Supply management uses a methodical eight-step process called passport review to make sure there is executive-level and business-unit buy-in at each stage of the sourcing process. "It's like a gated review: go-no go," comments Singer. Passport review is a tool set from the ACE quality program. "The real uniqueness is in how we apply it," says Singer. "We have fleshed it out with our own sourcing process. And it gets somewhat modified by each category manager."

Brittan says one of the most important aspects of the UT500 program is creation of company-wide policy. "For example, we run the travel business in-house. We work with a travel agency and we have a travel card. However, the big piece of travel is usage, or policy — who can fly first class or business class and when. The executive sponsor is responsible for the policy and tells the other divisions: 'This is the policy and we need your support.'"

Every direct report to CEO George David heads one of these teams. They lend support to other teams because they know they must run the gauntlet with their own projects.

Singer provides the staff and the tools to implement the programs. The supply professionals gather data across the enterprise, organize electronic auction events when needed, determine lotting sizes, and provide whatever professional purchasing expertise may be required. "The executive sponsors come out of the process with respect for the function and what we can do to support them," adds Singer.

The savings program is now being expanded to UTC's operations in Europe. "We have a complementary program called Euro 150," says Singer. The goal is to save 150 million euros (see Figure 12.3).

Two years from now, there undoubtedly will be a whole new set of goals and supply management programs at the Hartford, Connecticut–based industrial conglomerate. The UTC story is important because supply management became an integral aspect of overall corporate strategy. Supply management was viewed as a competitive weapon rather than an isolated operational function. Brittan used online tools to get attention and demonstrate impact, and then he lined up senior executives to champion supply change. The senior executives are actively involved on an ongoing basis. The

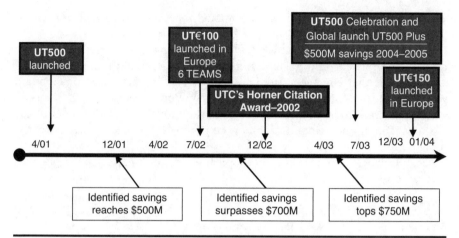

Figure 12.3. How UTC 500 rolled out. (Source: UTC)

fact that the metamorphosis took place in a highly decentralized company comprised of business units with long histories and strong character is even more impressive.

IV

The ABCs of Best-in-Class Practices

13

Strategic Sourcing
Your Most Important Tool

In the upcoming chapter on supplier relationships (Chapter 14), we note that the word "partnership" is often used casually in the business world when the speakers often means different things.

The term "strategic sourcing" can sometimes fall into the same trap. Simply adding a few bells and whistles to conventional purchasing, and then slapping the word "strategic" onto the process or the department name, is not the same thing as adopting the process that the authors have used in their careers to generate significant improvements in corporate financial performance.

What is strategic sourcing? It is a fact-based, rigorous process that involves substantial internal data gathering and evaluation, and extensive external data gathering and interactions, in order to select the most appropriate strategy and negotiations approach and ultimately select the right supplier. Strategic sourcing transforms conventional purchasing into a strategic process involving all appropriate stakeholders in a company and which can add significant value by reducing total costs relating to purchased goods and services. In a recent further evolution of strategic sourcing, the concept has expanded beyond adding value to a company's earnings to include adding value in other factors affecting return on assets or return on invested capital, such as improvement in payment terms and inventory programs.

To put strategic sourcing into perspective, it is one of three critically important elements in modern procurement (see Figure 13.1).

On a daily basis, there is a need for accurate and efficient transactional execution (often now referred to as just "purchasing"). Here, the focus is on easy and cost-efficient order placement (with suppliers that have been se-

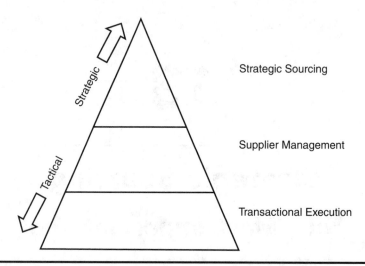

Figure 13.1.   Three interrelated elements of modern procurement.

lected by strategic sourcing), order follow-through and expediting (if needed), order receiving, and order payment. In the state-of-the-art company, the end user (not a purchasing professional) places an order into a system that is populated with approved suppliers and approved materials/prices using master agreements or contracts, and that system communicates directly through electronic media with the approved supplier. As opposed to traditional purchasing, in which the end user communicates his or her needs to someone in purchasing (by phone, fax, e-mail) and then that purchasing person communicates with the supplier, state-of-the-art purchasing involves the direct involvement of the end user and minimizes the nonvalue-added involvement of purchasing.

On an *ongoing* basis, there is supplier management, which involves the continuous and active supervision of the supply base. This includes evaluating supplier performance against criteria agreed to during the negotiations phase of the sourcing process, discussing opportunities for mutual process improvement, and resolving conflicts. Some of these ongoing activities are tactical in nature; others are strategic.

On a *periodic* basis, there is strategic sourcing. Intensive strategic sourcing efforts often occur every three to five years for a specific spend category, with active monitoring of the supply market in between those sourcing events. The distinction between the complementary functions of purchasing (the tactical and operational elements) and strategic sourcing can be described along three dimensions:

◆ **The primary mission/objective**: Purchasing is typically focused on the tactical day-to-day execution of orders, receipts, and supplier on-time delivery to meet the daily production demand and as a result is heavily transaction oriented. Classical purchasing textbooks talk about the goal of purchasing being the "three rights — the right parts, at the right time, at the right price." The primary objective of strategic sourcing is to become a competitive differentiator for the business. This is accomplished by employing a multistage process to understand supply markets, understand internal needs, identify qualified suppliers interested in your business, structure the right type of relationship, negotiate, and implement. Furthermore, strategic sourcing involves leveraging the corporate spend and partnering with a small, preferred supplier base, which is capable of achieving continuous (year-over-year) improvement in cost, quality, delivery, technology, and service.

◆ **The planning horizon**: Planning horizon for the purchasing function is 1 day to 12 to 28 weeks into the future (depending on the longest lead time in a company's supply base). Strategic sourcing activities are focused on long-term continuous improvement activities, but must also deliver near-term financial results. As a result, strategic sourcing planning horizons begin two to three months from today and can extend as far as five years or more in the future.

◆ **Organization structures and individual competencies**: As one might expect based on the differing objectives and planning horizons, the organization structures and competencies are near polar opposites of each other. The purchasing organization and its professionals need to be expert "firefighters" with extremely fast reaction times. Purchasing individuals must withstand tremendous "real-time" pressure and cannot become bored or intolerant of very intensive and repetitive daily transactional activities. The strategic sourcing process and activities must be organized cross-functionally to be successful with engineers, manufacturing and quality personnel, commodity managers, and financial analysts. These professionals must be competent in planning, project management, financial analysis, negotiation, and cross-functional operations.

In any organization, resources typically are pulled toward and consumed by the tactical activities. This is a natural outcome when you consider that failing to perform the tactical and transactional activities on a day-in, day-out basis can trigger immediate problems for an enterprise. The dilemma is that the greatest value add comes from the strategic activities. The challenge, then, is how to redirect and reallocate resources to strategic activities.[1]

Companies with significant experience and success in strategic sourcing often establish separate, dedicated resources or subteams for the tactical activities and the strategic activities. This makes sense because the objectives are different, the processes employed are different, and the skill sets are often very different. The tactical and strategic personnel can be viewed as subteams of an overall effort that is focused on achieving significant, breakthrough results, with ongoing and active supply management and utilizing efficient processes.

Strategic Sourcing: The Process

There are different variations of the strategic sourcing process. The shortest version the authors have seen is a five-phase process. A.T. Kearney's classic seven-phase process (shown in Figure 13.2 and which is the basis for the strategic sourcing description provided in this chapter) is well known among chief procurement officers; there are other variations that have more than seven phases. For the interested reader who wants to do a deep dive on the subject of strategic sourcing, there are entire books and seminars on the subject. What we provide in this chapter is a description suitable for the executive-level audience to understand the process, its rigor, and its potential.

Regardless of the number of phases in the individual design, the basic components and steps in true strategic sourcing are the same. Doing it well requires a meaningful investment in personnel and skills.

First, there is a need to define and profile the sourcing group. A sourcing group is defined as a group of purchased items that are likely to be sourced from the same subset of suppliers. Examples of sourcing groups are safety equipment and supplies (which is served by many manufacturers but a unique subset of major distributors within the supplier world), personal computers (again, served by a unique subset of manufacturers within the supplier world), and truck transportation (served by a variety of service providers serving various segments, such as flatbed, enclosed box, refrigerated, and tank). Obviously, within each sourcing group there may be many specific items, but the commonality we are looking for is that the group of items or services in a sourcing group is available from a distinct subset of suppliers. Other ter-

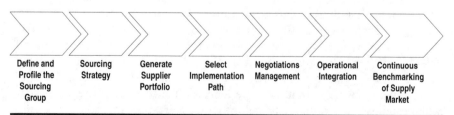

| Define and Profile the Sourcing Group | Sourcing Strategy | Generate Supplier Portfolio | Select Implementation Path | Negotiations Management | Operational Integration | Continuous Benchmarking of Supply Market |

Figure 13.2.   Classic strategic sourcing. (Source: A.T. Kearney, Inc.)

minology is often used. Some companies refer to these groups as "categories" and to their supervision as category management.

Profiling the sourcing group involves both internal data and external (supply market) data. The internal profiling is greatly aided by having the ability to analyze your spending detail. "Spend analysis" tools, described in Chapter 7, can be powerful aids to speed up the sourcing process, and provide the facts necessary for analysis, and to present the size of opportunity to suppliers that will be participating in the sourcing process. In addition to historical and projected volume data for the sourcing group, critical data include specifications, delivery requirements, technical support, and systems interactions (especially for direct materials involved in the production process). Delineating between "wants" and "needs" is also very important. More than one sourcing effort has been greatly aided by shortening the list of specifications to include only true "needs," thereby enabling more suppliers to qualify for participation.

External profiling of the sourcing group involves understanding the supply market, both currently and prospectively. Even historical studies of how markets can respond to various events and pressures can be extremely revealing in forecasting the future. Plastic resin markets, for example, react consistently to changes in gross domestic product, auto sales, or housing starts and swings in oil or natural gas prices (depending on basic chemical type). Preorders surge and inventories bulge in advance of expectations that resin prices really will rise. If you can develop forecasts for any of those events, you can develop a strategic sourcing plan for plastic resins that indicates contract versus spot buying approaches, which will save huge sums on purchase price and inventory costs. Very few buyers take adequate advantage of opportunities in spot resins markets.

Knowing today's market price (market intelligence) is not the same thing as fundamentally understanding the supply market (market knowledge). In fact, a comprehensive supply market assessment will involve assessing each component of Professor Michael Porter's "Five Forces" framework: suppliers, buyers, substitutes, new entrants, and internal market competition.

Furthermore, understanding the supply market involves determining whether the market is a global market, a regional market (e.g., North America), a national market, or a local market. Properly assessing the geographic scope of the markets, and whether or not the suppliers are capable of serving your needs on a global, regional, or national basis, is critical for designing an effective sourcing strategy.

Let's follow an example through the seven steps of the strategic sourcing process. Safety equipment and supplies are manufactured by a wide range of manufacturers, but the majority of the volume goes to the marketplace via a well-defined group of major distributors with extensive product and service ranges as well as a national or global presence. (All of the "Five Forces" are

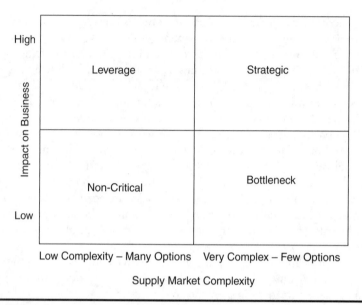

Figure 13.3. Assessment to determine the right sourcing approach. (Source: A.T. Kearney, Inc.)

at work in this marketplace, with post–September 11 awareness driving demand in many areas of this supply category.)

Second, there is a need to determine the likely sourcing approach, based on the sourcing group profile. This step often involves "positioning" the sourcing group in a 2 × 2 matrix, similar to Figure 13.3. The internal assessment from the prior step is noted on the "impact on business" axis, and the external assessment is noted on the "supply market complexity" axis. The value in positioning a sourcing group in this fashion is that it suggests appropriate sourcing strategies and can guide the data gathering in the next few steps.

For example, sourcing groups that fall into the "strategic" category are high-value groups where the supply market is difficult (i.e., the supplier has the negotiating advantage due to the supply market characteristics). In that quadrant, it is often best to focus on a strategic relationship or partnership approach, which can often involve long-term agreements, shared cost and quality targets, leveraging the supplier's expertise, and optimizing the operational and administrative processes between the supplier and customer.

Those that fall into the "bottleneck" category are also in difficult supply markets, but are lower value sourcing groups. Since these sourcing groups often do not have the visibility, due to smaller size, they have the potential to become problems for your business unless you devote time and effort to careful supplier selection and relationship structuring.

On the left side of the matrix, sourcing groups that fall into the "leverage" category are high-value groups where the supply market is very much in favor of the buyer. This is the classic opportunity to utilize your buying clout and the supply market to the advantage of your competitive sourcing effort.

Those sourcing groups that fall into the "noncritical" category are also easier supply markets that call for a competitive supplier selection process, but due to their smaller size also deserve attention to simplification and automation, including use of procurement cards with the selected suppliers.

It is important to note that this is a preliminary assessment of the appropriate sourcing approach. Further insights that develop as the sourcing process proceeds, including results from the request for proposal (RFP), will refine the approach.

Safety equipment and supplies is relatively low value, highly leverageable, and somewhat critical due to the sensitivity of properly protecting employees; it requires the supplier to have product application expertise to aid in specifying, substituting, and standardizing products to achieve lowest cost while assuring a high level of safety and personal protection.

Third, the focus is on generating a portfolio of qualified and interested suppliers. This starts with all current and past suppliers in that sourcing group, adds likely alternative suppliers, and also searches for nontraditional suppliers that might have the ability to grow into a qualified supplier role. Extensive database research, along with benchmarking with other companies, can help to identify all potentially relevant candidates.

Turning the list of potential suppliers into a shorter list of prescreened and prequalified suppliers requires two things: a carefully thought-out inventory of evaluation criteria and a good fact base regarding each potential supplier. It is at this stage that the sourcing effort often utilizes a request for information (RFI), which, if structured properly to ask the right questions, can not only be a powerful tool for understanding the strengths and weaknesses of each supplier, but also provide additional insight into the supply market.

Following the safety equipment and supplies example, high on the list of RFI considerations might be number of manufacturers represented, application services and training offered, and proximity of distributor locations to sites requiring service. After the sourcing team uses the criteria to screen the initial list of suppliers, there is a shorter list of prescreened potential suppliers to approach with the selected implementation path (step four). There may also be additional insight to confirm the preliminary assessment in step two, or to revisit that assessment as part of step four.

Fourth, the appropriate implementation path is selected. The appropriate path for approaching and selecting suppliers is determined by the position of the sourcing group in the 2 × 2 matrix, plus what has been learned so far in the first three steps of the sourcing process. As a general comment, the left-hand side of the matrix represents sourcing groups where the supply market favors a competitive supplier selection process. In other words, it is more of a buyer's market. Specific implementation path options include volume leverage (consolidating the number of suppliers), expanding supplier options (by developing new supplier alternatives), and aggressive negotiations that take advantage of the supply market's weakness.

The safety equipment and supplies spend category is clearly positioned on the left-hand side of the matrix, which favors a competitive supplier selection process. However, developing a longer term supplier/customer partnership will be necessary in order to capture and implement additional cost reduction opportunities in areas such as substitution, standardization, and new product development.

The right-hand side of the matrix represents sourcing groups where a competitive selection process might be inadvisable or even impossible, due to the more complex supply market situation plus the potentially critical importance of those categories to a business. In those sourcing groups, the effort might best be devoted to initiating a collaborative effort with the supplier, based on themes such as product specification improvement, joint process improvement, and — more fundamentally — a supplier/customer partnership. (For a more comprehensive discussion of supplier partnerships, see the next chapter.)

Fifth, there is a need to develop and execute a well-thought-out negotiations strategy. This involves, among other things, crafting an RFP to be sent to all prequalified suppliers, analyzing the RFP responses, and constructing and executing a negotiations strategy in accordance with best practices (see the section on negotiations in Chapter 17). The authors cannot stress enough that if the negotiations phase is allowed to proceed in an informal manner, a significant loss of potential value can occur.

Using the safety equipment and supplies example, it may be beneficial to segment the RFP by major usage categories such as breathing apparatus, face protection, hand protection, foot protection, etc. to determine relative buying power in each segment. Comparative information of this type can provide valuable insight for the development of negotiations strategies. In addition, this technique of revealing strengths in specific areas of a broad category of supply provides an opportunity to "identify the best fits" for unique requirements.

Sixth is operational integration. Once the negotiations are complete, the focus turns to transitioning to the new supplier or transitioning to a new business relationship with a retained incumbent. In the case of introducing a new supplier, this process often involves a testing period as part of a planned ramp-up. The testing should involve not only the purchased product or service but also the requisite administrative, operational, logistical, systems, and quality processes important to you as the customer.

Including key stakeholders as participants throughout the sourcing process can provide significant benefits, including ownership and buy-in at this stage of the process.

During this phase, the hand-off occurs between the original sourcing team and the ongoing implementation team and user community. The authors have found it very useful to include in the final report card of the sourcing team the success of the transition to implementation. That way, you avoid a sourcing team "throwing the contract over the wall" into the laps of unprepared users.

Seventh and finally, there is value in continuously benchmarking the supply markets in order to monitor changes in the supply market, be aware of evolution of the product or service, and ultimately be in a position to make an informed decision about updating the sourcing group strategy or the suppliers selected as part of that strategy. With regard to the chosen supplier, this can mean such things as the establishment and monitoring of agreed-to ongoing key performance metrics, timely updates regarding new products, and general market knowledge information that may be critical for demand planning.

The point here is that strategic sourcing is not a one-time event. It is a periodic event, with the periodicity a function of internal considerations and supply market developments. Without an explicit process to monitor the supply market, the timing of the "re-sourcing" decision might be left to accident or happenstance — and that would not be conducive to achieving the best financial results.

Strategic Sourcing: Determining the Priorities for "Waves"

Companies that have embarked on strategic sourcing often talk about their experiences in terms of the "waves" of sourcing teams. The first wave is composed of those sourcing categories that were determined to be the best spend categories to kick off the sourcing effort, the second wave is the "next best" spend categories, etc. What is best practice for selecting the categories for each wave?

The classic approach is to perform a high-level assessment of two factors for each potential sourcing category: the opportunity for reduction in total costs and the ease or difficulty in negotiating and implementing a new agreement. The opportunity assessment is greatly facilitated by having a comprehensive discussion and review of the market factors affecting that category. Depending on the quality of your team's pre-existing understanding of these market factors, it may require external research, including analyst or industry reports and input from parties that have previously studied that sourcing category (including consultants). The assessment of ease of negotiations and implementation is heavily dependent on the current supply market, the current contract, and internal issues and constraints that are important to your company. Those internal issues and constraints can include such factors as operational issues, systems issues, and even the willingness to consider a change of suppliers.

The results of this high-level assessment are then plotted on a diagram, similar to Figure 13.4. The top right-hand corner of the diagram, comprised of higher opportunity, easier implementation categories, becomes Wave One. The number of categories selected for Wave One will depend heavily on how many professional resources are available to staff the efforts. Note that the sourcing categories shown in Figure 13.4 are for *illustrative purposes only* and may have no relevance to the correct assessment of those categories for your company at any point in the future.

Depending on company culture and eagerness to change, it is not unusual for companies to select a small number of sourcing categories (perhaps four

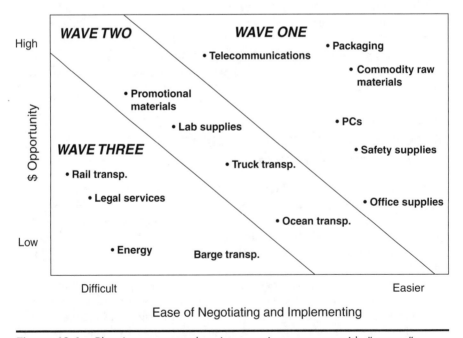

Figure 13.4. Planning a comprehensive sourcing program with "waves."

to six) to "seed" the effort in Wave One and prove that strategic sourcing works within their business culture. After initial successes with some easier, high-opportunity categories, an increasing executive commitment is made to the subsequent waves.

A few companies, either because of financial stress or because their culture is amenable to embracing significant change, proceed on a "tidal wave" basis. In that approach, the objective is to achieve monumental change in a shorter period of time, and a significant resource commitment is made from the very beginning. This resource commitment is often comprised of a cross-functional pool of high-potential employees from the procurement organization, operations, finance and accounting, R&D, and marketing who are plucked from their normal duties for a two- to three-year assignment to a "core team" that will drive the strategic sourcing process. Sometimes that core team is aided by outside consulting resources from one of the experienced procurement consulting firms.

Co-author Rudzki compiled data from six years of strategic sourcing experience at Bethlehem Steel in the mid to late 1990s. Those data reflected a fairly linear relationship between the amount of strategic resources dedicated to strategic sourcing and the resultant new annual cost reductions achieved. The data revealed a hard-dollar return of approximately $1 million per employee per year one year after the resource commitment was in place.

The decision to start slowly with a small first wave or start big with a tidal wave is heavily dependent on a company's culture, the commitment of the executives in the company to embrace change, and the leadership of the procurement organization. As important as the start of the process is, it is equally important to ensure that it becomes embedded in your business as a core business process.

Strategic Sourcing: Key Success Factors

There are a few absolutely critical success factors for strategic sourcing. First, strategic sourcing must be part of an overall, coordinated transformation plan as described throughout this book and as illustrated in Chapter 9. With that organizational support and context, strategic sourcing has a stronger chance to succeed as an initiative and has excellent prospects of becoming an embedded business process that serves your business well into the future. Without that support and context, strategic sourcing is likely to face an uphill battle.

Strategic sourcing must also have access to cross-functional talent and resources, either through ad hoc team members borrowed from key departments and locations or, even better, through the assignment of high-potential employees to a core team role lasting two to three years. This latter idea has served companies well in terms of both strengthening the sourcing process and providing valuable developmental experiences to employees viewed as having significant upward potential in their careers.

Another key success factor in strategic sourcing is avoiding the captive mind-set. When you self-constrain your consideration of alternatives, you have a captive mind-set. A practical way to avoid the captive mind-set is to construct teams that are composed of personnel who understand the reasons why something has been done a certain way in the past, plus personnel who have no such historical perspective but are simply focused on applying the sourcing process to a "new area" in order to achieve breakthrough results. The probing questions asked by the "naïve" team members often create highly productive working sessions.

The authors cannot say enough about the importance of stakeholder involvement throughout the sourcing process. In fact, one of the key success factors is identifying early in the sourcing process who the key stakeholders are, inviting them to play one or more roles in the sourcing effort, and regularly communicating with them as the sourcing effort proceeds. The final role of the stakeholder is often "signing off" on the negotiated results (and the calculation of benefits) and commissioning the implementation phase.

Beyond the role of stakeholders with specific sourcing teams, the executive officers of the company can assist by asking for periodic report-outs by the teams. In particularly challenging situations, the authors have found it to be very powerful for each executive officer to assume the role of executive sponsor of one or more sourcing efforts.

Another key success factor is recognizing that the conclusion of the sourcing effort may be that leverage and competitive bidding is not the right approach to supplier selection. A supplier relationship/partnership approach may be more appropriate.

Finally, the authors suggest selecting the sourcing team composition with an eye toward who may be necessary for the implementation phase. Why is that important? The ultimate benefit of strategic sourcing comes from effective implementation. Sometimes you are lucky, and the supplier and materials specifications are unchanged and only the commercial terms change. That's a relatively easy implementation. However, you must be prepared for the possibility that all key elements will change: supplier, specifications of what is being purchased and delivered, commercial terms, and operational integration. Since that is a possibility with every sourcing effort, the authors strongly suggest selecting team members for the sourcing phase with an eye toward which personnel will be crucial to successful implementation.

14

Supplier Relationships
The Advantages
of Partnering Well*

Over the years, there has been considerable discussion about the working arrangements that are possible between suppliers and their customers. "Partnership" is a term used often, and casually, by both suppliers and their customers to describe a wide range of working relationships. But are all relationships truly partnerships? And, more fundamentally, is a true partnership the appropriate form of relationship for every situation?

The short answers are no and no. If the authors had a dollar for every time a supplier's salesperson came through the door and began talking about "our partnership," they could have retired a long time ago. In the past, we might attend a dozen meetings and hear a dozen different ways in which the term is used. In many cases, "partnership" may be the label applied inappropriately to a transaction or a series of transactions: perhaps the regular purchase of copier paper or the one-off sale of a suite of software. Marketing impulses have expanded the term beyond reasonable scope, distorting the significance of minor relationships and devaluing the word partnership where it has true strategic importance.

As a result, resources can be misapplied. Partnerships that, properly managed, can add significant value may be shortchanged on funding, staff, and time. It may be crucial to layer in additional measurement processes or

---

* The original version of this chapter by Robert A. Rudzki appeared in the March 2004 issue of *Supply Chain Management Review* (www.scmr.com). Copyright ©2004 Reed Business Information, a division of Reed Elsevier, Inc. Reprinted with permission.

to open new liaisons between senior managers on each side, for example. Conversely, relationships that now or in the future are less critical may be oversubscribed. Most large corporations are well aware of the differences, of course. They have elaborate and proven mechanisms to drive procurement, supplier relations, sales, marketing, and customer relations. And they sometimes have sophisticated operations to drive alliances and other joint ventures.

But business pressures today are so great — and are rising so rapidly — that even the most sophisticated businesses may fail to realize the full potential of their current relationships and miss opportunities to build new ones. Even if they do maximize existing arrangements now, they may not reevaluate their objectives and achievements with enough rigor to ensure continued optimal performance. For companies that lack the expertise and resources to focus on relationship potential, the dangers are even greater.

With the competitive success of both the supplier and the customer at stake, there is value in stepping beyond casual and traditional approaches. At best, a traditional method gives you traditional incremental results. At worst, it can be counterproductive. Companies at either end of the supply chain can sharply differentiate themselves if they apply a disciplined structural approach to their relationships with each other. In other words, there is great benefit in developing and managing the right kinds of relationships. In some cases, those newly designed and implemented relationships can become the nucleus of an "extended enterprise" involving a network of businesses. That extended enterprise can offer enormous competitive advantages, as Thomas Stallkamp demonstrated at Chrysler Corp. in the early 1990s (see Chapter 10).

In fact, real partnerships are all about collaboration, not confrontation. With real partnerships, we often share future product and technology thoughts, market projections, and internal plans. When we do that well, as part of a well-thought-out relationship, we can maximize mutual performance and achieve optimal results for the entire supply chain and, in particular, for the end customers.

The Momentum Behind Supplier Partnerships

What's really driving the need for a new approach in dealings between customers and suppliers?

There is no debate that businesses everywhere face increasing competitive pressures. Capital moves immediately and massively around the world. Product cycles get shorter every year. Average product development time today — 16 months from concept to launch — is 12% less than in 2000, according to a recent survey by consultancy Deloitte. Businesses are innovating faster than ever; research shows that by 2006, 35% of manufacturers' revenues will come from products introduced during the three preceding years — up from 21% in 1998.

Increasingly, markets, sources of supply, and sources of competition are global in span. Everyone is aware of the extent to which American and European manufacturers have been locating or expanding their factories in China. And many U.S. and European manufacturers are locating *product engineering* far afield. Communications are denser and faster all the time. Sales grow more complex as customer expectations rise around the world.

The role that suppliers and partners can play to help respond to those market pressures cannot be overlooked. We are a long way from the vertical industry business models that prevailed in Henry Ford's day, when Ford Motor actually owned rubber plantations to supply the raw materials for the tires his own factories made.

Many organizations long ago learned about the transaction and coordination costs of managing long lists of suppliers. Many companies have worked hard to rationalize their supplier rosters so they can focus limited internal resources on fewer suppliers. At the same time, there has, in the last few decades, been much more attention devoted to other forms of relationships: joint research and development projects or co-branding initiatives, partial equity investments, and long-term strategic alliances such as the code-sharing initiatives run by many airlines. Sometimes a deeper relationship has been a pilot run for, or a precursor to, an outright merger or acquisition.

Spurring on the extension of relationships is a factor unknown to business until the 1990s: the Internet. Although telecommunications and computer networks have progressively extended and accelerated collaborative activity, the Internet has led to an explosion of commercial interactions of every type worldwide — and will continue to do so.

Partnership Pitfalls

All is not perfect when it comes to partnering. Information from a mid-1990s report by The Conference Board points out that as many as 40% of partnerships have typically failed or not realized their true potential. Failures are often attributed to factors related to "partner selection" and to "partnership implementation." In almost all situations, difficulties are rooted in very human factors: fear, mistrust, culture, power. Suppliers typically cite the following concerns:

◆ Fear of overdependence on the customer
◆ Different company cultures
◆ Inequitable "power" in the relationship
◆ Fear that the customer's emphasis will be on price and margins

Similarly, customers often have significant reasons for hesitancy. They cite lack of trust in suppliers, concern that there will be more risk than benefit (and certainly inadequate grounds for sharing of benefits and risks), and fears a relationship means relinquishing "control."

Other internal factors play out, too. Poor leadership very often gets the blame for failures of partnership implementation. And external factors, such as changing business climates, are cited as reasons for failures attributed to partner selection.

This means that those eager to establish and nourish the right supplier/customer relationships must attend to an array of "soft" issues. It is crucial for each side to occupy the other's shoes for the duration of a partnership. To put it another way, if you want to have a world-class supplier base (and realize the benefits from such an achievement), you will have to work hard to become a world-class customer yourself. This is a two-way street. There is no shortcut.

Are You Ready to Partner?

Taking your procurement and supply management practices to a best-in-class state will require an effective approach to designing and implementing supplier relationships. But are you ready? Table 14.1 identifies key issues that can help you assess your organization's readiness to be an effective partner.

A Foundation Framework

Let's turn now to a framework for thinking about, designing, and implementing relationships. Relationship structures can take many forms; the challenge is to select and develop the appropriate structure. What you see in Figure 14.1 are the dimensions of commitment level and involvement and a spectrum of supplier/company arrangements, from a simple purchase order to the highest level of commitment and involvement: full ownership of a supplier.

In fact, you can classify relationship structures into four major categories, with the level of commitment increasing from 1 to 4:

1. **Transactional relationship**: Noncritical, low value. The focus should be on the *efficiency* of the transaction.
2. **Basic partnership**: Noncritical but high value, involving areas that are not a core capability.
3. **Strategic partnership**: Important, high value. Used when there is a need for an exchange of technology or other core capability, for ex-

**Table 14.1. Assessing Whether You Are Ready to Be
an Effective Partner**

You're Probably Not Ready If...	*You May Be Ready If...*
You believe that suppliers have nothing to offer beyond a rock-bottom price	You believe suppliers have expertise that can supplement your in-house talent
You believe that "churning" the supply base for annual price cuts is the best way to manage suppliers	You believe that there is greater value in structuring long-term relationships with shared objectives
Your culture is one where ideas must be "invented here" for the ideas to have credibility	Your culture actively searches for the best ideas regardless of who might contribute them
Your culture insists on controlling all aspects of its supply chain activities	Your culture is comfortable with delegating activities to qualified parties
You view suppliers as part of the problem	You view suppliers as part of the solution
You believe in holding information "close to the vest"	You are willing to communicate plans to your key suppliers so that they can better serve you
You believe that only suppliers should have objectives	You believe that to maximize value from a key relationship, both customer and supplier should have objectives

Source: Greybeard Advisors LLC

ample. Valuable when acquisition is not possible or desirable, such as in cross-border situations or when there are financial limitations.
4. **Acquisition/equity stake**: Critical, very high value and worth having an equity position in.

As one might expect, the level of complexity, both *negotiating* complexity and *implementation* complexity, increases as the relationship becomes more strategic. Negotiations in a straightforward transactional relationship typically revolve around price, terms, delivery, and order-processing issues. In a strategic partnership, however, they will extend to include factors such as levels of risk and reward sharing, managerial structure and team makeup, levels of contribution, ways to balance cultural differences, and methods of conflict resolution.

It is much the same with implementation complexity. Whereas a simple transactional relationship may have a single point of contact (the traditional buyer/salesperson interface), a strategic partnership will involve many more disciplines and points of contact, at all levels. At the highest levels, it will

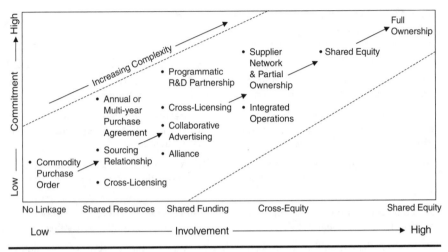

Figure 14.1. The range of relationships.

sometimes bring in the chief executive. You might think that this seems intuitive, but it is often not how relationships play out in practice. It is not uncommon to see transactional relationships where a whole team from the supplier will show up. On the other end, with more strategic relationships, it is too often the case that a single representative from the supplier (a midlevel manager or, at worst, a sales representative) attempts to carry the ball for his or her whole organization. It just doesn't work.

What is needed is an objective, value-driven framework. The framework can help identify the right relationship structure for the objectives required and the constraints that apply.

Conventionally, purchases might have been analyzed along simple Pareto lines, focusing on the 20% of transactions that comprise 80% of spending. Newer methods of thinking, however, are focused on a spending "portfolio" to be arrayed in a matrix that has value (or spending) on one axis and market complexity on the other (see Figure 14.2).

Commodities (and we use that term very broadly) located in the top right quadrant are characterized by few supply options (and thus a more complex market from the procurement perspective) and significant spending. They are often critical to your company's competitiveness. From the buyer's point of view only, commodities in this quadrant should be managed using joint ventures, strategic alliances, and value-added arrangements.

At the other end of the matrix, the "noncritical" end, are those types of spending characterized by multiple supply options and relatively small spending, such as office supplies. In this quadrant, the buyer's view is to simplify

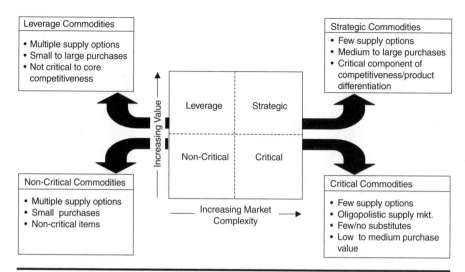

Figure 14.2. Partnership development framework.

and automate as many of these functions as possible. Procurement cards, often known as P-cards, can be an ideal solution.

In the upper left, the "leverage" block, as the name implies, represents types of spending with relatively sizable spending and fairly uncomplicated markets. We are talking about a "buyer's market." Here, the buyer believes it is best to expand the use of minimum specifications for opportunity purchases, to increase concentration with the right suppliers (sourced globally), and to make only short-term commitments.

"Critical" includes the relatively low-spend items that can often become bottlenecks. Examples might include motors, bearings, and power transmission units. One way to deal with that market complexity is to rely on distributors that can provide value-added services (matching motors and transmissions, for example) and broader buying efficiencies. Buyers will also work to manage critical commodities using tactics such as buying consortia, longer term agreements, hedging, and lumping together for leverage.

Fitting Viewpoints to the Framework

To properly assess the right form of relationship between a customer and a supplier, it is necessary to evaluate *both* perspectives. Within each quadrant, the buyer and the supplier have their own unique viewpoints, which become the drivers or, in some cases, the constraints in developing the relationships (see Figure 14.3).

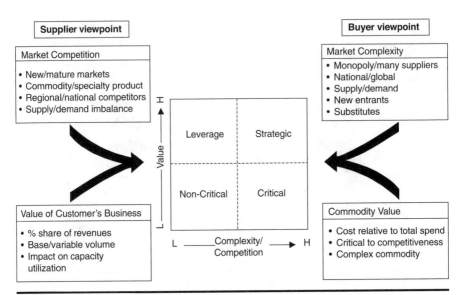

Figure 14.3. The supplier and buyer viewpoints.

In Figure 14.3, we have layered in the supplier's considerations when viewing the relationship with the customer. The supplier would look at market competition on the x-axis and the value of the customer's business along the y-axis. Properly used to capture the perspectives of the supplier and the customer, the grid can quickly expose significant similarities or differences in the viewpoints of the prospective partners. Let's look at an example for rail transportation, where there is plenty of room for differences of opinion.

In Figure 14.4, the buying organization, denoted by "B", may view rail transportation as a commodity of relatively high market complexity, so its view would be reflected on the far right on the matrix. But the supplier (the railroad), denoted by "S", may well see it as a low-competition situation, especially if it is the only rail supplier serving that customer. Thus its view would show up on the far left. Similar exercises with other customer/supplier pairings can highlight convergence of viewpoints. The chart clearly pinpoints the closeness or distance between the viewpoints of the prospective partners and thus is valuable to help determine the type of relationship that will work best.

Whether or not you use a graphical tool, understanding the degree of overall alignment of the supplier and buyer viewpoints is important to selecting the right relationship framework. What we are suggesting is that it is not enough to look at the relationship in your own terms; when you examine both viewpoints, you can more ably assess the likely value of partnering and

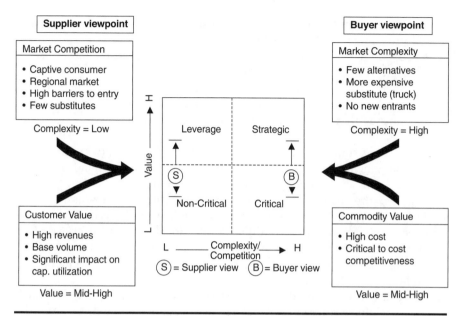

Figure 14.4. Rail transportation example.

at what level. Indeed, the very act of sitting down with the other party to work through the framework in itself bolsters the relationship.

One Company's Experience

So how does this all work in practice? The experiences at Bayer Corp. provide useful insight.

First we need to be clear about terminology. Not long ago, Bayer, like many organizations, could have fielded a range of definitions for the term "partnership." As a result, the procurement council decided to nail down what it wanted that term to mean. It was not a long and elaborate exercise, but it was an absolutely vital one that led the company to develop a discipline for framing relationships with suppliers. The conclusion was that the term "partnership" should be reserved for those special relationships where (1) the supplier maintains a leadership position in technology, service, and cost and the customer maintains a receptive attitude to the supplier's ideas and (2) there is an appropriate consideration for the amount of business the customer directs to the supplier.

Bayer's basic partnerships were defined to be long-term, mutually responsible business relationships that are the result of tangible effort and attention to factors such as:

- Joint commitment to information exchange, planning, continuous improvement, and cost reduction
- Encouraging a more interactive and trusting environment
- Agreed-upon measures of key performance factors
- Sharing of risk to achieve mutual benefits
- Working to prevent problems from initially occurring, solving problems as they occur, and preventing their reoccurrence

Bayer successfully implemented several "basic partnerships" with significant results, including reductions in total cost of ownership and inventory savings to bring about more effective use of working capital. Some partnerships are in the maintenance, repair, and operating supplies arena, using single-source suppliers for a wide range of products and services where the supplier provides, among other things, professional and technical expertise, inventory management, and continuous improvement. The benefits from these arrangements have been quite significant over the years — literally in the millions of dollars in some cases.

Bayer also implemented a few relationships that truly meet the tough definition we have offered for "strategic partnerships." They meet all of the standards applied to basic partnerships and are additionally characterized by long-term supply/purchase commitments, as long as 10 years, and by significant sharing of risks and benefits.

It is typical for strategic alliances to feature innovative pricing/cost approaches. One example is gainsharing, or mutual cost reduction programs. Bayer has worked on the indirect purchase side with distributors that commit to collaborate on cutting total costs over a multiyear period. The cuts can come from product substitutions, vendor cost savings, or gains in transaction efficiencies. Such strategic partnerships oblige the distributor to devise new ways of trimming costs, and they require us to be receptive to those ideas.

Strategic partnerships often will be steered by joint operational integration teams and be subject to rigorous ongoing performance measurement. It goes without saying that they will have been screened for a close cultural/philosophical fit.

The Importance of Measuring Performance

We are all familiar with the saying "You get what you measure." The corollary is: "Measure what you want to achieve." Unless you and your supply chain partners apply detailed and sustained performance monitoring and measurement, you will have no way to know for sure if your partnerships are effective. You may not even know if they are a net positive or negative on your resources. If you don't have a scoreboard, you certainly won't have a way to track trends.

Three interdependent dimensions determine success in supplier partnerships. There is an operational dimension common to all forms of partnership, a cultural dimension that is also pervasive, and a strategic dimension that applies to deeper enduring relationships of high value to both parties.

In terms of operations, you want to find ways to gauge the flow of information and the compatibility of the partners' processes. Typically, you will have checklists to spot and eliminate duplicate activities and to improve transparency of information. You will assemble joint teams to implement improvement programs and resolve problems, and you will have mechanisms for periodic joint performance reviews. Ideally, one team member will be designated to lead the measurement effort and to devise effective ways of not only continually gathering the right data but conveying the data to supply chain decision makers.

On the strategic level, the metrics will focus on the degree of business integration necessary for a continued strategic fit and on the characteristics vital for a long-term partnership. Key dimensions to monitor include linked business goals with specific targets, jointly defined performance standards, pay that relates to performance, and cost transparency. However, we have found that the area most likely to contribute to the success or failure of partnerships is cultural. That's the area that is most difficult to change. If supplier and customer start far apart culturally, you have to question whether partner selection was done properly. To test for cultural affinity, the "dashboard" has to indicate commitment, compatibility, and cooperation toward continuous improvement and growth. For example, one gauge may measure mutual assistance in problem resolution, while another tracks continuous improvement processes, and still another weighs compatibility of management styles. This last measure is especially important when there are significant management changes at one partner or if one comes under new ownership.

It is crucial to get a sense of the cultural fit as soon as possible. Ideally, it should be assessed fully before there is any mutual commitment in the first place. If the ratings are low, the success of the partnership is in serious doubt.

Partnerships, Supplier Development, and Supplier Diversity

Closely related to the subject of supplier relationships and partnerships are the topics of supplier development and supplier diversity. Companies at the leading edge of obtaining value from their procurement practices give serious attention to supplier development and supplier diversity because it is both good business and common sense. Supplier development is about developing future outstanding suppliers by investing your organization's time and resources today in a mentoring relationship that helps those suppliers understand your business and understand how to become a top-tier supplier. Supplier diversity is often linked to supplier development and introduces the additional perspectives of addressing expectations of your local community regarding awarding business to companies that represent local demographics and assisting in economic development objectives. For more on these important subjects, see Chapter 15 on supplier diversity. Finally, for a fascinating story about two fundamentally different approaches to dealing with suppliers, see Chapter 10.

Businesses can no longer afford *not* to partner where it makes sense, and they cannot afford to partner poorly. At best, the companies that put minimal effort into their customer and supplier relationships will miss opportunities that their more committed competitors will seize. At worst, partnership laggards will find it harder and harder to turn in satisfactory financial performance.

The stakes are already too high for substandard partnering initiatives, and they are getting higher as cost pressures intensify and innovation cycles accelerate. We are entering an interconnected era in which the global corporation will be eclipsed by the more massive and complex "global enterprise" — an ever-changing mesh of business entities and the relationships between them. The global enterprise will be a natural evolution from today's network of strategic linkages.

Consequently, supply chain leaders will take into account not only their own companies' core competencies but also those of current and potential supply chain partners. They will have to look well beyond investments in their own facilities, infrastructure, and resources to include those of their key partners. This calls for a much broader vision of what constitutes supply chain value and requires that supply chain managers move rapidly from a transactional orientation to a strategic orientation to help develop their companies' competitive value-added supplier networks.

A structured analysis can help select the appropriate relationship framework and thus minimize the potential for failures. But the analysis and the framework are only the earliest steps. Supply chain managers must use those tools, and tailor them to their own needs, to wholeheartedly rethink their whole approach to supply chain value. As such, they must rework business processes, performance tracking and measurement systems, and incentives. It will not be easy, but it will be well worth it.

15

Supplier Diversity and Supplier Recognition

Expanding Your Base and Building Momentum

Supplier Diversity: The Business Case

Supplier diversity programs began in the 1960s as a response to social issues and were deemed social programs. Over the last 25 years, supplier diversity has become a business imperative for many companies. Diversity fits into overall corporate programs for social responsibility, which have become front and center in the wake of high-profile corporate scandals.

A strong business case can be made for supplier diversity programs. Clearly, the government still promotes the model that sets goals for spending with minority- and women-owned suppliers. However, financial services, automotive, and many consumer-based companies now recognize the strategic importance of a robust program. Demographics are shifting; minority groups are growing rapidly and are projected to grow even more rapidly in future years. With this in mind, many companies have concluded that sourcing with minority businesses makes sense because these groups represent an ever-expanding customer base. The current definition of a minority or women's business enterprise (MWBE) is a company that is at least 51% owned, controlled, and operated by one or more minorities or women.

A 2001 study by the National Association of Purchasing Management, now called the Institute for Supply Management, indicates that there are approximately 3.25 million minority-owned businesses that generate $495 billion in sales revenue and employ four million people. It is noted that over $60 billion in goods and services were purchased from diverse suppliers in recent years. A report by the Corporate Executive Board's Procurement Strategy Council in March 2004 indicates that MWBE spend has increased 79% from 1999 through 2003.

The increased interest is attributable to several factors/benefits:

◆ Expectations from major customers (e.g., federal, state, and municipal contracts often require a certain percentage of minority "content" and automotive customers have clear guidelines of what they expect their suppliers to accomplish in diversity purchasing)
◆ Set-aside programs (e.g., California programs, Utility Market Access Partnership in energy)
◆ Corporate awareness and sensitivity to local demographics
◆ Desire to build customer loyalty and brand
◆ Long-term value in encouraging new entrants in supply markets and helping new suppliers become established competitors
◆ Opportunity to take a public leadership position in doing the right thing

What are the key attributes of a good supplier diversity program? First and foremost is senior executive support. Second is building the business case so that it makes sense to the people in the organization who are executing the plan. Third, it must be built into the business metrics so that it is not viewed as a special initiative.

Senior leadership support, particularly from the CEO's office, is critical. CEOs at United Technologies and Raytheon have lent their full support to supplier diversity programs. Senior executives not only backed the program but also became actively involved with the major minority advocacy organization, the National Minority Supplier Development Council, by becoming the chairmen of the organization. This action sent a very strong message to all employees as well as to the supplier community, recalls co-author Shelley Stewart, Jr., who held senior leadership positions in supply management at Raytheon and UTC. Additionally, at Raytheon, the CEO has led the supplier diversity council and participated actively in the awards program that included recognition of minority suppliers.

Benita Fortner, director of supplier diversity at Raytheon, feels that supplier diversity should be an integral part of the source selection decision and supply base rationalization decision.[1] Supplier diversity at Raytheon is being integrated into the complete supply chain strategy, which includes creating a competitive advantage in technology design and total cost considerations. At Raytheon, the CEO is involved through the use of customer satisfaction objectives because key customers have a supplier diversity focus. As mentioned earlier, many customers, both commercial and government, are driving a focus on supplier diversity.

Building a strong business case for supplier diversity is not difficult. Corporations spent over $60 billion with women-owned minority businesses in 2004. Minority groups in the United States are expected to grow to 37% of the populace by 2020. This means that these groups have, and will have, even more significant buying power. There are many methods that corporations and, in particular, the chief procurement officer and the supplier diversity leader can use to build their case. Today, in many corporations, because of the significant rationalization of the supply base, which basically is to reduce the number of suppliers and move to larger suppliers, it is critical to have a plan to maintain and grow this area of spending.

Companies are doing this in several ways. Some are increasing performance by assigning specific goals for spend targets. Some corporations are identifying specific commodities where there is a concentration of diversity suppliers. Others are finding opportunities by requiring their larger suppliers to drive second-tier spending for specific contracts. Kodak has reduced its overall supply bases by 76% over the last four years. However, it has pushed through to its Tier One suppliers a diversity requirement which has actually increased its spend with diverse suppliers. This creates an opportunity, but is oftentimes difficult to track.

The automotive manufacturers are also helping grow some of their suppliers in areas where they want minority participation. Corporations are also working with suppliers that consider joint ventures, or joint bidding strategy, between MWBEs and majority firms. Many corporations make a concentrated effort to work with their existing diversity suppliers by mentoring and training them in continuous improvement areas such as Six Sigma and developing technology assistance programs. These tools are often taken for granted by major corporations, but small businesses can use them to expand and become more efficient. These are all ways in which good companies assure they are taking full advantage of a thriving minority business community.

Measuring the performance of a supplier diversity program is a critical component of a well-run program. Measuring and tracking diversity spend should take on the same importance as any other corporate metric. Creating key performance indicators and using the right tools to drive performance are typical of good corporations. Start with the creation of a supplier diversity database. These tools can be found in existing ERP platforms or stand-alone systems, which will allow the buying community to have a clear understanding of what MWBEs the company is doing business with and what their capabilities truly are. These tools will allow for the creation of a good baseline by which improvement plans can be built and tracked.

Typically, when tracking diversity purchases, they are usually measured as a percent of a corporation's total sourceable spend. It is not unusual for corporations to create diversity performance scorecards that monitor spend quarter over quarter, as well as cost, quality, and delivery. The key for many corporations is not to allow the nontraditional spend opportunities to be pushed to the majority suppliers just because there are no current diverse suppliers. In this case, metrics or goals and objectives should be set up for a supplier development model that increases creation of viable diverse suppliers. Goals truly need alignment up and down the organization. It does no good for the senior executive to have a portion of his or her bonus linked to achieving supplier diversity goals if the day-to-day buyers are not similarly linked to those goals.

An example of how not to do it comes from a major U.S. utility that established top-level goals for its senior executives. Those goals are even mentioned in its annual proxy statement to stockholders. One of the goals relates to achieving significant increases in all areas of diversity, including supplier diversity. A big portion of the executives' bonus is dependent on achieving those diversity goals. You would think, therefore, that those execs would ensure that everyone in the chain of implementation would be aligned with those goals. Not so. The natural gas procurement desk, which makes the actual decisions to award business each day and each month, has NO objectives linked to the executives' diversity objectives. Not surprisingly, the gas group is not achieving anything meaningful with regard to supplier diversity.

Corporations are also targeting specific areas of opportunity for MWBEs, such as temporary labor and IT, because there is an abundance of firms in these areas. Oftentimes, these smaller MWBE firms are brought under the umbrella of a larger majority firm in the same type of business. These enterprises often can get things done more efficiently because of their size.

Chief procurement officers are supplementing traditional approaches to supplier diversity with a supplier development model or approach. The customer identifies a new minority supplier with the capabilities to grow into a sizeable supplier in a major spend area and works with that supplier in a mentoring/development relationship. Both parties set well-defined expectations, where goals and objectives are aligned. For example, the MWBE supplier must achieve competitive terms (i.e., within 1 to 2% of market pricing) with comparable service and delivery performance. This creates a level playing field where the company can dramatically increase minority spend on competitive terms, with less investment and time.

In terms of the length of time it takes for a supplier diversity effort in a corporation to really gain traction, factors ranging from the issue of receptiveness within the organization to whether management "gets it" determine the speed at which a program truly becomes viable. In a recent paper, Gwendolyn Whitfield, Ph.D., a professor at Pepperdine University, examines the relation between organizational culture and supplier diversity.[2] Whitfield points out that a strong culture for diversity maintains productive interpersonal relations among people with different backgrounds and stresses the accomplishment of individual and organizational goals. Basically, the belief system from the buying community that supplier diversity is important to the business is a critical factor in the success of every program.

There are many organizations that exist to assist corporations in their quest to identify qualified MWBEs. The National Minority Supplier Development Council is the premier organization and brings major corporations together with MBEs. Others are the Hispanic Chamber of Commerce, Women's Business Enterprise National Council, and U.S. Small Business Administration. They can all be helpful for corporations that want to become leaders in this area. The Institute for Supply Management, in its social responsibility document, also indicated the importance of supplier diversity.

The National Minority Supplier Development Council (NMSDC) will help ensure that companies meet the criteria for minority business through a certification process. Corporations may find it difficult to attract the right diverse suppliers. Use of company supply management Web portals creates an excellent opportunity to explain your goals and requirements.

Recent advancements internationally in supplier diversity reflect the importance of this area to some major corporations and have been accomplished through the support of the NMSDC. Corporations have begun to push the supplier diversity concept globally. The European Union has begun to focus on social responsibility and specifically the economic impact on the many ethnic minorities in Europe. NMSDC programs have been established in Brazil and Canada. Corporations such as United Technologies, IBM, and Chrysler are behind the push to expand supplier diversity concepts globally, with potential opportunities existing in the United Kingdom and South Africa. Each of these regions of the world presents a difficult set of issues regarding supplier diversity; however, with the support of major corporations, the local supplier base, and in some cases government agencies, there is great potential for program growth and the expansion of opportunity for minority business owners. These opportunities do not necessarily stem from the "social program concept," but rather the various economic and business-related issues in each region of the world.

Great corporations have "great supplier diversity programs." They lead, not follow, in this area. Ray Jensen, director of supplier diversity development at Ford Motor Co., has been running Ford's efforts in this area for many years and has created the "Billion Dollar Roundtable." This group of companies has a targeted spend of $1 billion annually. Many other corporations, such as IBM and P&G, have robust programs and are constantly challenging their organizations, making this a critical business imperative. Gillette has launched a supplier diversity advisory board in the Boston area, made up of its local minority suppliers. Kern Grimes of Grimes Oil, one of the oldest African

American oil companies in the United States and a member of this group, believes that being able to influence Gillette from inside has been extremely helpful to the program.

Doing business with MWBEs makes good business sense. Recognition of the growing buying power of minorities in the United States and abroad is becoming more evident every day. Supplier diversity is an integral part of creating and managing a robust supply chain strategy. It is not a stand-alone concept; it is not a "social program." It is good business, and what it needs is everyone's attention in the company, including the CEO!

Supplier diversity is an important cornerstone of an overall corporate program of social responsibility. In 2004, the Institute for Supply Management unveiled a program aimed at boosting awareness of social responsibility in the supply chain. Social responsibility is defined as a framework of measurable corporate policies and procedures and resulting behavior designed to benefit the workplace and, by extension, the individual, the organization, and the community in the following areas: (1) community, (2) diversity, (3) environment, (4) ethics, (5) financial responsibility, (6) human rights, and (7) safety.

Policies on social responsibility have been part of the culture at some companies such as Hewlett-Packard virtually since their founding. "One of our company's objectives right up there with profit is global citizenship," comments Dick Conrad, senior vice president, global operations supply chain at Hewlett-Packard. "To ensure our global citizenship commitment is clear to employees, customers, partners, and suppliers, we created standards of business conduct for HP employees and a code of conduct for suppliers. We also have policies in human and labor rights, environmental health and safety, and supply chain SER [Social and Environmental Responsibility]."[3]

One example is HP's design for environment program, which started in the early 1990s. "It's underpinned by the premise that the environmental performance of our products and services is largely determined in the design stage," comments Conrad. One outcome is that more products are designed with snap fits, eliminating the need for solvents and making them easier to dissemble for recycling. HP engineers also built a prototype of a printer made from maize, a biodegradable polymer.

Suppliers have become a major part of HP's SER policy because more than 80% of its products are manufactured through alliances and partnerships. Conrad is requiring HP's largest suppliers to sign a code of conduct statement indicating they are in compliance with laws and regulations covering areas such as child labor, environmental issues, and other social concerns. If they won't sign, they are required to show steps they are taking toward compliance. Conrad expects that suppliers representing 95% of all purchases will be in compliance.

The Institute for Supply Management hopes such programs will become commonplace. "We know that many companies have their own standards in place for corporate-wide behavior, but ISM's principles focus specifically on supply management's role in fostering good corporate citizenship," comments Anthony Nieves, who spearheaded the drive when he was chairman of the Institute for Supply Management board of directors. Nieves is also senior vice president of supply management at Hilton Hotels. "We launched this initiative to provide tools, information, and best practices for the development of a social responsibility program for supply management professionals and their companies."[4]

Increasingly, social responsibility programs, ranging from supplier diversity to environmental issues, are good business. Now they are becoming mandatory to just stay in business.

Supplier Recognition: Building the Momentum

By following and implementing the suggestions in this book, you will have set the stage for outstanding performance in cost reduction, working capital and asset management, and supply chain effectiveness. But how do you build the momentum and keep it going?

We have described most of the key ingredients for building and maintaining momentum throughout this book: exceptional leadership in your procurement function, the right role for procurement, a structure that does not complicate matters, continuing to invest in your people and their processes and technology, measuring the right things and setting the right goals around which everyone is aligned, and senior management being actively and appropriately involved. Do all these well, and you have set the stage for exceptional, best-in-class performance for your company.

There is another key factor for success, a factor that many companies, in their focus on internal processes, often ignore. It is a simple idea that, if implemented properly and creatively, can yield powerful results. That idea is to recognize your best suppliers on an annual basis.

It takes serious time and effort to recognize suppliers well. The benefits, however, are substantial:

◆ It reinforces your company's expectations that suppliers must perform well against the metrics that have been established for their relationship with your company.
◆ For the selected suppliers (the "best of the best"), it creates a powerful incentive to work even harder in the current year so that they can "repeat" their win at the next annual event.

- For the rest of your supply base (the 99% that were not recognized), a visible, well-promoted supplier recognition event can serve to improve their focus on improving their performance in order to win your public praise in the future.
- Finally, as more suppliers vie for this recognition, the "performance bar" begins to rise, which in turn benefits your company.

Most supplier recognitions for one calendar year occur in April or May of the following year. This is due to the time required to assemble final performance data for the year just ended, time needed to consider all potential nominees, time to prepare the nominations and review them against established criteria, lead time to advise the selected suppliers (typically six to eight weeks in advance of the event itself), and lead times to prepare program materials, print ads for publications, arrange for photographers, facilitate the attendance and travel logistics of the supplier representatives, etc.

The objective is to have a recognition ceremony (the "awards ceremony") that in itself is memorable for your selected suppliers. The ceremony, combined with press releases and selectively placed print ads that publicly recognize your premier suppliers, will generate enormous goodwill with your chosen premier suppliers and give them strong incentive to work hard to earn an invitation to return the following year.

At its first-ever premier supplier event, held in the mid-1990s, Bethlehem Steel recognized nine suppliers as the "best of the best" from among its active list of thousands of suppliers. The day-and-a-half program started with a reception and dinner, sponsored by then Chairman and CEO Hank Barnette at Bethlehem's private Weyhill Guest House. At that dinner, Barnette and Chief Procurement Officer Rudzki welcomed the guests, outlined the performance that earned each of them the recognition as a premier supplier, and thanked them for their contribution to the company's performance.

The next morning, a two-hour business meeting allowed members of Bethlehem's executive team the opportunity to describe the company's strategy and challenges and engage the nine supplier CEOs in a wide-ranging discussion on business issues. After the business meeting concluded, everyone relocated to the corporate auditorium — already filled with employees and invited guests — for the official awards ceremony. That ceremony was videotaped and photographed for later media use.

In an awards ceremony which lasted slightly more than half an hour, the performance and contributions of each premier supplier were detailed, and each supplier CEO was presented with an award by Bethlehem's chairman and handed the microphone to make brief comments to the audience. During those personal and heartfelt remarks, all nine executives accepted the award on behalf of their employees, expressed their appreciation to Bethlehem for honoring them with the award, and many promised to "be back next year." In fact, some of the executives who knew each other challenged their compatriots in front of the audience to win the recognition two years in a row.

The follow-up to the awards ceremony included a "local event" held at the headquarters of each of the premier suppliers for the benefit of their employees, who had in fact won the award. A member of Bethlehem Steel's procurement council represented the company. While each supplier designed a local program that made sense for its employees, many used the videotape of the official awards ceremony as one way to let their employees participate in the excitement of the official recognition at Bethlehem's corporate headquarters.

Follow-up also included a formal press release listing each of the nine premier suppliers and a full-page color ad in *Purchasing* magazine which touted the premier suppliers recognized by Bethlehem Steel. Intel consistently followed a similar annual program.

Finally, a letter was sent by Bethlehem's chief procurement officer to all active suppliers, outlining the supplier recognition program and providing a copy of the event's program brochure, press release, and a reprint of the color ad.

The response of the original nine premier suppliers was exceptional at the time of their recognition. In the months following, most of those suppliers made an extra effort to add further value to their relationship with Bethlehem Steel. Even though most did so, only three of the nine returned the second year. The reason: the performance bar had been raised by the efforts of many other suppliers to win Bethlehem's recognition. And since the program measured suppliers' performance against not only expectations but also the relative performance of other suppliers, only the "best of the best" each year would be invited.

What happened after this first supplier recognition was truly beyond anyone's expectations at the time. Within days of the press release, suppliers began approaching their Bethlehem procurement contact to learn more about the supplier recognition program and what they needed to do to improve their chances of being recognized in the future. Some suppliers very specifically asked: "What do I need to do to win the award next year?" Procurement personnel were coached in advance about how to answer anticipated questions. The end result was that a large number of suppliers immediately began to take their performance to a higher level, generating real benefit to the customer.

16

Low-Cost-Country Sourcing

Today's Game-Changer

Tyco International launched a three-year program (2004–2006) to save $3 billion through "Operational Excellence." The cornerstones are Six Sigma, strategic sourcing, real estate, and working capital. One of the pillars of strategic sourcing is use of suppliers from low-cost countries. Tyco's spend with low-cost-country sources was 10% of its direct materials spend in 2003 and totaled about $800 million. Tyco expected to source $1.9 billion or 23% of direct spend in 2005, with a goal of $2.3 billion in 2006. In an example tied to manufacturing, one of Tyco's businesses moved production of high-performance butterfly valves from Houston, Texas, to Chennai, India, and sourced all components in India. There was a 29% cost reduction on eight models, yielding $636,000 in annual savings. As a topper, sales rose 40% because the valves were more cost competitive.[1]

Co-author Shelley Stewart, Jr., vice president of supply chain at Tyco, and his team launched buying teams in China and India for tooling, electronics, metal forming, and chemicals. In 2005, Tyco will begin to ramp up teams in Eastern Europe, Latin America, and Southeast Asia. An enterprise-wide ("One Tyco" in Tyco talk) sourcing team in Latin America, created in 2004, delivered $8 million in savings.

The trend toward low-cost-country sourcing is most dramatic in electronics. One producer (a household name) sourced 70% of its direct spend from China by the end of 2004. Some consumer products companies became major buyers in China and other low-cost countries, but their original motivation wasn't strictly cost driven. They developed large markets for their products in developing nations and sourced products there as they grew.

Technology adoption, particularly electronic reverse auctions, was the big sourcing story of 1999–2002. Since then, the big story has been low-cost-country sourcing. As one white paper indicates, "published research suggests that companies can generate average incremental cost savings of between 15 and 25 percent" in certain categories by focusing on low-cost countries.[2] What are the facts? Is "low-cost-country sourcing" fact or fantasy? Is it best practice or a fleeting fad?

There is no simple answer. Let's examine a few examples to see why low-cost-country sourcing is a complex topic that deserves more than a superficial go/no-go decision.

Everybody in the information technology and procurement worlds has heard that there are major savings to be found by outsourcing IT support to India. Whether for call centers or software development, India has a large pool of highly trained IT professionals, and the country's wage scale has been low in comparison to the United States and Europe. Technical expertise plus low wages make India an ideal candidate for IT sourcing.

In an experiment designed to evaluate the *total cost and implications* of outsourcing IT development to India, a U.S. company found that the hourly wage advantages were substantially eroded by poorer productivity (i.e., more man-hours to accomplish the same project scope), plus higher complexity (and costs) associated with managing a satellite operation 12 time zones away.

In a further indication that low wages are not the best basis for making an outsourcing decision, Dell started to return some of its India-based call center activity to the United States, based on customer service consider-ations.[3] If you conclude from these two examples that low-cost-country sourcing is not worth pursuing, you are reading too much into the examples. What these two examples highlight is that the decision to source purchases from, or to outsource production to, a low-wage-cost country must take into account the total costs and implications of that decision. It is just like the disciplined process of strategic sourcing, with an added twist: identify and quantify all of the unique complications of selecting a source of product or service from another country. And that list of complications may be different from country to country.

These unique complications generally fall into the following categories:

- Country risk (i.e., the risk of local turmoil that affects the supplier you chose)
- Supply disruption risk (relating to any number of reasons)
- Extended lead times
- Extra inventory required

- Difficulty in assessing creditworthiness
- Difficulty and time required to confirm supplier capabilities
- Differences in business practices and business ethics
- Productivity differences
- Costs relating to shipping (landed cost)
- Trade regulations and the expertise required to ensure no mistakes are made
- Technical differences
- Foreign currency issues
- Up-front negotiations process can be more difficult due to language, customers, document and legal issues, and time zones
- Differences in local customs, including in some countries the expectation of "gratuities" to facilitate deals
- Legal domain for enforcement of disputes
- The in-country infrastructure and staff needed to manage the program locally

In some cases, there may be an additional complication: a country may "encourage" countertrade or offset discussions as part of an overall business discussion. Countertrade sometimes comes up when a U.S. manufacturer is trying to *sell* excess inventories at a discount outside the normal markets. In order to facilitate sales into emerging markets, and not adversely affect its pricing in its primary markets, the U.S. manufacturer may be asked to accept, in lieu of monetary funds, products manufactured locally. That is the typical manner in which countertrade is raised with U.S. and European companies.

With a procurement or manufacturing presence in an emerging economy, a U.S. or European company may be asked to facilitate countertrade discussions with other companies or even facilitate access to U.S. or European products not normally sold into that country's local markets. As noted above, the right decision cannot be based solely on price considerations. Successful low-cost-country sourcing involves all of the normal strategic sourcing steps, plus a careful identification and assessment of those unique considerations (listed above) for doing business in that country.

Many companies are using a three-pronged approach to study potential low-cost-country opportunities. First, they conduct a strategic assessment that entails understanding maximum spend for potential candidate categories. Next, they identify the right geographical location and supplier candidates. That is followed by risk/benefit reviews.

This results in the business case and an actionable plan. Then the participants would develop the execution strategy, which entails developing the specification, or organizing the proper documentation, and supplier identification. The next step is development of the global supplier negotiation concept depending on the part of the world. Postnegotiations are critical, as is the development of a detailed implementation plan which includes an analysis or review of total landed cost. Ongoing supplier management is critical to assure quality and delivery because of the number of risk factors associated with the distance and the cultures involved.

In 2004–2005, it was becoming apparent that the logistics issue was emerging as a major complication in Asian trade. Port traffic approaching Los Angeles was a major bottleneck. Traffic in India to specific ports was slowing shipments. While it was conventional wisdom that China sourcing was an absolute must, some chief procurement officers couched that statement with "yes, if you are expert in logistics."

Furthermore, a successful low-cost-country sourcing program needs to constantly monitor the evolving economics around the world. Today's low-cost countries for certain materials or services (see Table 16.1) might become tomorrow's medium-cost countries, due to a variety of factors, including too many buyers all chasing suppliers in the same country, plus foreign currency valuation changes.

Table 16.1. Sample Expertise of Low-Cost Countries

China	Molded plastics
	Electronics
	Textiles
	Household appliances
	Toys
	Furnace coke
	Increasingly — just about everything
India	IT — software development
	Specialty chemicals
	Pharmaceutical R&D
	Textiles
	Call centers
South Korea	Semiconductors
	Liquid crystal displays
Taiwan	Personal computer assembly
	Textiles
	Tools and dies
Poland	IT — software development
	Coal and coke
	Machinery
Russia	Raw materials
	Steel
Czech Republic/Slovakia	Castings, forgings, tooling

Table 16.2. Offshore Sourcing: The Options

Alternative	Advantages	Disadvantages
Traveling employees	◆ Utilizes your own internal experts, who intimately understand your needs ◆ No sizeable setup costs ◆ Can begin immediately	◆ May take longer to achieve desired results ◆ May not be familiar with local customs
Hire a third-party IPO	◆ Once selected, quick to begin work ◆ In-country presence and familiarity with local customs	◆ Evaluation of their capabilities takes time
Establish your own IPO	◆ Your own experts on the ground, in the local market	◆ May lack necessary technical expertise ◆ Investment of time and money ◆ Costs to shut down in the event country economics change ◆ May be difficult to encourage employees to accept the assignment and relocate

Finally, a successful low-cost-country sourcing program requires either a presence in the target country (sometimes referred to as an international procurement office, or IPO), access to a third-party IPO service provider, or a few talented employees who don't mind a lot of international travel. There are trade-offs among these three paths, as detailed in Table 16.2. You might wonder whether the "traveling employee" option can generate real results. It can, and the following is an example that combines low-cost-country sourcing with supplier development.

In the mid-1990s, the steel industry was faced with the prospect of another price spike in one of its critical raw materials: high-quality furnace coke. Furnace coke is an intermediate product made by heating coal in special ovens. The coke is in turn used to produce molten iron, which is subsequently converted into steel. In the mid-1990s, the high-quality furnace coke market was dominated by the Japanese steel mills because they made the best quality furnace coke for export purposes.

The purchasing department at Bethlehem Steel did not want to simply ride the wave of another price spike, but the conventional wisdom was that there was nothing that could be done. The only "exporters" of high-quality furnace coke into the global market were the Japanese producers. (Ironically, much of the Japanese coking coal came from West Virginia and western Pennsylvania, where coking plants, such as those in Clairton and Hazelwood, were under environmental siege.) Other sources of coke were poorer quality, which had a negative economic consequence in the iron- and steelmaking process.

A member of the Bethlehem Steel raw materials purchasing team, Lou Benedict, was an internationally recognized authority on coke making. He believed that the Chinese, who were at the time interested in selling their coke on the world market, could substantially improve their coke quality by selecting different coals as input to their excellent coke-making facilities. Up to that point, the Chinese coke producers had been using the coal mined closest to the coke plants, for a variety of reasons including logistics. Benedict proposed that a small team from Bethlehem Steel, including himself, visit the Chinese coke producers and the Chinese coal mines and work with them to improve their coke quality.

Over a several-year period, the Chinese coke makers began to test alternative Chinese coals. Their coke quality began to improve. Continuing to accept input from Dr. Benedict and his Bethlehem Steel colleagues, the Chinese coke producers achieved world-class quality in coke making within four years and substantially altered the competitive dynamics of world coke procurement. This is an excellent example of the benefits of low-cost-country sourcing combined with a dedicated effort in supplier development.

The "traveling employees" option can be an excellent, quick way to begin. If necessary, you can supplement your own team with a focused engagement of local experts to provide the local expertise in business and cultural customs. That is what the Bethlehem Steel coke team did. Truly global companies, which have a physical presence in many countries, have a natural opportunity to set up their own IPOs using employees already situated in the local country. If needed, the local employees can be supplemented with technical or procurement experts brought in from the sourcing country, either as traveling resources or transferred resources on assignment for a few years.

It should also be noted that for many companies today, the most important issue about China is not sourcing — it's marketing. China is, or will be, the largest market in the world for just about everything. You need a position there to understand the local market and become a factor. While you are manufacturing for the local market, develop sources that make you more competitive in the rest of the world. Procter & Gamble worked that approach like a charm and now has more than 100 sourcing people based in China. Chinese suppliers are treated like real partners and are given opportunities to participate in new product design, such as the Crest Spin Brush.

To summarize, low-cost-country sourcing is an important, but complex, tool in the arsenal of best-in-class companies. It requires a strong foundation in strategic sourcing, plus strong global and regional market knowledge, an ability to monitor changing economics worldwide, a careful identification and assessment of all cost factors (to ensure a correct economic evaluation is made), and a willingness to invest time, people, and money to convert the *possible* economic advantages of sourcing from (or outsourcing to) a new country into *realized* benefits.

17

Negotiations Management

Homework and Preparation Pay Big Dividends

One of the greatest challenges for corporate purchasing is described in the following comment by one chief procurement officer to peers at a conference:

> Everyone in an organization has bought things for their personal lives. Whether it's the CEO, his executive assistant, or the blue-collar guy on the loading dock, everyone buys things every week in their personal lives. And, in fact, most people are very proud of their buying skills. Why not? After all, ever since someone spent his or her first dollar as a young person, that person has done a lot of buying, and they probably believe they do a good job at it. That's our biggest challenge — everyone sees themselves as a buyer.

Ask someone who has bought a house, gotten a mortgage, or bought a car whether they "got a good deal." Most people would speak passionately about the fine job they did. But how do you measure whether you "got a good deal"?

In fact, there are three major phases to successful negotiations, and most people in their personal lives, and many corporate purchasing departments, only focus on the last phase:

- Build a fact base
- Develop a carefully thought-out and appropriate strategy
- Negotiate/buy

Strategic sourcing (explained earlier in Chapter 13) is a modern, disciplined, fact-based, and rigorous process. Why should the negotiations phase of strategic sourcing be anything less? In fact, to avoid losing the benefits of the entire sourcing process, the negotiations management process must be equally rigorous and fact based in its development and execution.

Table 17.1 contrasts "old style" negotiations to the new negotiations paradigm along several critical, revealing dimensions. Notice that it includes some new terms:

- **Most desired outcome (MDO)**: The best scenario that the negotiating team feels is possible. The MDO is our "want" and defines the best-case outcome from the negotiations.
- **Least acceptable agreement (LAA)**: The minimum outcome that the team will accept. Although not optimal, the LAA is considered an acceptable outcome. LAA reflects the minimum needs.

Table 17.1. The Difference Between "Old Style" and "New Paradigm" Negotiations

"Old Style"	"New Paradigm"
Lone-ranger buyer, hard bargainer	Multidisciplinary team representing you as the customer, and *speaking with one voice*
Get a good deal	Targets based on extensive research to determine most desired outcome, least acceptable alternative, and best alternative to a negotiated agreement
The supplier knows the market	The purchasing organization makes extensive use of market intelligence to build a fact base
One round of negotiations	Multiple negotiating rounds until predetermined objectives are reached
Off-the-cuff discussions	Extensive preplanning, scripting, and role playing
Meetings happen	Preplanned agendas, preplanned communications
Don't offend the other party	Drive the discussions to an impasse
One-step process	A multilevel approach in which the actual face-to-face negotiation is only a small segment

- **Best alternative to a negotiated agreement (BATNA):** Reflects our fall-back position. It is the preplanned course of action if we are unable to fashion a negotiated agreement. BATNA represents a unilateral course of action on our part. The objective in negotiations is to reach an agreement that is better than the BATNA.

In addition to the critical dimensions outlined in Table 17.1, successful negotiations involve the entire organization (not just purchasing) realizing that *every conversation or contact with a supplier, no matter how innocent or "technical" it might appear, is part of the negotiation process.*

As a result, the organization must develop discipline about "speaking with one voice." Speaking with one voice involves having a clear point of contact for all supplier interactions with your company, identifying all points of potential contact within your organization that a supplier might access (to bypass your negotiations team), giving everyone a clear message about their role (or nonrole), and planning all meetings and conversations.

One of the authors has the following story to tell about a CEO's support of the principle of speaking with one voice:

> We were at a very difficult and delicate stage of negotiations with one of our railroad suppliers. Our CEO received a call from the CEO of that railroad, a person our CEO knew fairly well as a result of their common membership on various executive councils. *Before returning the call to the railroad CEO, my CEO asked me what was under way with the railroad, and then he requested that we develop specific messages — consistent with our negotiations strategy — that we wanted him to insert in the conversation with the railroad CEO. We provided the requested "scripts," he used them effectively, and the negotiations progressed out of their "stuck" phase toward a very successful conclusion.* The best part of the story is that my CEO told this story at our next corporate management meeting (all the officers were present), and everyone got the message: if the CEO can "speak with one voice," they can too.

Organizations that are really serious about developing and embedding best-in-class negotiations management processes often utilize worksheets to guide the strategy development and execution process. For example, with regard to negotiations strategy, the following items might be assessed and documented on a strategy worksheet:

- Evaluation of each supplier's benefits from obtaining our business
- Hot-button issues for each supplier and benefits if we address those hot buttons

- Each supplier's likely receptivity to our MDO
- Identification of the supplier's various objectives (i.e., what the *supplier's* MDOs and LAAs are and which are likely to be most important to the supplier)
- Key messages we want to utilize during the opening phase of negotiations and reinforce during the later stages of negotiations
- Identification and assessment of our leverage points
- Relative position of one supplier vis-à-vis competitors that also want to earn our business
- Plan for the negotiating session(s)
- Overall communications plan

Negotiations effectiveness is affected by several basic factors:

- Strong support and, as needed, involvement of senior executives
- Selection of a creative, multifunctional, authoritative negotiating team
- Doing your homework (your own needs and wants, the needs and wants of the other side)
- Boiling the MDOs, LAAs, and BATNAs down into a well-planned and scripted strategy and communications plan
- Avoid common mistakes (e.g., win-lose attitudes)
- Carefully listening to, and writing down, everything the other side says during negotiations and evaluating those details later
- Willingness to drive to impasse (useful to force creative thinking by the other side; often triggers breakthroughs)
- Follow-through on the details (have the same team that negotiated the deal put the concept on paper and also be involved in implementing the arrangement)

18

Contract Management

Apply Supplier-Centric Strategies

Chapter 7 reviewed contract management from the technology perspective. Here we will take a look at the underlying reasons to adopt contract management as a best practice in your organization and the benefits which can result. We will also take a look at how good contract management, combined with modern strategic sourcing, can create extra value through a process we refer to as *supplier-centric strategies*.

To illustrate some of the underlying reasons to adopt contract management best practices, consider the following real-life examples.

Reduce Time in Contract Creation and Get Better Negotiations Results

Upon starting his job as the new chief procurement officer of a large company, one of the co-authors commissioned a team to study the total cycle time of sourcing efforts in that company. He was curious how long it took to go from forming a new sourcing team to realizing the benefits of that sourcing effort and what the principal obstacles to reducing that cycle time dramatically were.

The team's data gathering and analysis revealed a total cycle time that was longer than desired, but its main value was in identifying the time spent on each major component of the sourcing process and the reasons underlying those time lines. Contract creation was identified as one of the top three reasons for the longer than anticipated sourcing cycle times at this company. The team found that it could potentially reduce the sourcing cycle time by as much as 8 to 12 weeks by doing two things: having a repository of contract templates to speed the contract creation process and including those draft contracts in the request for proposal, so that the suppliers were bidding with full knowledge of the contract terms. The first change not only improved the speed of contract creation but helped to standardize new contracts around certain critical best-practice contract features. The latter change not only significantly speeded up the negotiations process, but also effectively eliminated the tendency of some suppliers to try to whittle away at contract terms that are presented to them *after* they are told they "won the bid."

Reduce Maverick Buying and Optimize the Value of New Contracts

The following example highlights the value of both spend analysis and contract management. Shortly after its implementation of a spend analysis tool, the procurement council at a major company sat through a live demo of how to use that new tool. After the basic how-tos during the demo, one council member asked to see the spend analysis for the category "office supplies." His rationale for selecting that category was that office supplies had a corporate-wide contract that had been in place for several years, the benefits associated with that contract were compelling, and the spend analysis tool should readily show the extent to which that contract was eagerly adopted by all locations.

The information that appeared on the projection screen caused everyone around the table to roar. While the "corporate contract" vendor was in fact number one on the list of office supply vendors, *over 150 other vendors* regularly received office supply business from this company's locations, and the total amount of business given to those "nonapproved" vendors was significant. Because of weak contract management, significant amounts of spend were not benefiting from the contract terms of the corporate contract, and the company actually risked being in violation of its commercial terms to award most of its business to the corporate contract vendor.

Properly Prepare for Outstanding Strategic Sourcing and Contract Negotiations

One of the mind-sets in old-style purchasing is that the supplier negotiation process is an annual process, often initiated before Thanksgiving and wrapped up before Christmas each year. As we now know, there can be significant benefits in progressing beyond this "annual mating dance" and constructing multiyear relationships with well-selected suppliers.

A key ingredient in approaching sourcing and negotiations in a more strategic manner is to plan ahead. Sometimes that means initiating the market analysis phase of strategic sourcing *far ahead of* the contract expiration.

Good contract management includes information that allows you to know with certainty the expiration dates of all commitments to every supplier, provides easy access to the commercial terms of current contracts, and enables you to plan ahead. Not having that information, or not using it effectively, puts you in the position of initiating a sourcing effort without adequate time to prepare and also puts you in a weaker negotiating position than if you had begun early.

Few chief procurement officers haven't heard the following words at least once in their career: "Boss, we just realized that the Acme contract expires this month. What do you think we should do now?" That's a costly position to be in.

Strategic Sourcing Kicked Up a Notch: Supplier-Centric Strategies

Shortly after instituting a contract management tool, an American manufacturer convened a cross-functional team to study the contracts in place and make recommendations. It is important to note that virtually every contract in the database had been negotiated after the manufacturer had implemented strategic sourcing some years earlier. These were good, solid, state-of-the-art contracts, resulting from category-specific sourcing efforts.

One of the surprises that came out of that review was the size of some of the supplier relationships. Keep in mind that the sourcing efforts had been driven by a spend category focus, fairly typical of strategic sourcing, in an environment where there was no mechanism to catalogue and manage contracts or supplier relationships. As a result, no one had taken a strategic view of the total relationship that was developing with each of the suppliers that had won business in discrete sourcing efforts. In one case, a major raw materials supplier had won contracts for seven separate commodities, and that relationship amounted to well in excess of $100 million per year.

In addition to the other benefits outlined in this chapter, contract management gives you the perspectives needed to go the next step in strategic sourcing: supplier-centric strategies. With supplier-centric strategies, a company seeks to add additional value to its supply management activities by optimizing the total relationship with key suppliers. It does so by shifting the focus from individual category-specific contracts to a holistic view of the current relationship with that supplier, plus the areas where the supplier might grow its involvement with the company. With regard to the raw materials supplier noted above, after realizing the extent of the current relationship, the customer approached the supplier to discuss the total relationship. The supplier sheepishly acknowledged that it had itself only recently realized the extent of the total relationship with the customer, believed that it should not be managing the relationship merely on a product line basis, and also felt that it was time for a comprehensive, strategic discussion about the current state and future direction of that relationship. With that conversation behind them, the parties began to talk in earnest about ways to further optimize their strategic and operational interactions for mutual benefit.

Follow-Through After the Contract Is Signed

After the contract is signed, it is important to ensure that contract commercial terms make it into purchase orders and into the accounting system. This is an area for potential loss of significant value, and having discipline and a process is invaluable.

How many times has your internal audit department identified a disconnect between the negotiated contract terms and the issued purchase orders or between the negotiated terms and the invoices received from the supplier?

Beyond the obvious embarrassment, real money can be lost by poor follow-through, and this is an additional reason to make contract management a priority for your company.

19

Risk Management

When — and How — to Hedge Your Bets

Most senior executives are aware of the term "risk management." However, there is evidence to suggest that being aware of the term is a far cry from understanding the strategic process of risk management, avoiding the pitfalls, and capitalizing on the opportunities.

In 2001, Ford Motor Co. announced a $1 billion write-down of palladium inventories. There was considerable negative press about that earnings surprise and considerable second-guessing regarding Ford's risk management process.

Remember the notoriety earned by Bankers Trust Company in the 1990s? Several of BT's high-profile clients lost hundreds of millions of dollars on "hedging" and accused BT of failing to explain the pros and cons of the particular hedging tools they bought.

These two examples point out just a few of the pitfalls in managing risk. There are other pitfalls as well, and there are also opportunities to add tremendous value to your company.

A common way for companies to begin to focus on the subject of commodity price risk — and to have an unpleasant first experience — is when a massive run-up in commodity prices occurs. This event typically results in *two* unpleasant outcomes. The first is that it creates an unfavorable financial variance to business plan that attracts top management attention. The second unpleasant experience results from the reaction to the first: it often spurs those companies to begin hedging right away, often at (in hindsight) what turns out to be the peak of commodity prices. Inevitably, in a short period of time, they see their hedging programs begin to report unfavorable variances to market prices as commodity prices retreat away from their recent peaks. At that point, if it has not occurred sooner, the finger-pointing begins.

But let's take a step back and first review the fundamentals of risk management. Risk management is much more than just the use of hedging tools to lock in commodity prices. Risk management is the process of analyzing possible exposures to loss and reducing loss potential. Risk management recognizes that some loss potentials may be avoided, others can be modified to limit their financial consequences, and not all risks must be accepted as they first present themselves. When properly understood and managed, risk can be controlled and minimized within a range of financial exposure that a business finds palatable and consistent with its appetite for risk.

That "appetite" for risk, or alternatively, aversion to risk, is the starting point for a successful risk management strategy. Sophisticated companies define and assess the "value at risk" (VAR), which is another way of saying they identify what portion of their earnings is at risk for certain types of exposures. This VAR analysis, which can be very quantitative and sophisticated or can be fairly high level and simple, is a critical starting point. It is followed by an explicit management discussion regarding the company's risk appetite or risk aversion. In other words, how much of our annual earnings, in the current business environment, are we willing to have "at risk" due to risk factor x?

For example, many process industry companies (e.g., chemical and steel companies) utilize large amounts of oil and natural gas in their daily operations. A VAR analysis might indicate that X dollars of annual earnings would be eroded by a 20% rise in energy prices. Management, in conjunction with its market experts in procurement, would assess the likelihood of that 20% increase in energy prices and determine its willingness to retain that exposure or its interest in transferring some or all of that risk (at a cost) to a third party through hedging.

So we want to do a VAR assessment and have an internal discussion about risk aversion in our company. Do we immediately focus on high-profile commodities? If we do just that, we are missing some very critical risk categories.

Every corporation is exposed to several fundamental types of risk (see Table 19.1). Often, the focus is just on purchased commodities, but the discipline and the process of risk management should be applied to all types of risk. While the "ownership" of each risk probably falls in a different part of your organization, the risk management process should be consistent.

There can be considerable variability in the potential frequency and magnitude of those risks. A comprehensive risk management strategy will pay

Table 19.1. Types of Risk and Management Alternatives

Risk/ Exposure Type	Example	Management Alternatives	Insurable/ Hedgeable
Market	◆ Volume ◆ Pricing	Business strategy and tactics	Uninsurable
Social/ political	◆ New environmental regulations ◆ Health care regulations	Public advocacy	Uninsurable
Property	◆ Physical damage ◆ Business interruption	Loss avoidance, loss control	Generally insurable
Casualty	◆ Third-party injury ◆ Director and officer lawsuits	Loss avoidance, loss control	Generally insurable
Employee	◆ Injury/disability/ death ◆ Departure	◆ Safety programs ◆ Compensation and benefit packages	Some are "insurable"
Financial	◆ Net income and liquidity ◆ Impact resulting from all the above types of exposures ◆ Interest rate risks ◆ Commodity price risks ◆ Foreign currency risks ◆ Credit risks	Financial strength Interest rate hedging Commodity hedging Foreign currency hedging Credit insurance	Some are "insurable"/ hedgeable

attention to each fundamental area of risk outlined in Table 19.1 and employ a risk management process for each area.

As noted in Figure 19.1, the process for managing risk is essentially the same regardless of the risk type. First, you must identify and assess the specific risk. This involves understanding the potential for loss with each event or incident and the potential frequency of occurrence. Sometimes historical data can be a good indicator. In other cases, particularly with new business activities, historical data are not relevant or do not exist, and you must acquire benchmark information or, if that is not available, go through a candid appraisal of the potential risks.

The second phase is to evaluate and select risk management options. In general, the choices are to avoid the risk (not always possible), retain the risk,

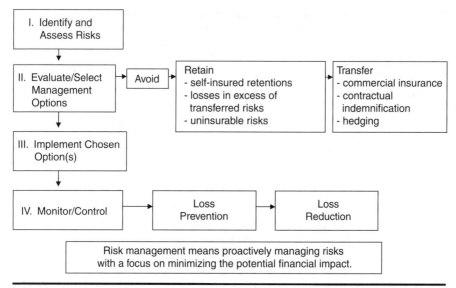

Figure 19.1.   Risk management: the process.

or transfer the risk to someone else. It is in the transfer alternative that you evaluate hedging tools, insurance tools, or contractual means of transferring risk.

The third phase is to implement the chosen options. This is followed by a rigorous monitoring/controlling stage which focuses on constantly evaluating the effectiveness of the risk management plan, encouraging loss prevention, and when losses do occur, focusing on loss reduction or containment through swift management action.

Successful risk management involves proactively identifying and managing risks with a focus on minimizing the potential financial impact on the corporation. For each corporation, there is some level of risk which that corporation is willing and capable of assuming (sometimes referred to as the corporate risk retention level). The capability of the corporation to assume risk is heavily influenced by its capital structure, liquidity, and business outlook. An investment-grade company that has strong earnings and cash flow can retain much more risk than a below-investment-grade company that has poor liquidity and marginal earnings performance.

Companies that jump to a narrow implementation of hedging tools, without the benefit of strategically considering their VAR, their appetite for or aversion to risk, and a thorough risk management process, are likely to be disappointed — and perhaps catastrophically surprised — at some point in the future.

Let's focus now on financial risk management, or hedging as it is typically called. It is probably appropriate for every corporation, regardless of financial condition, to do certain amounts and types of financial risk management to reduce risks and to add value. Hedging represents a way to reduce risk as well as to add value. Hedging should play a prominent role in financial risk management, especially in the areas of interest rate exposures, commodity price exposures, and foreign currency exposures.

What Exactly Is Hedging?

Hedging is a strategy used to offset (and thereby reduce) risk, generally accomplished with options (caps), swaps, or costless collars. The principal attributes of these hedging tools are listed in Table 19.2. A perfect hedge is one which eliminates the possibility of future (additional) gain or loss by exactly offsetting the exposure being hedged. Most hedges are imperfect to varying degrees.

A customer that buys a fixed-price swap (Figure 19.2) locks in a known price regardless of what happens to the market price. A customer that buys a call option (Figure 19.3) buys a "ceiling" beyond which the price will not rise. If the market price falls, the customer participates fully in that price drop. The difference between the price paid and the market price reflects the premium paid to have the "insurance" protection of the call option. If a customer is mainly interested in ensuring that the price paid falls within a price "band," a zero-cost collar merits consideration (see Figure 19.4).

It should be noted that the use of "excess inventories" to *physically* hedge a future price exposure is often an option, though not the focus of this discussion. In the case of physical hedges, an analysis of the holding costs associated with the physical hedge must be considered. In addition, there may be practical limitations to the extent of physical hedging possible. The market's ability to allow you to acquire the desired amount of physical inventory in a short time span may severely limit the usefulness of a physical hedging

Table 19.2. Attributes of Different Hedging Tools

Call Options	Collars	Fixed-Price Swaps
♦ Specific, up-front cost (like buying insurance) ♦ Ceiling price established ♦ Unlimited downside price participation	♦ Often no up-front costs ♦ Upside cost is capped (ceiling) ♦ Downside price is set (floor)	♦ No up-front costs ♦ Single, fixed price ♦ Full protection from higher prices ♦ No ability to participate in price decreases

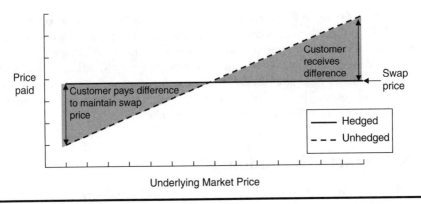

Figure 19.2. Customer buys a fixed-price swap.

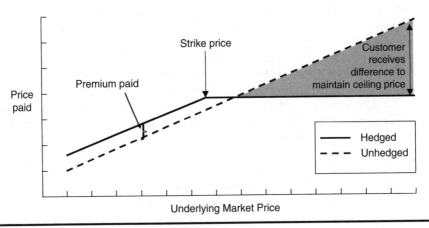

Figure 19.3. Customer buys a call option.

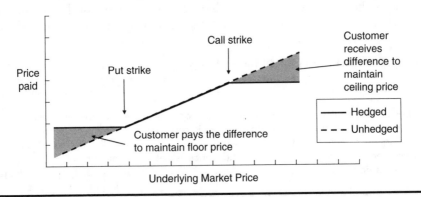

Figure 19.4. Customer buys a zero-cost collar.

program. Space limitations at the manufacturing plant may make it impractical to achieve a desired 6- to 12-month hedge for a critical material. Physical hedging is a very common tactic by plastics processors that build inventories one month in advance of expected price increases. Such strategies are short term and not high risk. At the other extreme was Ford's purchase of palladium. Ford worried that supplies, such as those in Russia, were subject to extreme price volatility. Its buying spree actually pushed up prices to higher levels than market forces dictated. When Ford withdrew from the market, prices collapsed. Other major buyers used different tactics, including financial instruments, and were not exposed to the same risk. Thus, financial hedges, which are not space limited (but may be limited by your credit capacity), may be a more flexible way to proceed.

The benefits of financial hedging include:

◆ Decrease financial risk, by reducing volatility of:
  ◇ Cost of raw materials
  ◇ Interest rates
  ◇ Foreign currency exchange rates
◆ Increase competitive advantage by offering more pricing alternatives:
  ◇ Export sales
  ◇ Offshore procurement
◆ Enhance purchasing flexibility by separating the physical supply (quality, delivery) from the achievement of pricing objective (via financial hedge)
◆ Improve likelihood of achieving business plan by establishing known price of product components
◆ Improve working capital management and increase liquidity by:
  ◇ Eliminating need for physical inventory hedging

Financial hedging itself is not without some risks or disadvantages. The risks include:

◆ Counterparty credit risk (potential inability to realize the value of the hedge because the other party to the transaction, the "counterparty," fails in its obligation).
◆ Underlying exposure being hedged is eliminated (e.g., hedge two million pounds of product based on business plan, but need only one million pounds), resulting in a speculative position and an immediate financial reporting requirement.
◆ For certain commodities, and for certain hedging mechanisms or markets, an imperfect correlation may exist between the underlying exposure (e.g., the specific commodity needed) and the hedging instrument available for use.

◆ If the market price for the hedged commodity drops after the hedge is put in place, the hedge will appear to have been an expensive choice compared to remaining unhedged.

On this latter point, we must remind ourselves that the primary objective of hedging is to reduce volatility and earnings at risk. In many cases, companies that hedge do so to "lock in" prices at or near their business plan levels. On occasion, the result of hedging may be that the prices you pay are higher than if you had remained unhedged. But that hindsight does not alter the prime objective of hedging: to reduce volatility as you look forward. That reduced volatility by itself adds value to your business in the eyes of investors.

Price risk management of commodities represents an opportunity to lock in prices consistent with business plan assumptions and reduce earnings risk. It is also an opportunity to separate pricing decisions from the physical supply decision and to potentially reduce the amount of capital tied up in physical inventories.

But the fiascos of the 1990s highlight that an effective risk management program requires a number of key components to be in place:

◆ Assess the value or earnings at risk (discussed above)
◆ Explicitly assess the company's risk appetite or risk aversion (discussed above)
◆ Acquire market knowledge, understand the factors that drive the market, and have a strategic outlook/view for the commodity
◆ Adopt a risk management strategy for the commodity (including specific objectives and price boundaries)
◆ Have a consolidated (single) strategy across all business groups (desirable, not required)
◆ Follow an approved financial risk management policy ("hedging policy")
◆ Identify knowledgeable, engaged stakeholders (i.e., a "steering committee") who are willing and able to make prompt decisions
◆ Employ knowledgeable experts in applying risk management tools
◆ Specify clearly delineated roles for treasury, procurement, and business groups relating to:
   ◇ Determining acceptable instruments for hedging
   ◇ Determining acceptable counterparties
   ◇ Determining acceptable credit exposures
   ◇ Establishing strategies, consistent with policy
   ◇ Executing strategies, consistent with policy
   ◇ Auditing transactions
◆ Implement audit controls and ensure compliance
◆ Have a process for evaluating and approving counterparties

◆ Insist on a close working relationship between procurement, treasury, and accounting
◆ Develop useful management reports

Finally, it is imperative to keep your board of directors informed about your hedging policies and practices.

20

Consortium Buying

The Good, the Bad, and the Internet

As we have outlined already, pooling your own internal needs and then approaching the supply base in a coordinated, strategic sourcing effort is the smart way to go. But what about pooling your needs with those of other companies? Can "consortium buying," as it is called, be a best practice too?

In theory, it's a good idea. In practice, it generally hasn't worked. The idea of online exchanges that pooled buying exploded in 1999–2000 in the dot-com boom.

Leaving the Internet out of the equation for the moment, let's explore the issues by following one company's evolving experiences with consortium buying. In the mid-1990s, B Company was invited to attend a kickoff meeting in Chicago, organized by one of its competitors, for the purpose of discussing whether this group of competitors wanted to do some "joint buying" for their plants in the Chicago area. On the surface, the meeting made a lot of sense. These were plants with a lot of common needs and buys, and pooling their needs could create significant efficiencies for both the buying organizations and the prospective winning suppliers.

The meeting coordinator properly suggested that each company send one attorney. After all, even a *preliminary* discussion about the *possibility* of establishing a consortium would require careful legal advice and involvement, due to potential antitrust considerations. Everybody was suitably proper about the process, and the first meeting actually had in attendance more lawyers than businesspeople. As everyone knows, when you have more lawyers than businesspeople present, success is assured.

The concept eventually moved from talk to pilot efforts involving several areas of "indirect spend" relating to plant supplies. About a year and a half after the initial meeting, B Company dropped out, feeling frustrated with the lack of meaningful progress. Eventually, A Company, another large player, dropped out as well.

What happened? In hindsight, this well-intentioned effort was doomed from the beginning because of several design flaws. Yes, there were more lawyers than needed, but that wasn't the biggest difficulty. First, direct competitors are typically not good candidates for forming a consortium, due to a natural reluctance to share basic information and best practices with each other and a lack of trust among fierce industry competitors. Second, the initial participants were at different stages of purchasing sophistication. Some were practicing strategic sourcing, and others did not even know what the words meant. It proved difficult to get everybody on the same page regarding a business process for the consortium to follow. Third, the quality of data that the participants had regarding spend was vastly different — partly related to their degree of purchasing sophistication. Without quality data about what each company needed to buy, the job of putting a consortium together became a virtual Mount Everest. As an example, a major consortium drive by consumer products companies in 2000 uncovered the problem that each defined common items such as "box" and "film" in different ways. Much time by highly paid people was spent defining simple terms as a first step toward aggregation.

Intrigued by the idea of consortium buying, and convinced that it could be successful, Company B entered into a joint buying agreement with two other large companies near its headquarters location. The three companies were from different industries and were at approximately the same stage of procurement sophistication. This small group decided to focus on safety supplies, office supplies, fax machines, and copiers. They had several successes, but found it to be a challenge to develop commonality of needs, even in some of the "indirect" spend categories selected. They also concluded that a group of three companies was not quite large enough to achieve the desired efficiencies.

One year later, trying a slightly different tack, Company B launched a consortium buying effort for off-road tires on behalf of itself and several of its major in-plant service providers and contractors. The combined effort was limited to purchases used at Company B's plant sites. It created a pool of spend three times larger than Company B alone. It also resulted in better costs for all participants and better efficiencies for the selected supplier — a clear win for all parties.

Later that same year, Company B was approached by A.T. Kearney's Leveraged Sourcing Network (LSN) to participate as a founding member of a consortium group spanning multiple industries. In early discussions with

LSN, and based in part on Company B's experience, it was agreed that candidate participants would:

◆ Be center-led or centralized procurement organizations
◆ Be relatively sophisticated in their procurement practices
◆ Be from different industries (no direct competitors)
◆ Represent diverse markets
◆ Have good-quality (apples-to-apples) spend data

The initial focus of this group was indirect spend, and it proved its value over time, though not without some growing pains. As of early 2005, that third-party managed consortium had contracts in place covering over 60 sourcing categories in indirect spend, for the benefit of its 26 members.[1]

One of the successes in this group was office supplies. Company B, on its own initiative prior to the formation of the consortium, had conducted a very successful strategic sourcing effort for office supplies, resulting in a 20% cost reduction (and a change to a new supplier). As a result of the consortium's pooled effort, Company B saw its costs drop a further 25% and in the process returned to its original supplier!

In summary, consortium buying *has the potential* to increase efficiency significantly and thereby reduce costs for both the customer and the selected supplier. It has the potential to achieve better service and quality levels for the consortium partners.

It requires participants that have similar degrees of sourcing sophistication and have good-quality data on their spend. Participants must also be able and willing to commit meaningful amounts of spend to the consortium effort. Successful consortium participation also requires a serious commitment of leadership, time, and resources.

Consortium buying with other companies makes sense if you meet all the requirements of the preceding paragraph *and you have already done a good job with internal pooling of your spend*. There is no point talking about external consortium buying until you have done a first-rate job on consortium buying (pooling) inside your company.

Numerous examples could be provided of effective consortia. One is Corporate United, which was formed in 1997 by a group of northeastern Ohio corporations to pool expenditures for office products. Their businesses covered a wide gamut: financial services, energy, manufacturing, and retail. The consortium represented 58 companies across the United States in early 2005. Clients included Capital One, Progressive, Eaton, Toro, Best Buy, Sherwin-Williams, and American Greetings. There were 21 contracts in place covering pharmacy benefits management, temporary labor, office products, safety supplies, and office equipment. One client, Sherwin-Williams, estimates savings of 15% plus improved terms with the same supplier as a result of its participation in the consortium. Gerard C. Hourigan, vice president of purchasing at Charter One Bank in Cleveland, Ohio, adds: "Corporate United has helped drive significant costs out of our operation through their innovative formula. In our first year with Corporate United we realized a six-figure savings that went right to the bottom line."

Consortia that were developed as Internet projects often were not as successful. This reinforces our earlier point that organizations must have solid sourcing practices in place before launching electronic initiatives of any type. One example of a bad consortium was covered in Chapter 10: Covisint, the huge automotive exchange established in 2000 by General Motors, Ford, and Chrysler. Covisint suffered many problems:

1. Solid purchasing fundamentals were not in place.
2. It was founded by competitors. As a result, it was almost impossible to establish standards or common ground.
3. Suppliers viewed Covisint as a hostile money grab.
4. Many suppliers had already invested in portal and other technology and had no interest in ceding this power to the automotive giants.
5. Officers of Covisint just plain tried to do too much too fast.

Consortia are a good idea to the extent that leverage is power. But you must have your own house in order first. Not many companies do.

21

Asset Recovery
Why the Scrappies Drive New Caddies

Some years ago, a group of purchasing professionals was having an impromptu conversation at the coffee machine when the subject of steel scrap dealers came up. One thing led to another, and then a comment was made which surprised most of the folks listening. The scrap buyer observed that every scrap dealer he had met in his many years of dealing with scrap dealers drove a new Cadillac. That comment surprised the others in the conversation circle because they had the impression that the dirty business of scrap trading was a low-profit business.

The conversation grew more interesting as others joined the discussion and noted that used equipment dealers also seemed to prefer (and be able to afford) new Cadillacs in their line of business. There are other examples where a similar pattern emerges: knowledgeable intermediaries in the "used" market profit handsomely from their expert knowledge and their connections, often by focusing in areas that are below the radar screen of professional procurement groups. The question becomes how to manage this activity for better results.

Asset recovery is a term that applies specifically to the effective management of idle plant and equipment. Done well, it can have a meaningful impact on return on assets, on capital spending, and on cash flow.

Traditionally, when a plant facility has an idle piece of equipment, someone in the plant declares that equipment "surplus." It is often subsequently written off for accounting purposes (or written down to some assumed scrap value), and then it is stored somewhere and forgotten. That happens much too often. In a slightly better scenario, after the write-off occurs, someone in the plant seeks out a scrap dealer or a used equipment dealer and asks for a proposal, happy to obtain anything close to the written-down amount left on the books. If the equipment was completely written off, scrap value would often be viewed as an acceptable result.

In either one of these two common scenarios, particularly at a large plant or a multiplant corporation, an amazing phenomenon might be occurring. Someone might be ordering a brand-new piece of equipment, similar to the equipment declared surplus at the first location. The opportunity to avoid an unnecessary capital expenditure is lost because of a lack of knowledge and the absence of an effective, coordinated management of the equipment process (new and used).

With effective asset recovery, you can sometimes avoid unnecessary "full-dollar" purchase of new equipment by effectively matching internal surplus equipment with new needs at other locations. If within some reasonable time period there is no match, effective asset recovery shifts its focus to the next step: monetizing the surplus asset in a best-in-class manner. Companies that focus on asset recovery find that it becomes a dependable way to minimize full-dollar capital spending on new equipment, can be a regular source of cash flow (through equipment monetization if there is no internal need), and can assist in the achievement of return on invested capital objectives as well.

Successful asset recovery programs are built around the following key success factors:

- An accurate and up-to-date database reflecting all idle or surplus plant and equipment (with reasonably detailed descriptions, asset history, and, ideally, photos of the asset from various views)
- Access to that database for all internal users
- A responsible person at each major location (or, at very large facilities, at each major operation within the facility) who is designated the asset recovery "point person" for that location and who also functions as part of the internal network for asset recovery management
- A professional who is responsible for overseeing the program, the database, and the network of internal contacts
- Connection between the asset recovery process and the process for ordering "new" plant and equipment
- Internal policies (management and accounting) that facilitate the fair value transfer of idle equipment among internal company locations
- Access to market expertise for used equipment or idle real estate (often accomplished via a master agreement that was the result of a strategic sourcing effort to select an appropriate service provider)

♦ Use of the master agreement service provider to determine fair value for internal transfers and to monetize the asset in a best-in-class manner where no internal transfers are appropriate

Asset recovery may not be one of the sexier topics in modern procurement, but done well, it can be a recurring producer of value for your organization. It is a particularly appropriate topic in today's world because the drive to manufacturing outsourcing has created significant idle capacity in North America and Europe. Many sophisticated tools and services, many of them Web based, have been developed to assist in the task.

22

Consultants

To Use or Not to Use —
That Is the Question

In 1997, a book about consultants was published, and it sent ripples through the consulting industry and corporate America. Titled *Dangerous Company: Management Consultants and the Businesses They Save and Ruin,* it was both a practical guide for the effective use of consultants by potential customers and an exposé of the consulting industry's business development and consulting practices. It also pointed out that the lack of active management by the client company can result in large consulting bills without discernible benefits.

Three of the four authors of *Straight to the Bottom Line*™ have used consultants during their careers. Their experiences confirm that consultants are not inherently evil, but can be very effective under the right circumstances, for certain subjects, and if properly and actively managed. Let's explore all three of those points.

What are the right circumstances for using consultants? Table 22.1 identifies basic considerations regarding using — or not using — consultants. The classic, good reasons to consider using consultants include a desire to jump-start change and improvement, a need to introduce and embed new best-in-class business processes such as strategic sourcing, a need to acquire expertise that is lacking within your organization, a desire to leverage all the prior experiences of the consulting firm, and a need to supplement internal resources with the talented resources that a qualified firm can quickly muster for a major engagement.

The classic, worst reason to use consultants is that your organization lacks a leader in the functional area, you are unwilling to make a change to intro-

Table 22.1.   Factors to Consider Regarding Use of Consultants in Procurement

Unnecessary to Use Consultants	Consider Using Consultants
Benchmarks confirm that your internal processes/results are best in class	You lack benchmarks and are uncertain how good your processes and staff are
Company is able to make ongoing investments (people, systems) to achieve and remain best in class	Not able to make ongoing investments to achieve and remain best in class
Best-in-class category/market expertise	No particular internal strength
No urgency to achieve significant cost reductions	Time is of the essence for achieving improvements
Best in class already and still reaping new benefits each year	Not generating new benefits each year
Internal staff able to effectively deal with internal politics	Internal politics constrain achievement of cost reduction objectives; a "third party" might have credibility
Your organization lacks a leader, and you hope the consulting firm can fill that gap	You want to supplement your internal talent for a defined time period

duce true leadership, and you hope the consulting firm can fill the gap. Never let consultants run a project or run a part of your business. That is a cop-out in terms of your responsibility to identify the right internal leader and opens the door to the very real possibility of countless, run-on assignments.

Consulting firms have been providing significant assistance in procurement since the mid-1980s, when "strategic sourcing" matured into a best practice. Today, procurement consulting firms are ready to offer assistance in a number of areas and scopes: assessing the current state-of-the-art in a company compared to best-in-class practices, designing an overall procurement transformation plan, performing spend analysis as a prelude to effective strategic sourcing, training and implementing strategic sourcing and all of its subprocesses (see Chapter 13 on strategic sourcing), training and implementing good practices in negotiations management (as an integral component of a best-in-class strategic sourcing program), and helping to structure a steering committee process or governance structure that works for your company's culture. A few consulting firms are also willing to roll up their sleeves and get involved in implementing the conclusions coming out of their procurement strategy consulting. Appendix B provides specific information about procurement and supply chain consulting firms.

An important starting point in considering whether or not to use consultants is to clearly define what it is you are trying to accomplish and then to perform a candid assessment of your internal ability to accomplish those objectives on your own. It all boils down to deliverables and timing (no matter who does the work), access to the needed amount of the right talent to do the specified work, and the leadership of change.

The most dangerous consulting firms utilize their personal relationships with senior corporate executives (the C-level audience) to short-circuit the necessary internal review alluded to in the prior paragraph, which is further detailed below. The "superstars" in a consulting firm are those who have nurtured high-level contacts with C-level executives, can utilize those relationships to open the door to a sales pitch that often ignores the relevant functional executive, and can achieve a "handshake" understanding with the naïve C-level executive on a new consulting assignment that lacks specific deliverables and a well-negotiated fee schedule. At some consulting firms, that's a superstar. Fortunately, other consulting firms place a high value on involving all stakeholders and also strive to reach a clear and crisp understanding about deliverables. As one senior consultant told a co-author, "the best client knows exactly what they want as an outcome, and works with us to describe the specific deliverables that the joint client-consulting team will focus on."

The best way to successfully approach the subject of consultants in procurement, or virtually any topic, involves the following steps:

◆ Make sure that you have a true internal leader involved in the area being evaluated (see Chapter 5 for more on this topic).

◆ With the active involvement of the leader and the C-level executive team, define exactly what is desired (i.e., the expected outcomes over a one-year, three-year, and five-year horizon). The more specific and quantifiable you can be about your targets, the better.

◆ Compare those internally generated targets to the achievements of best-in-class companies, to make sure that you are setting sufficiently aggressive objectives. Sometimes that comparison can be achieved by confidential benchmarking visits, and in other cases it can be an area of value-add by a consulting firm. In the authors' experiences, most of the qualified consulting firms in procurement are willing to assist in this benchmarking phase (sometimes referred to as "opportunity assessment") at no charge — as long as there is an understanding that they would be given strong consideration should a consulting firm be hired.

◆ Once there is a clear description of the opportunities and how they translate into specific deliverables (e.g., $200 million of new cost reductions in three years), the next stage is to assess the internal processes and resources available to do the job in the desired time frame. This can often be done in conjunction with the opportunity assessment.

◆ If the conclusion is to retain consultants to supplement internal resources (not to run the project, but to supplement your internal talent and perhaps co-lead the effort during its initial phase), the consulting engagement letter should include the following points:

1. Specific deliverables (quantifiable objectives, linked to a time line).

2. Incentives if deliverables are exceeded and consequences if deliverables are not achieved (e.g., 20% of fees are at risk).

3. Agreed-upon methods to measure or calculate the results.

4. Customer's right to interview and approve each consultant placed on the project, including the consultant's project manager. You want to avoid having the "A team" sell you on using the firm and then have the "B team" show up on-site to do the work.

5. A project steering committee that involves both your senior executives and the consulting firm's senior executives or an alternative governance structure and process.

6. Agreed-upon fee structure for each level of consultant that is utilized (e.g., partner, manager, senior consultant, consultant, analyst, etc.). This typically is expressed in a dollar rate per day for each level of consultant.

7. Agreed-upon mix of consultants (how many of each level) for the project.

8. Rules regarding expense reimbursement. Some consulting firms like to charge a flat percentage of their professional billings to cover travel and other expenses. Do not agree to this practice. Best practice in this regard is to specify that only actual costs will be reimbursed, that they will not exceed x% of the billings on a monthly or quarterly basis, and that the customer retains the right to audit the expense details of the consulting firm's project team. Some client firms insist that consultants utilize travel policy guidelines consistent with the travel rules which their employees must follow (e.g., no first-class airfare, no luxury hotel suites, etc.) and also use their corporately negotiated travel arrangements for airlines, hotel, and rental cars.

9. Invoice detail should be sufficient so that you understand exactly how the monthly invoice is charged. Don't tolerate a consultant (or a law firm, for that matter) that is unwilling to provide that detail.

10. A ramp-up schedule, and a ramp-down schedule, showing the number of consultants joining and departing the project during each month of the prearranged time frame for the assignment.

Beyond the consulting engagement letter, success will require the periodic involvement of your executive team in the project steering committee or governance process, as well as in regularly supporting the project in a visible manner.

The final point to be made is that the success of any consulting engagement can be measured not only on how the specific project deliverables are achieved, but also on whether your organization is able to continue the momentum after the consulting personnel depart. In other words, have knowledge and best practices successfully migrated to your own organization? The co-authors have on occasion incorporated "embedding the new process into the client organization" as one deliverable upon which the consultant's final true-up compensation depends. For example, if the organization demonstrates within three to six months after the consultants depart that it can carry on without loss of momentum, then the consulting firm has helped to achieve that final deliverable. In reality, good project management by both the client executive and the consulting partner-in-charge will ensure that new processes are embedded well before the project begins wrapping up. This is facilitated through ongoing training and reinforcement during the project and may even include a follow-on training session after the project is "finished." The evidence of success or failure in embedding new processes often will be transparent well before the last consultant walks out the door.

In spite of the notoriety afforded consultants in *Dangerous Company*, there is nothing inherently evil about consultants; they just are not often managed well by the client. The client should do its homework and carefully select the consulting firm for its niche of expertise, carefully task the consultant, properly compensate the consultant with well-thought-out at-risk incentive arrangements, and manage the program/project engagement actively. If the client does all of these things, real benefit can result for both parties.

23

Outsourcing

When and Where
It May Make Sense

What is business process outsourcing (BPO), and when might it be worth considering?

BPO is typically defined as "the delegation of one or more IT-intensive business processes to an external provider that in turn owns, administers, and manages the selected process based on defined and measurable performance criteria" (Gartner definition). As we will see shortly, current developments in procurement BPO are causing that long-standing definition to look a little out of date.

BPO has been receiving increasing press coverage in the last few years, as major BPO contracts have been awarded by household-recognizable companies. Ingersoll-Rand, Goodyear Dunlop (Europe), Deutsche Bank, and Avaya (one of the AT&T spin-off companies) are just a few of the large companies that have awarded sizeable BPO contracts in procurement to experienced BPO service providers.

While the press coverage, and the term BPO itself, have been relatively recent developments, BPO has actually been in practice for many years in one form or another. Perhaps the earliest example in the procurement arena is in travel. There are two approaches which have emerged. Some companies do their own deals with hotels, airlines, and rental car companies, but utilize a credit-card provider that administers the use of the program. This amounts to "partial outsourcing" of travel. In other cases, companies have effectively outsourced their entire travel program (supplier selection and negotiation, supplier performance monitoring, and travel operational execution) to a professional travel services firm. The benefits of doing so have been straight-forward: you can leverage the market expertise of a firm whose entire business is devoted to understanding the intricacies of the particular marketplace and also achieve operational efficiencies by employing the service provider's technology/systems in-house. Today's BPO services providers suggest that the benefits of BPO in procurement include these two basic benefits plus other benefits as well (more on that later).

By most accounts, the early "big-ticket" area of BPO focus was information technology outsourcing. This was a natural development, given the huge investments in capital and people required for any company to "stay current" in the IT arena. Ross Perot's Electronic Data Systems (EDS) was essentially a business built on the concept of IT outsourcing to an expert firm that had the necessary capital and people resources. In fact, when Bethlehem Steel Corp. decided in the mid-1990s to outsource its entire IT function to EDS in a 10-year deal, the rationale included wanting to avoid ongoing capital spending on IT infrastructure (by leveraging the significant base of EDS) and a desire to stay current in a fast-changing field that was not Bethlehem's core competence. Once Bethlehem became comfortable with the implications of "giving up control" of its IT operations, the challenge then became how to structure and manage the IT outsourcing service provider. Bethlehem solved that problem by establishing an "IT governance" group comprised of almost 20 professionals to oversee and manage the sizeable EDS relationship.

The history of BPO is heavily geared toward IT outsourcing, but in recent years BPO has seen significant activity in other "IT-intensive" and administratively heavy "back-office" functions. Human resources, finance, and accounting have all been very active BPO focal areas during the past decade and continue to grow at a significant pace. In each of these areas, the value proposition for the client is straightforward: cost reduction through head count reduction. That head count reduction is typically accomplished through technology (e.g., tools that allow employees to directly access and manage their human-resources-related files and accounts) and also offshoring some or all of the back-office functions to take advantage of wage rates in low-cost countries.

Estimates of the size of the BPO market in 2004 (cumulative value of contracts awarded up through that date) exceeded $100 billion, with torrid growth rates forecast for the foreseeable future.

Procurement BPO has been a late comer to the game, for several reasons:

◆ It was initially not a focus of the "recognizable players" in BPO, which tended to devote their attention to the other functional areas where the value proposition was simple and fairly straightforward: cost reduction through head count reduction.

♦ The initial service offerings in procurement outsourcing were not clearly defined, and the technology platforms were immature.

♦ Many of the target customers were achieving substantial cost reductions pursuing strategic sourcing and advance procurement on their own — and often saw little benefit and potential risks in handing over this lucrative source of cost reductions to an unknown service provider.

♦ Procurement BPO represented a distinct departure from the prior BPO service offerings in one important respect: procurement contained both a strategic component as well as the "back-office" operational component. Until a BPO service provider could offer a coordinated proposal encompassing both pieces, with suitable and credible metrics for performance in both areas, there was less rationale to award a comprehensive BPO contract for procurement.

These shortfalls began to disappear shortly after the turn of the century, and procurement BPO started to gain acceptance. The business was accelerated by several important players, including Accenture, A.T. Kearney, IBM, Ariba, ICG Commerce, and CapGemini. As the technology platforms matured and became more integrated, the field acquired credibility as a serious topic for consideration in the right circumstances.

When does procurement BPO make sense? Is it as simple as knowing that procurement BPO works in certain industries, or for certain size companies, and not for others? No. The relevance and effectiveness of procurement BPO are principally dependent on the structure and the maturity/sophistication of each company's existing procurement operations. They are also dependent on the role the company's executive team has given to procurement.

General factors that typically influence the decision to use a procurement outsourcing provider include the state of systems in the company, the ability to invest in people and systems, the urgency in achieving new savings, and the skill level and geographic reach of the internal staff. Factors that influence the decision to outsource a particular spend category are outlined in Table 23.1. These are all company-specific factors, and the assessment should be done by major category of spend. Thus, the assessments for big-ticket, strategic commodities (e.g., raw materials) may be significantly different from the assessment for so-called "indirect" categories of spend (e.g., PCs, cell phones, office supplies, and services). If all your responses are in the left-hand column for a category of spend, it is probably better to retain that category responsibility in-house. If some of your responses are in the right-hand column, then a closer look at procurement outsourcing may be in order.

The reason procurement outsourcing is growing is that increasing numbers of companies have been assessing their internal state of affairs and have concluded that procurement outsourcing makes sense for certain portions of

Table 23.1. Factors to Consider Regarding Outsourcing Specific Categories of Spend

Retain Spend Category In-House If	Use Outsourcing Provider If
Spend category is viewed as strategic differentiator for the company	Spend category is not a strategic differentiator for the company
Company is able to make investments (people, systems) to achieve and remain best in class	Not able to invest as needed or to focus resources
You already have best-in-class category/market expertise	No particular internal strength
Company has significant scale/leverage of spend	Lack significant scale/leverage
No urgency to achieving significant cost reductions	Time is of the essence for achieving improvements
Already have high-quality processes and systems/technology	Processes and technology not best in class
Consistent, integrated systems and processes	Disparate systems
Best in class already and still reaping new benefits each year	Not generating new benefits each year
Internal staff able to effectively deal with internal politics	Internal politics constrain achievement of cost reduction objectives

their spend base as a way to achieve aggressive new objectives. Some common scenarios that drive a company to outsource include a need to drive rapid cost reduction, a desire to focus scarce resources on strategic categories and outsource others, and a desire to upgrade systems and people across the enterprise (step change). A few companies have concluded that outsourcing makes sense for the bulk of their procurement operations (e.g., Deutsche Bank outsourced its worldwide procurement operations to Accenture).

Some companies attempt a "do-it-yourself" approach to outsourcing, by pooling resources with one or more partners to create a third-party service provider. Ingersoll-Rand did this in 2001 when it formed The 21st Century Supplier with two other companies, specifically to focus on managing the many small supplier relationships that tend to be ignored. This new company initially served the interests of its founding partners, with the intent to eventually expand its business activities by signing up additional customers.

While it is possible to embark on a "do-it-yourself" approach, most companies that conclude that outsourcing makes sense for one or more areas of their spend want to proceed quickly in order to obtain the benefits of the service provider's pre-existing large-scale and technological expertise and also want to benefit from the "on-demand" nature of utilizing the existing infrastructure of an established third-party service provider.

If a decision to proceed with outsourcing has been made, the critical success factor then becomes *managing the service provider.* Success in outsourcing, whether it be outsourcing of procurement, IT, human resources, or finance and accounting, cannot be achieved by a "dump-and-run" approach. "Set it and forget it" may apply to certain types of kitchen appliances, but not to outsourcing.

The probability of success can be enhanced by establishing appropriate, quantifiable objectives for the relationship (including objectives and responsibilities for both the service provider and the customer) and constructing a governance or steering committee process to provide support and remove obstacles.

While the specific contractual arrangements with procurement BPO providers are confidential, BPO service providers typically are willing and able to structure their contracts to reflect the internal needs and realities of the customer. For example, gainsharing approaches are often popular with chief procurement officers and provide incentives for all parties to work closely together to achieve mutual objectives. Other clients may prefer a "pay-by-the-drink" model (transaction fee basis). The ultimate design and structure of any long-term outsourcing arrangement will depend on the nature and scope of activities that are outsourced, the objectives for that outsourcing, and the respective roles of all parties.

Epilogue
A Few Final Words from the Co-authors

Robert A. Rudzki

There comes a time in life when, for many people, thoughts turn toward sharing your accumulated learning with others. That sharing can take many forms: mentoring, advising, speaking at conferences, consulting, publishing an article, or even writing a book. One of the book projects that I felt was long overdue is *Straight to the Bottom Line™*. Let me explain why.

I have been very fortunate in my corporate career to have had interesting and important assignments in diverse settings. I have been through all parts of the financial office and ultimately had responsibility for treasury, have led strategic change in procurement and logistics, have been in charge of business development and e-business, have had profit-and-loss responsibility for an exciting group of companies, and have also been a board member of several high-tech and low-tech companies (an activity which I continue). Through these activities, I have had the opportunity to interact with hundreds of companies of all types. Thinking about all of those experiences, I can tell you that one of the greatest drivers of business performance is procurement and supply management, and it is also one of the best-kept secrets in business.

As I reflect on the truly great business success stories, one theme that those outstanding companies have in common is their devotion to creating and sustaining a world-class procurement and supply management practice across their entire organization. But because this topic is often misunderstood and overlooked by most senior executives, only a few companies have truly mastered it and turned it into a competitive advantage. The purpose of *Straight to the Bottom Line™* is to reveal this opportunity and provide a roadmap to success for all senior corporate executives, whether the CEO, COO, CFO, or the person directly in charge of procurement.

Since I was the originator of this project, one of my responsibilities was to identify the rest of the team: the right co-authors and the right publisher. My first task was to identify two other corporate executives who had transformed the procurement and supply management practice at multiple companies into something special. The first two CPOs that I approached were Mike Katzorke and Shelley Stewart, who I have known for several years through our mutual involvement on the editorial advisory board of *Purchasing* magazine. When I described the book's concept, they each said yes without hesitation. As a result, the rest of my CPO invitation list never had the chance to know I also had them in mind for this project. Among Mike, Shelley, and myself, we have led more than eight successful business transformation efforts that generated over $5 billion of total benefit to our organizations. I felt confident that we had a critical mass of relevant experience to share.

As Mike, Shelley, and I were finalizing the outline for the book, and getting ready to put fingers to keyboard, Doug Smock advised me that he was leaving his job as editor-in-chief of *Purchasing* magazine to pursue several new ventures, including freelance writing. I quickly touched base with Mike and Shelley, and we all agreed to invite Doug into the project. We did so not just because we knew Doug to be an experienced editor, but because over the years he had shown himself to be a keen observer of best practices and the value of procurement and supply management. When Doug heard the concept for the book, he eagerly said yes.

Drew Gierman, publisher of J. Ross Publishing, has been involved in several "supply chain" books during his publishing career and was also well aware of the strengths and weaknesses of the books in print in this arena. He saw *Straight to the Bottom Line™* the way our co-authors envisioned it: filling a vital need for executives — both inside and outside of procurement — to realize the opportunity presented by procurement and supply management and helping executives understand specifically what they can do in their organizations to trigger dramatic improvements in business performance.

Since I am listing people who were important in making this book project happen, I cannot fail to mention the role and support of my wife. Over the years, Nancy has encouraged me to share my accumulated learnings in business with others and has supported my efforts to do so. This book on procurement and supply management is just the latest manifestation of our personal commitment to help organizations succeed, which continues through my advisory firm, Greybeard Advisors LLC (www.greybeardadvisors.com).

Of course, excellent procurement and supply management is not the only reason that businesses succeed or fail in the long term (more about that subject in my next book project). However, it is a necessary and critical component. Without excellent procurement and supply management, a company cannot hope to excel in meeting the tough performance expectations of today's unforgiving business world.

Doug Smock

The big idea in this book for me is to improve the competitive position of American business through more intelligent and efficient management. I grew up in the Monongahela Valley near Pittsburgh, just over a hill from the steel mills in Braddock, Pennsylvania. Most of the mills in that area are now shopping malls or office parks. As a very young business reporter for the *Pittsburgh Post-Gazette*, I heard all of the reasons why the American steel industry should be protected — as if its very existence and right to make a profit (and pollute) were a birthright. The mills had the political clout in western Pennsylvania to make sure many people agreed with their view of the world.

As a slightly more mature adult, I have (hopefully) a bigger view — one more closely aligned with classical economic theory, some of which I learned as a student at Case Western Reserve University in Cleveland. Economic protectionism of almost any sort is harmful to the long-term interests of any economy. Manufacturing or IT activity or whatever should take place in the lowest cost, highest productivity venue. That was often the United States in the 1960s, when we enjoyed high growth, abundant and relatively inexpensive resources (particularly oil), and a skilled workforce.

Through implementation of outstanding management practices, much of them learned from American experts such as W. Edwards Deming, Japan moved strongly to the forefront in the 1970s and 1980s. Then it was Mexico and Taiwan. And today, it's China. There will be more of a tilt to India in coming years because of its powerful educational foundation, such as the Indian Institute of Technology. Twenty years from now, there may be a different paradigm, possibly one not even geographically based.

For the next 10 years, businesses in America and Europe must constantly innovate and improve to survive. That includes an acknowledgment that manufacturing may not be an internal activity. America's high-tech companies quickly spun off manufacturing assets in the 1990s, beginning the outsourcing wave. As we have pointed out in this book, that is a paramount reason why supply management (formerly known as purchasing) must be a critical part of management planning. Other than a few exceptions, it has not been. Those companies that have embraced the concept (e.g., Procter & Gamble) are highly profitable and are category leaders.

These ideas became apparent to me in my second stint at *Purchasing* magazine, when I served as chief editor from 2000 to 2004. In my first tour of duty at the magazine, starting in 1977, none of these ideas were apparent or even talked about. No one at that time also had any inkling of the potential of computers, digital analysis, and advanced mathematics to dramatically improve supply management techniques right when they were most needed. The talk then was of issues that seem odd today. For example, in the late 1970s, it was accepted wisdom that we would see chronic double-digit inflation. I most remember that comment from E.F. (Andy) Andrews, who was a purchasing executive at Allegheny Ludlum Steel and one of the real developers of and believers in the National Association for Purchasing Management's Manufacturing Index, which now is a key indicator of the American economy. It was one of the few things Andy was wrong about.

When Bob Rudzki approached me in June 2004 to become a co-author of a book written for C-level executives, I was eager to participate. It was a pleasure to also work with my friends Shelley Stewart, Jr. and Mike Katzorke. The ideas and approach of the book evolved as it moved from concept to keyboard, but the central idea was always the same: the need for corporations to make supply management more strategic, with strong CEO involvement. Developing those ideas became a personal journey for me. As a reporter, I was always on deadline and never had time to really sit back and analyze the avalanche of information flowing through my Royal typewriter and later computer. I went back and reread and restudied the thinking of professionals I tremendously admire in the supply management field. Two stand out: Gene Richter and Tom Stallkamp.

I first met Gene at my inaugural editorial advisory board meeting at *Purchasing* magazine. He had led teams that won *Purchasing*'s Medal of Professional Excellence three times: at Black & Decker, Hewlett-Packard, and IBM. He was a tremendous visionary who embraced the importance of strategic sourcing, executive involvement, and the role of the Internet. He was way ahead of his time. His greatest characteristic was his wonderful treatment of people. I became especially close to Gene during a series of Procurement Executive roundtables sponsored by SAS Institute of Cary, North Carolina, that were held around the United States. Gene and I gave keynote talks, led workshops, and spent evenings together. I once asked him to indicate the single most important attribute to look for in a chief procurement officer. He didn't blink: it was great people skills. Gene built a team of leaders at all three companies, and particularly at IBM, who became the top professionals in the field. I was greatly saddened when Gene died unexpectedly in August 2003, on a personal vacation. I am very grateful to his widow, Nancy Richter, for making Gene's speeches and presentations available for use in this book.

Tom Stallkamp may be even better known than Gene outside of purchasing because he became president of Chrysler after a highly successful run as its top buyer. His story is outlined in "A Tale of Two Spenders" in Chapter 10. Tom also is a great "people" person and was very fondly remembered by commercial and technical professionals at Chrysler whom I interviewed for that chapter. He always made himself very accessible to discuss his views and now spends a significant amount of his time teaching his ideas to business students.

In the course of my work on this book, someone asked "Why include Richter and Stallkamp? They did most of their great purchasing work in the 1980s and 1990s. They may be dated now." The answer: they stand for principles and values that none of us must ever forget.

Even though much of my career has been spent writing about plastics technology (which I still love), I have developed a passion for better supply-side management and will continue to spread the word through Web-based writing (www.globalcpo.com), books, and freelance writing. Thanks to my best friend and wife, Nancy, I can do that.

Michael Katzorke

As I look back on my work life, I am truly grateful. I am grateful first of all to my best friend and wife of 36 years, Julie, who was my best source of counsel and common sense and who tended to the home front while I engaged in the corporate world learning and helping to develop and deploy many of the topics of discussion in this book. I am grateful to my three sons, who gave much of the motivation for the work. I am grateful to my many teachers and mentors, like Ken Stork, Dr. Bill Lee, Mike Smith, Charlie Johnson, Keki Bhote, and Tom Hoogervorst, who guided me along the way at various junctures in the journey and helped a young man learn and do more than he thought he could, because somebody else thought he could. I am grateful for my country, where we are free to pursue our dreams and anything is achievable and, above all, to Almighty God from whom all these blessings come.

For me, this book is the product of much sharing, much experience, and many mistakes. A fancy word for sharing is benchmarking. After a while, those who share a lot know that they are not going to find a mother lode in any given sharing event, but they will get a nugget here and there. And when all those nuggets are pieced together, we have a better process and better results more rapidly without having to suffer through the consequences of all the same mistakes and lessons again and again. So, I am also grateful to organizations like CAPS, ISM, APICS, AME, and MAPI for providing a forum for the initial sharing and the personal network building that facilitates the sharing that has been so instrumental in my personal thought process development in the supply chain arena.

In my early years in supply chain leadership roles, there was always a battle for the resources needed to approach the strategic aspects of the process that ultimately yield the greatest and most lasting fruits for the business. It was always the tendency to blame the "head shed" for lack of understanding and short-term management. Over the years, however, experience has taught that if you are not getting the support you need from the board, it's probably because *you* are not doing a good enough job of selling.

Today, some corporate boardrooms understand the leverage the supply chain process brings to improving and sustaining a corporation's competitive posture. They understand that over 50% of their cost in most cases is in things they buy and that a dollar saved in supply chain is an additional dollar of profit, whereas another dollar of sales is maybe $.15, and that 3 to 15% of their cost is direct labor on the average. They also understand that the first one to the marketplace with a better value mousetrap wins and that the integration and ideas of their key supply chain partners are paramount in making winning this race a reality. Thus, boards that understand this are very interested in investing in supply chain in a major way today. They just need leaders to provide them with a clear business case. We are grateful to pioneers in strategic supply chain like Xerox, IBM, and Motorola that back in the 1980s proved the business case for the investment.

For me personally, I have been in leadership roles in major corporations for over 25 years. I've had a lot of laughs — and a few tears. But for me, the only real joy is the legacy I may have of helping the next generation grow and watching it succeed. To this end, we have written this book.

Shelley Stewart, Jr.

As I reflect on my career, the most fortunate event for me was landing in the field of supply chain. Unlike many young people today who select supply chain as a career focus, I took a more circuitous route. I found myself in the purchasing department of an aerospace company because no one quite knew what to do with an employee's overeducated son. How's that for luck! The job fit me perfectly. I applied my communication and negotiation skills and was quickly able to learn the art of the deal.

I often think about the young people I recruit and hire. They now have the wonderful advantage of actually studying supply chain management, which enables them to start out fully equipped and ready to hit the ground running. I am also pleased to see that enlightened leaders of many organizations now recognize what supply management can become: the secret weapon that drives cost and quality.

When my co-authors and I first thought about this book project, we felt that we needed to appeal to an audience of senior management who did not quite understand how to harness the true opportunities right under their noses — their supply chains. Teaming up with my co-authors and sharing our collective knowledge with each other and with our readers has been an eye-opening experience for me. Although our career paths may have been somewhat different, our knowledge, experience, and opinions about supply chain management are very similar. We share the collective view that if positioned properly in a company, with the right leadership and with top-down support, the opportunities are limitless for supply chain management to bring benefits to any company.

As I reflect on this project, it is the combined experiences of Rudzki, Katzorke, Smock, and myself which have helped illuminate a subject that should be front and center in every CEO's mind. A great deal of thanks is owed to my co-authors for their ability to take these experiences and bring together a collaboration of this breadth despite our busy schedules.

In addition, I am particularly thankful to my wife, Ann, and my children, Shelley, III and Sydney, who selflessly afforded me the additional space to spend the time needed to work on this project.

My hope is that our message about good execution of purchasing/supply chain management strategies will go a long way in helping to improve the bottom-line performance of companies.

Appendices

Appendix A
Supply Management Software Vendors

The following brief profiles of several leading vendors of supply management software are provided as a service, and the co-authors make no claims concerning the completeness or accuracy of the statements, which were provided by the vendors. In some cases, they have been slightly edited to remove marketing assertions or puffery. The term ASP which appears in several of the profiles is typically defined as application service provider. Some companies declined to provide profiles or failed to provide profiles by the deadline. It should be noted that this information changes constantly and often dramatically. A major shakeout and consolidation of this business has been under way. Check the Web-Added Value™ Download Resource Center at www.jrosspub.com for changes and additions.

Ariba, Inc.

Contact Information: 807 11th Avenue, Sunnyvale, CA 94081, phone: (650) 390-1000, e-mail: info@ariba.com, Web: www.ariba.com

Representative Clients: Ariba has more than 500 global customers including over half of the Fortune 100 and over 100 of the Global 500. They include Alcoa, Bristol-Myers Squibb, DuPont, FedEx, HP, Merrill Lynch, Motorola, Novartis, Pfizer, and Royal Bank of Scotland.

Scope and Type of Services Offered: Ariba, Inc. is a leading provider of spend management solutions — both software and services, to help successful companies around the world and in every industry realize rapid, sustainable bottom-line results. Ariba spend management solutions:

◆ Enable enterprises and public sector entities to efficiently manage the purchase of nonpayroll goods and services
◆ Uniquely integrate software applications, spend management expertise, professional services, and network access and deliver a closed-loop spend management process
◆ Are designed to provide technology and business process improvements to better manage spending and save money

Ariba spend management solutions streamline and improve business processes that identify suppliers, negotiate terms of purchase, and manage ongoing purchasing and settlement activities. This includes suppliers of commodities, raw materials, operating resources, services, temporary labor, travel, maintenance, repair, and equipment.

Key Strengths/Expertise: Three capabilities are essential for spend management success: speed, sustainability, and coverage. Ariba delivers on all three, empowering organizations to fully realize the promise of spend management.

Speed: Extensive services, intelligence, and rapidly deployable solutions support faster rollout and greater traction in undermanaged spend areas, generating results in weeks instead of months or years.

Sustainability: A high level of information transparency drives improved spend performance throughout the enterprise. Platforms and systems with built-in best practices and templates help organizations capture and institutionalize crucial spend management processes and knowledge, facilitating widespread compliance and self-sufficiency and ensuring that identified savings can be realized long into the future.

Coverage: Broad category coverage and expertise, combined with powerful technology, drive efficient sourcing and procurement from supply markets across the globe, regardless of category complexity. Integration to multiple ERP and legacy systems, along with outstanding visibility and control, expands spend management value to all users and transactions across the enterprise.

Service Model: Ariba's solutions are available for a perpetual license, term license, or as managed services. Ariba's professional and knowledge services are available using a combination of bases, including per project, time and materials, and "pay for performance."

Compensation Structure: Ariba's software solutions can be purchased as:

1. Up-front, one-time license fee based on the number of employees, with an additional annual maintenance fee
2. One- or three-year term license

3. Subscription fees based on the amount of spend and number of named users

Ariba's professional and knowledge services are available using a combination of per project, time and materials, and "pay for performance."

Target Customers: Ariba's complete spend management solutions serve Global 3000 customers and Fortune 2000 enterprise customers. Ariba also serves government sector entities requiring complete spend management solutions. Ariba procurement solutions serve Global 3000 and leading government sector entities. Ariba's sourcing solutions address the purchasing needs of Global 10,000 companies. Ariba Supplier Network serves global suppliers of all revenue size. Ariba's managed services solutions deliver a turnkey service for a specific spend category, a spend management process step, or the complete spend management for Global 3000 customers.

Case Study: PPG Industries had more than $5 billion in spend across more than 15 business units offering products from industrial coatings to insurance. The company knew it had considerable leverage with suppliers if it could establish a centralized, controlled procurement discipline backed by comprehensive information and analytics. To achieve that goal, the company developed a strategy of consolidating its global spend information in a single data warehouse, which it would leverage to aggregate spend within commodities for aggressive renegotiation. Additional objectives included improved data classification, enhanced spend information available online, supplier rationalization, and maverick spend reduction.

To increase its productivity and savings potential, PPG turned to Ariba to provide targeted spend management capabilities, including an easy-to-use dashboard-like ability to drill down into and navigate the data in the warehouse. In late 2003, the company rolled out Ariba Analysis™, Ariba QuickSource™, and the SoftFace data cleansing application (integrated into Ariba Data Enrichment since the Ariba acquisition of SoftFace in March 2004).

Today, PPG has 95% of its indirect spend under central visibility and control with the help of the data warehouse initiative and Ariba's spend management solutions. Every PPG buyer also has access to spend data. More than $200 million has been sourced through the Ariba solutions to date, resulting in 90% supplier reduction and 10% savings in overall costs.

CombineNet, Inc.

Contact Information: Fifteen 27th Street, Pittsburgh, PA 15222, phone: (412) 471-8200, e-mail: info@combinenet.com, Web: www.combinenet.com

Representative Clients: Procter & Gamble, Siemens, U.S. Postal Service, H.J. Heinz

Scope and Type of Services Offered: CombineNet's cost and profit tools can change the way companies make strategic sourcing decisions. REV, CombineNet's flagship product, is described as a fast, easy-to-use, highly configurable Web-based application that allows sourcing and procurement professionals to reduce their total cost of ownership by driving inefficiencies out of the supply chain.

REV's proprietary combinatorial optimization engine provides analysis capabilities that enable supply chain professionals to embrace complexity and quickly identify the award allocations that best meet the needs of their supply chain. That means managers can now make critical decisions with the ease, speed, and confidence that create real competitive advantage, says CombineNet. And they can use these same systems to document, justify, and present their decisions to stakeholders and management peers. More than 45 Global 1000 companies have added hundreds of millions of dollars to their bottom line by reducing enterprise-wide strategic sourcing costs with REV.

Key Strengths/Expertise:

Expressive Bidding: Suppliers are encouraged to offer alternative, creative bids that make sense for their business, creating a win-win situation by driving inefficiencies out of the supply chain and reducing your total cost of ownership.

Iterative Scenario Analysis: Unlimited, on-the-fly "what if" scenario analysis capabilities enable sourcing teams to uncover hidden savings and learn the trade-offs between potential identified savings and *implementable* savings by understanding the cost impact of business rules against award scenarios.

CombineNet's REV optimization engine uses proprietary, patented methods of problem definition to translate real-world situations into streamlined formulas that can be solved by advanced combinatorial optimization.

Service Model: ASP, on demand, and/or enterprise-wide license

Compensation Structure: Offers three types of payment options:

- ◆ Access fee plus professional services as incurred (enterprise or per-project basis)
- ◆ Fixed fee (based upon spend size and complexity of project)
- ◆ Gainshare — percentage of unconstrained savings realized as a result of the expressive bidding aspect of CombineNet's system

Target Customers: Global 1000 companies with emphasis on industrial manufacturing, consumer products, chemicals, etc.

Case Study: A Fortune 100 company in the consumer goods industry used CombineNet to implement a new sourcing strategy for one of its largest indirect material sourcing spends: in-store product displays. Procurement of in-store displays had been a process closely managed by marketing managers responsible for different product categories. Based on individual product promotion schedules and display requirements, marketing managers typically used incumbent suppliers to deliver turnkey solutions that included design, production, and assembly of displays for easy in-store setup.

CombineNet and the client's project team developed and executed a sourcing implementation plan designed to combine their annual display spend across a more efficiently used supplier base, while improving the reliability and quality of display production and services.

The new data model identified requirements and costs of individual display components in all four of the client's product categories, providing benefits for suppliers and buyers. CombineNet's unique Expressive Bidding format allowed suppliers to bid in their own terms, including volume discounts, bundled pricing, and alternate products or services. CombineNet's robust Scenario Builder tool allowed buyers to quickly and easily consider a large number of "what if" scenarios when analyzing the larger, more complex set of data.

Project Results:

Cost savings
◆ 45% implementable savings versus previous spends = $75 million
◆ Analytical results generated in seconds versus days
◆ Annual combined procurement cycles consolidated to eight weeks

Insight
◆ Gained more accurate measurement of business decisions and trade-offs
◆ Gained clarity concerning market competition and innovation

Best practices
◆ Established combined sourcing model for annual contract awards
◆ Implemented collaborative supply chain practices that increased efficiency for suppliers and business

Emptoris, Inc.

Contact Information: Edmond Macri, Product Marketing Manager, Emptoris, Inc., 200 Wheeler Road, Burlington, MA 01803

Representative Clients: American Express, Bank of America, Exostar, GlaxoSmithKline, ICG Commerce, Owens Corning, Quadrem, Syngenta, Toro

Scope and Type of Services Offered: Emptoris is a provider of powerful enterprise supply management solutions for Global 1000 companies. Through Emptoris 5, a suite of Web-based supply management solutions, enterprises are able to drive millions of dollars in bottom-line savings, execute savings initiatives faster, and improve the productivity of their procurement and supply management teams. By incorporating in-depth spend, category, and supply base knowledge with Internet negotiation applications, optimization technologies, and an enterprise-deployment framework, Emptoris provides the first closed-loop enterprise supply management solution that automates the entire process from up-front strategy development through tracking of savings capture. Utilizing Emptoris's comprehensive set of features which integrate spend analysis, negotiation, supplier performance management, contract management, and compliance tracking, enterprises can:

- Automate spend analysis to ensure quick identification of new savings opportunities
- Provide insight into how suppliers stack up to spur supplier innovation and drive down total cost
- Create a holistic view of supplier performance that can be factored into all decisions
- Link spend analysis, category strategy, sourcing execution, compliance tracking, and supplier performance to ensure greater control
- Access an enterprise-wide view of spend, supplier, and category knowledge to drive reuse
- Track internal and external compliance to guarantee savings capture

Key Strengths/Expertise:

- *Advanced analytical decision-support technologies*: Including full-spectrum spend analytics, optimization-based bid analysis, and supplier assessment analytical models, to make better decisions, faster
- *Advanced buyer/supplier collaboration*: Via the Emptoris Smart Data Framework, which allows suppliers to compete on all elements of value, not just price, and incorporates supplier innovation into the bidding process
- *Data source agnosticism*: Enables Emptoris solutions to work with all ERP and legacy systems to aggregate data and provide a "source of truth" across the enterprise
- *Ease of use and breadth of application*: Via a Web-based, global solution that integrates spend analysis, supplier negotiation, optimization-based bid analysis, compliance, and supplier performance management processes

Service Model: Software license model

Compensation Structure: Emptoris offers both perpetual and term license options.

Target Customers: Emptoris targets enterprises that are looking for solutions designed to manage the strategic aspects of the supplier engagement from up-front savings and supplier identification, evaluation, selection, negotiation, and contract to postcontract supplier performance evaluation and compliance management. These enterprises typically have revenue of $500 million and up. This market includes vertical sectors that allocate a significant portion of their costs to procuring goods and services from suppliers. This includes but is not limited to the following industries: pharmaceuticals, retail, consumer packaged goods, high-tech electronics, diversified manufacturing, energy, automotive, aerospace and defense, and mining.

Case Study: GlaxoSmithKline, a $32 billion global pharmaceutical company, was looking to improve efficiencies across the enterprise to direct as much funding as possible into its R&D pipeline. A key component of this strategy was to improve internal efficiencies and reduce overall spending on goods and services. The company called upon Emptoris to provide a supply management solution to meet its aggressive goals. Procurement experts at the company wanted a solution that could handle their entire process, including spend analysis, negotiation, supplier management, and contracts and compliance. The company embarked on an implementation strategy to support the global procurement group's management of direct and indirect goods and services across the company's 47-country global footprint. After implementing Emptoris's strategic enterprise supply management platform, the company achieved positive return on investment within a few weeks of implementation from the savings of just three supplier negotiations. Over three years, the solution has realized an average annual return on investment of 150:1 by managing thousands of sourcing events with more than 10,000 suppliers — more than 80% of GlaxoSmithKline's core supply base. In total, GlaxoSmithKline has saved more than $300 million while enhancing its supplier relationships and improving the quality of both its supply base and the goods and services sourced.

Frictionless Commerce, Inc.

Contact Information: Don MacLennan, VP Marketing & Product Management, phone: (617) 495-0180, e-mail: sales@frictionless.com

Representative Clients: MetLife, Florida Power & Light, Aetna, Bristol-Myers Squibb, Wachovia, TDS, Alticor, Telewest Communications, CIGNA, Philip Morris U.S.A.

Scope and Type of Services Offered: Frictionless SRM is a suite of modules focused on spend analysis, supplier profiling, sourcing, contract management, and supplier performance management. Its focus is on the person-to-person processes that establish and deliver value. The Frictionless mission is to double the value its customers deliver through SRM every three years or less. To achieve this, customers leverage the combination of Frictionless services and the collected experience of its customer community to ensure that Frictionless SRM is fully adopted and the mission is achieved.

Key Strengths/Expertise: The software's flexible architecture enables companies to model the unique needs of their organizations, without any custom coding, says Frictionless. This capability becomes critical in the face of changing business needs over time, enabling them to sustain adoption and achieve expected SRM value.

The infrastructure enables "on-the-fly" changes to the system structure, mass customization to model business processes, and a highly adaptive structure that can be changed even after deployment.

- Easily modified, with just point-and-click from the browser
- Mass customization to model the complexities of numerous business processes
- No limit to the number of modifications that can be made, such as roles, processes, business objects, data feeds, etc.

Service Model: Frictionless offers both licensed software (that can be deployed behind the firewall and hosted through a Frictionless-managed data center) and a subscription-based, hosted on-demand offering.

Compensation Structure: Customers have the option of purchasing an annual or multiyear subscription or perpetual license. The on-demand offering is available as an annual subscription.

Target Customers: Focus is on Global 2500 purchasing organizations. The solution supports the cross-category requirements of numerous industries such as discrete manufacturing, financial services, process manufacturing, utilities, and communications services.

Case Study: MetLife is one of the largest U.S. insurers and is a member of the Fortune 100. The company began an enterprise-wide initiative to support sourcing best practices, fulfill e-sourcing and e-procurement needs, increase efficiencies, and achieve greater savings. Frictionless SRM is deployed throughout the company to capture and analyze all activity in both the supplier selection and supplier management processes. These processes include analyzing contracts, auditing contracts and ongoing projects, overseeing the request for proposal process, and managing more than 1300 suppliers.

Using the tools provided by Frictionless, MetLife has consolidated enterprise-wide purchasing into a single system to both increase efficiency and improve quality. In addition, MetLife has achieved:

- Expenditure analysis to improve managerial review and control of expenses
- Supplier selection process to negotiate the best value
- Contract management and compliance

I-many, Inc.

Contact Information: Dennis Wong, Director of Marketing, phone: (650) 226-1535, e-mail: dwong@imany.com

Representative Clients: Worldwide, I-many has 280 customers, 25% of which are Fortune 50 companies. All of I-many's customers fall within the company's three lines of business: contract and compliance management, revenue commitment management, and health and life sciences. Some of I-many's customers include Procter & Gamble, Honeywell, Scripps Health, RJ Reynolds, Dr. Pepper, Simplot, Otis Spunkmeyer, RONA, Sicor, and Wockhardt.

Scope and Type of Services Offered: I-many delivers the most advanced and comprehensive enterprise contract management solutions available, which when separate or combined allow any organization to automate one, some, or all of the contract management process. I-many's business solution suites consist of products and services in the following areas:

- ◆ *Contract and Compliance Management Solution*: Enables enterprises to create, store, edit, and manage any type of business contract and to ensure transaction compliance for the terms agreed to in those contracts.
  - ◇ Sell side: Enables enterprises to create, store, edit, and manage any type of contract and manage the associated commitments.
  - ◇ Buy side: Improves purchasing power by automating the source-to-spend process, including full contract creation and commitment management.
- ◆ *Revenue Commitment Management Solution*: Enables enterprises to maximize cash flow by lowering days sales outstanding and minimizing operational expenses. I-many's best-of-breed solutions combine transactional compliance capabilities, comprehensive dispute, deductions, collections, returns optimization, and contract management products to provide the best solution for the revenue commitment cycle.
- ◆ *Life Sciences Contract Management Solution*: Designed to meet the unique needs of the life sciences industry, paying special attention to the delicate interaction of legal terminology, market dynamics, and information systems in the life sciences industry.

Key Strengths/Expertise: I-many solutions provide business process benefits as well as hard-cost return on investment, allowing customers to easily justify projects. Traditionally, any automation of the contract process has largely been confined to only certain parts of the process (i.e., contract creation, storage, or contract rebate management). In fact, contract management is a broad function, and very significant benefits can be realized through automating many parts, if not all of the process. I-many's Enterprise Contract Management solutions provide what customers truly need: the ability to automate the entire enterprise contract management process.

Service Model: Hosted and installed

Compensation Structure: License and subscription

Target Customers: I-many targets enterprise customers in any industry. Since the company's inception in 1989, I-many has developed areas of expertise in several vertical industries:

- ◆ Aerospace and defense
- ◆ Computer hardware and services
- ◆ Consumer packaged goods
- ◆ Financial services
- ◆ Food services
- ◆ Health and life sciences
- ◆ Manufacturing
- ◆ Retail
- ◆ Telecommunications
- ◆ Transportation services
- ◆ Utilities

Case Study: With operations in over 60 countries, the Procter & Gamble Co. has extensive global purchasing needs. This $39 billion company makes product purchases and commitments based on contract agreements that directly impact the company's bottom line. The average Fortune 1000 company now has between 20,000 and 40,000 contracts, up 20% in five years, according to the National Association of Purchasing Managers. P&G realized that its ability to effectively manage its contracts was a critical business concern.

P&G's Purchases group turned to I-many for its ContractSphere solution. I-many ContractSphere is used by more than 700 P&G employees worldwide to draft, negotiate, amend, renew, and manage contracts. I-many ContractSphere has reduced P&G's financial exposure from noncompliance issues and unantici-pated contract expirations by helping it closely monitor performance and contract compliance. It also helped the P&G Purchases group standardize all its global procurement and contracting practices, as well as monitor contractual informa-tion and activities at every location.

I-many ContractSphere has also helped streamline contract creation, facilitate internal and external collaboration, accelerate negotiation and approval, increase contract visibility, and enhance reporting and control for P&G's business units around the world.

Ketera Technologies

Contact Information: 3965 Freedom Circle, 10th Floor, Santa Clara, CA 95054

Representative Clients: Maytag, Delta, United Airlines, GAP, Avnet, HMS Host, ServiceMaster, Wrigley, CNF, Newmont Mining

Scope and Type of Services Offered: Ketera says it is the lowest cost on-demand spend management solution that reduces and controls corporate spending for direct and indirect goods and services.

Spend Analysis: Ketera Spend Analysis enables companies to find savings through gaining a complete understanding of their spending and identifying areas for reducing costs. It enables companies to analyze spending without the need to implement enterprise software or invest in expensive consulting projects.

Contract Management: Ketera Contract Management enables sourcing and purchasing professionals to keep savings by providing a single repository for contracts, decreasing contract cycle time, and enforcing contract compliance. It delivers comprehensive support throughout the contract management life cycle.

Procurement: Ketera Procurement supports decentralized use but maintains centralized control over access to preferred suppliers and negotiated prices. The expertise of Ketera Supplier Services delivers supplier catalogue management, transaction routing, and project management services.

Services Procurement: Ketera Services Procurement provides a single repository for all service-related purchases and interactions with suppliers. It manages project time lines and costs for all services areas including professional, consulting, IT, facilities management, and human resources management.

Sourcing: Ketera Sourcing automates the entire sourcing process and can significantly decrease both sourcing time and unit prices.

Key Strengths/Expertise:
Why are Ketera solutions compelling?

- Ketera's on-demand model provides a stronger return on investment with five to ten times less investment.
- *Inexpensive*: A comprehensive solution at a fraction of the traditional cost.
- *Fast*: Implemented within 30 days of project kickoff.
- *Easy to use*: Order online as you would from paper catalogues from both new and existing suppliers.
- *Effective*: Eliminates noncompliance spending (typically 30% of all spending) by controlling access to specific suppliers, catalogues, and prices.
- *Flexible*: Distributed access allows for both central office and business unit approvals.

Service Model: Ketera Technologies is a leading provider of on-demand procurement solutions, enabling companies to control and reduce corporate spending at a low cost of ownership. Ketera creates a "source-to-pay" loop to identify, capture, and sustain bottom-line savings with spend analysis, sourcing, procurement, contract management, and supplier performance.

Compensation Structure: Ketera's pricing proposal meets the objective of maximizing return while minimizing risk through a structure that self-funds, avoids negative cash flow, and delivers benefits on or before fees. It is a subscription, "pay-as-you-go" model.

Target Customers: Ketera's target market includes both enterprise customers (defined by a 1000-employee size) and mid-market customers (defined by a 50- to 999-employee size). Ketera's customers come from a variety of industries including manufacturing, distribution, airlines, transportation, electronics, computer and technology, retail, media, and professional services. As of March 2005, Ketera had enabled more than 60 clients and has processed more than $150 billion through its spend analysis solution.

Case Study: Kennametal is the market leader in North America in metal cutting tools and is second in Europe and worldwide. With four business units and more than 25 manufacturing plants, Kennametal executives realized that significant savings could be achieved by centralizing contracts with suppliers, reducing maverick spend, and streamlining the source-to-pay process across the organization.

Before Ketera, fragmented supply base and lack of standards systems resulted in 20 to 25% maverick spend. There was wide variability in prices paid by business units and the procure-to-pay cycle was paper intensive and costly.

Kennametal went live with Ketera Spend Management in August 2002. The following results have been achieved:

- ◆ 150% return on investment generated after one year. Achieved payback on solution investment within six months. On track to achieve 500% return on investment within three years. Maverick spend has been reduced by 90%.
- ◆ 10 to 15% cost savings were achieved as business units shifted spending to preferred suppliers.
- ◆ Improved compliance with strategic contracts from 30% to 70% since 2002.
- ◆ Live with Ketera within 45 days; 360+ users and 10 suppliers enabled.
- ◆ Minimal resources required for project. One full-time equivalent required during deployment.

Oracle

Contact Information: Corporate Headquarters, 500 Oracle Parkway, Redwood Shores, CA 94065, phone: (650) 506-7000, Web: www.oracle.com/applications/procurement/intro.html

Representative Clients: GE, Alcoa, Citi, Cisco, University of Pennsylvania, Ingersoll-Rand, Reuters, NCR, TUI, Gap

Scope and Type of Services Offered: Oracle Advanced Procurement is described as the integrated suite that dramatically cuts all supply management costs. Oracle Advanced Procurement is a critical component of Oracle's eBusiness Suite.

Reduce Spend on Goods and Services: Oracle says it reduces costs at every stage of procurement, from spotting and exploiting new savings opportunities to enforcing contracted pricing. Packaged spend analysis spots opportunities such as nonsourced spending or contract leakage. Online negotiation increases sourcing bandwidth and effectiveness. Because sourcing is integrated, negotiated savings are reflected on every order. Oracle streamlines all procurement processes. With an extremely robust transaction backbone, Advanced Procurement provides complete procure-to-pay automation. Configurable automation executes routine transactions, freeing procurement professionals for strategic activities. Employees can place self-service requisitions. Structured online supplier communications through a Web portal and the Oracle Supplier Network reduce errors, lag time, and processing costs.

Enforce Policy Compliance: Paper-based procurement processes are slow, expensive, and create barriers to enforcing policy. Oracle builds compliance right into the system. Exception-based enforcement reforms behavior with configurable approvals that escalate exceptions for scrutiny. Budget-based procurement eliminates cost overruns by ensuring that funds are available. For total procurement visibility, Advanced Procurement drives compliance in real time.

Key Strengths/Expertise: Oracle Advanced Procurement is comprised of the following modules:

- Daily Business Intelligence For Purchasing
- Sourcing
- Procurement Contracts
- Purchasing
- iProcurement
- Services Procurement
- iSupplier Portal
- Oracle Supplier Network

Together, with Oracle payables, they provide a complete procure-to-pay automation designed to deliver for sustainable savings. Oracle Advanced Procurement is integrated to the Oracle eBusiness Suite for seamless flows between purchasing and accounts payable, project management, and supply chain planning, as well as design and engineering.

Service Model: Oracle Advanced Procurement is available as licensed software on a term or perpetual basis. Optionally, customers can choose to utilize hosting or technical implementation services from Oracle or its partner organizations. Business services for strategic sourcing (e.g., category expertise) are available through partner organizations such as A.T. Kearney, BearingPoint, and IBM.

Compensation Structure: Most customers choose to license Oracle's software and pay annual maintenance. Term licenses are available on a "pay-as-you-go" basis.

Target Customers: Oracle has a long history in serving organizations with revenue in excess of $100 million. Oracle has success in and focus on the following industry sectors: services (including financial services and public sector), industrial manufacturing, travel and transportation, telecommunications, high tech, health care, and retail.

Case Study: Since the time the University of Pennsylvania implemented Oracle applications, it has saved more than $70 million on purchases of products and services. In 2002, the university launched an integrated procurement and financials system based on the Oracle E-Business Suite. Online transactions now account for approximately 72% of the procurement dollars spent by the university. Invoice-processing time has been reduced by 40% and invoice-processing costs by as much as 98%. Approximately 1700 users take advantage of online procurement, which has lowered procurement prices by as much as 35%.

Perfect Commerce

Contact Information: 850 NW Chipman Road, Suite 5050, Lee's Summit, MO 64063, phone: (816) 448-4444, Web: www.perfect.com

Representative Clients: ITT Industries, First Energy, HR Block, Federal Reserve Bank, UCLA, Yellow Roadway, Con Ed, BellSouth, American Italian Pasta, Eli Lilly, eFunds

Scope and Type of Services Offered: Perfect Commerce is a leading supplier of on-demand supplier relationship management solutions and provides connectivity to trading partners via The Open Supplier Network℠ (The OSN℠). The company has more than 500 clients (51 in the Fortune 500), 160,000 users, and 8500 suppliers.

Perfect Commerce provides deep supplier-facing capabilities for the complete sourcing-to-settlement process. The company enables businesses to achieve sustainable supply management by simplifying the complex challenges of spend management, sourcing, contract management, services management, procurement, and electronic invoice presentment and payment.

- *The OSN℠*: 8500 suppliers, 21+ million SKUs, 160,000 users
- *Perfect Source*: Event manager, contract manager, event management services, collaborative sourcing, category solutions
- *Perfect Procure*: Search manager, catalogue manager, procurement manager, managed content services, supplier enablement
- Workforce management, vendor management, program management
- *Perfect Insight*: Benchmarking services, market intelligence, analytics, Accutrack
- *Perfect Finance*: Invoice manager, payment management services

Key Strengths/Expertise: Perfect Commerce's complete offering addresses the entire source-to-settle process. The OSN℠, on-demand delivery, along with deep supply chain expertise are what sets the company apart. By providing an OPEN network and solutions that are delivered outside the firewall, companies have improved their processes, increased efficiencies, and reduced costs.

Service Model: On demand

Compensation Structure: Pay as you go and subscription based

Target Customers: Fortune 1000 companies, across all industries

Case Study: Using an online reverse auction, FirstEnergy realized savings of 43% on its corporate copier contract covering several hundred copy machines.

Opportunity: Hoping to duplicate its success from previous online auctions, FirstEnergy needed help in sourcing and negotiating a contract for supply and maintenance of several hundred digital copiers.

Solution: FirstEnergy turned to the auctions services team from Pantellos, now Perfect Commerce, to determine cost savings objectives and design an online auction that would produce the desired results. The auction services team worked with FirstEnergy throughout the auction process, including defining requirements, developing a request for quotation, assisting in the selection of suppliers to bid in the auction, and finally, conducting the auction event itself.

Results: The copier auction saved FirstEnergy 43% based on the starting reference price. Ten bidders took part in the auction, driving the lowest bid below FirstEnergy's best-case expectations. As an added benefit, the entire auction process, from planning and training to conducting the actual event, took about five weeks from start to finish. The auction itself lasted less than two hours.

According to company executives, FirstEnergy is committed to deploying the tools needed to maximize the impact on earnings per share. The company uses auctions to assess current market conditions in real time while reducing the overall bid development and assessment cycle. FirstEnergy leaders believe that auctions, when used as part of an overall program, are an integral component of its supply chain success.

FirstEnergy uses online auctions as a regular part of its strategic sourcing plan. Auctions help buyers achieve the best possible market prices on goods and services while reducing procurement cycle time. FirstEnergy has saved millions of dollars by using auctions to source and procure commodities in several different categories.

Procuri, Inc.

Contact Information: Andrea Soltysiak, phone: (404) 720-1153, e-mail: asoltysiak@procuri.com

Representative Clients: Procter & Gamble, Eastman Kodak, ITT Industries, KLM Royal Dutch Airlines, Rio Tinto, U.S. Steel, Kohler, Newell Rubbermaid, Georgia-Pacific, Scientific Atlanta

Scope and Type of Services Offered: Procuri says it delivers functionally rich, online strategic sourcing solutions that empower enterprises to automate sourcing processes, to institutionalize best sourcing practices, and to make best-value sourcing decisions that improve bottom-line results. Because the solutions are Web based, there is no software to buy and install, PCs to be configured, or IT departments to slow the process down. Procuri's solutions are designed to be desktop applications that enable buyers to conduct sourcing events without the need for expensive consulting services.

Procuri provides functionality that fulfills the buyer's fundamental needs:

♦ *Supplier Qualification and Performance Analysis*: This functionality provides evaluation tools that allow buyers to establish rating categories to be used for comparing supplier capabilities and performance.

♦ *Collaboration, Coordination and Two-Way Information Exchange*: Procuri's collaboration tools foster a streamlined communication process with suppliers by capturing communications and storing them in a central location.

♦ *Competitive Bidding and Negotiations*: Once suppliers are qualified and the specifications are finalized, buyers collect pricing through an electronic bidding process.

♦ *Decision Analysis and Optimization*: Procuri provides a decision analysis capability that enables the user to select winners and record RFX results.

♦ *Performance Analysis and Reporting*: With Performance Analysis and Reporting, users can retrieve, analyze, and report on almost any data in the system.

Key Strengths/Expertise: Procuri describes itself as a proven and successful strategic sourcing solutions provider that delivers rapid, measurable business results through its dedication to functionally rich, online strategic sourcing. Procuri enables an immediate and measurable impact to processes and empowered decision making for buyers through its comprehensive and extensible solutions. Organizations achieve rapid self-sufficiency without dependence on outside consultants by leveraging and elevating the expertise of their staff. By incorporating input from procurement professionals, Procuri has developed its solutions with the buyer's needs in mind. Easy to use and cost effective, Procuri's on-demand solutions can be quickly and easily deployed to immediately begin improving processes.

Service Model: Procuri's solutions are delivered through an on-demand model.

Compensation Structure: Procuri's solutions are sold as an annual or multiyear contract on a fixed-price subscription.

Target Customers: Procuri targets Global 2000 enterprises.

Case Study: Bank of America knew that its lease origination process needed some work. Cycles times were too slow and there was a problem with getting the most competitive lease rate factor. Looking internally for a solution, Bank of America discovered that its supply chain management department successfully used Procuri's solutions to streamline processes. It decided to utilize Procuri's technology to create business competition and streamline processes to obtain the lowest lease rate factor.

Bank of America was extremely pleased with the effortless functionality of Procuri's solutions and the total control it had over the event. The leasing team has uncovered unprecedented savings and a more streamlined department by implementing Procuri's solutions. Through the events conducted, business partners have experienced significant lease payment reductions. Bank of America also discovered that the request for information process and the information gathered from it proves itself as a very powerful analytical tool.

"Implementing Procuri's solutions for bidding out leasing opportunities results in the ability to find lease savings through not only reducing lease rate factors but also reducing the price of equipment while also saving time *and* delighting its business partners. All of this makes the investment in Procuri's solutions well worth it," said Michelle Selk, assistant vice president at Bank of America.

SAP AG

Contact Information: Dr. Manfred Heil, Senior Vice President of SRM, SAP AG

Representative Clients: Alfa Corp., Ericsson Corp., FMC Kongsberg Subsea AS, Hero Honda Motors, Pemex Gas, Polish Security Printing Works, Sea Containers Ltd., Seattle Public Schools, Steelcase, University of Toronto

Scope and Type of Services Offered: mySAP SRM is described as a comprehensive purchasing solution that helps companies integrate supply management activities to achieve sustainable savings and generate enduring value. By closing the loop between sourcing and procurement, mySAP SRM enables a cohesive form of supply management that helps enforce purchasing policies in order to realize the cost and quality advantages secured through negotiated contracts. Instead of making one-off deals with random suppliers to secure the day's lowest price, companies can achieve the kind of repeatable savings that reduce unit costs over the long term. mySAP SRM also enables higher levels of overall supply value by helping companies improve margins, reduce supply risk, and more easily take advantage of supplier innovation. Because its flexible processes extend across multiple business units and spend categories, mySAP SRM enables business change, helping companies adapt to new developments in the marketplace with greater ease, agility, and success.

Key Strengths/Expertise: mySAP SRM is complete, integrated and connected, says SAP. It is described as the only solution which can close the loop between sourcing and procurement, within departments inside the enterprise (integration with product life cycle management, supply chain management, and ERP solutions) and across the entire supply base. This gives SAP a functional advantage over offerings by best-of-breed vendors.

mySAP SRM is built on SAP NetWeaver, an application and integration platform. SAP NetWeaver provides extensibility without requiring modifications to deliver a lower total cost of ownership. Including a platform with the depth and breadth of SAP NetWeaver gives SAP a competitive advantage over offerings by ERP vendors.

Service Model: License

Compensation Structure: Purchase

Target Customers: mySAP SRM is aimed at companies with more than $300 million in revenue and can be used to manage both direct and indirect spend.

Case Study: Pemex Gas is the exclusive provider of natural gas to consumers and businesses in Mexico, but the government will soon open the market to other companies. To better position itself to face competition, Pemex Gas is improving its performance through better procurement processes. The company is using mySAP SRM to enable these processes and is seeing shorter cycle times, lower inventory, and other measurable benefits. Results achieved between July 2003 and June 2004 include:

◆ Reduced prices on one-year contracts by 6% on average
◆ Lowered cycle times covering release order decision to order placement by 72%
◆ Reduced release order placement process costs by 20% and improved productivity by eliminating 64% of activities and automating 60% of manual processes
◆ Lowered bidding process costs by 13% through electronic collaboration
◆ Reduced inventory of purchased items by 25% and maintenance inventory costs by 9%
◆ Contributed to benefits for suppliers, such as a 70% reduction in cycle time for the sales process and a 50% reduction in manpower needed to develop products

SciQuest

Contact Information: Kristi Lee, SRK Communications, phone: (919) 754-9511, e-mail: kristi@srkcommunications.com

Representative Clients: Biogen Idec, GlaxoSmithKline, Pfizer, Roche, Schering-Plough, Arizona State University, Indiana University, University of Michigan, University of Nevada, Reno, University of Pennsylvania

Scope and Type of Services Offered: SciQuest's on-demand solutions help organizations gain greater control over their spend through content-driven spend management solutions. By providing spend management on demand, customers are able to deploy solutions more rapidly and at a dramatically reduced cost. Through its open supplier network, SciQuest aggregates access to detailed supplier content and enables supplier connectivity, allowing customers to increase contract compliance and user adoption to reduce costs. By outsourcing content management and automating procurement processes, customers can improve efficiency and bring more spend under management.

Key Strengths/Expertise:

♦ By aggregating access to detailed supplier content and supplier connectivity, customers can increase contract compliance and user adoption to reduce costs.
♦ By outsourcing content management and automating procurement processes, customers can improve efficiency and bring more spend under management.
♦ By providing spend management on demand, SciQuest can deliver its solutions more rapidly and at a dramatically reduced cost.

Service Model: On demand

Compensation Structure: Pricing is based on subscriptions that are determined by the size of the organization and the amount of spend going through the system.

Target Customers: Key target markets are:

♦ *Higher education research institution*: For example, the University of Pennsylvania used SciQuest solutions to connect to more than 100 suppliers and realized $2.3 million in savings in the first year of implementation.
♦ *Top-tier life science organization*: For example, GSK used SciQuest solutions to increase contract compliance from 49% to 71%, resulting in $2 million in savings in the first year of implementation.

Case Study: University of Pennsylvania
Key Challenges: To extract even more value out of the Penn Marketplace, the university's successful supplier exchange, purchasing services needed a solution that could increase user adoption while improving contract utilization. The University of Pennsylvania needed a solution to:

♦ Enable a critical mass of supplier content with minimal IT resources ·
♦ Configure catalogues to promote preferred suppliers and campus "best buys"
♦ Leverage existing technology investment in Oracle iProcurement suite

SciQuest Solution: The University of Pennsylvania licensed SciQuest's Spend Director solution with additional content packs to enable key suppliers. Spend Director was integrated with Oracle Corporation's iProcurement software. Prior to the adoption of Spend Director, the university achieved integration with 31 suppliers. Now the system's 1850 software users are currently able to access 97 of the university's strategic contract suppliers' online catalogues in key commodity groups, of which 21 are classified as diversity suppliers. Using Spend Director, the university currently directs approximately 70% of campus purchase transactions through participating Penn Marketplace contract suppliers.

This technologically advanced e-procurement solution has resulted in stronger relationships for participating suppliers. In calendar year 2003, individual Penn Marketplace suppliers realized an increase of 16 to 42% in purchase dollars spend placed with the company versus the previous 12-month period. The University of Pennsylvania also experienced an increase in on-contract spend of 21% between fiscal year 2004 and fiscal year 2003 due to the Penn Marketplace.

The University of Pennsylvania experienced a tremendous increase in the speed it was able to integrate suppliers using the SciQuest Spend Director solution. Ralph Maier, Director of Purchasing Services, attributes the speed of implementation to two main factors:

1. SciQuest provides a Content Management Tool that greatly decreased the time and effort for the supplier to provide catalogue content.
2. "No cost to supplier" SciQuest business model eliminates an important barrier to integrating with suppliers that other SciQuest-competitive providers still exercise.

Verian Technologies

Contact Information: 8701 Mallard Creek Road, Charlotte, NC 28262, phone: (704) 547-7301, fax: (704) 547-7304, Web: www.verian.com

Representative Clients: Allstate Insurance Company of Canada, American Medical Response, Americold Logistics, Branch Bank & Trust Corporation (BB&T), GNC Corp., Main Street America Group, Phillips-Van Heusen, Regions Financial Corp., The Warnaco Group, Whayne Supply

Scope and Type of Services Offered: Verian Technologies is a leading provider of spend management technology solutions to mid-sized organizations. Verian's software and services help clients cut costs in the key areas of purchasing, invoice management, enterprise asset management, and travel and expense management. Most clients earn between $100 million and $3 billion in revenue. Included in the ProcureIT product suite are Purchase Manager for procuring goods and services through an automated ordering system, Invoice Manager for processing invoices that do not originate with purchase orders, Expense Manager for creating and routing online expense reports, and Asset Manager for managing the life cycle and ownership costs of fixed assets. ProcureIT, the company's flagship product, typically yields savings that are three times greater than the price of the solution within a year.

Key Strengths/Expertise:

1. *Application Programming Interface (API)*: Integration capability that does not require access to source code.
2. *E-mail Approvals*: Managers can approve or deny requisitions on a line item basis via e-mail without logging into the system.
3. *Buyer Separation*: Requisitions are automatically split according to each buyer's specialty.
4. *Integrated Expense Reporting*: Expense report and reimbursement tool shares database and user interface/work flow with purchasing and invoice management tools.
5. *Integration Expertise*: Verian employees have experience writing integrations with hundreds of other systems in various development environments.
6. *Spend Management Reporting/Analysis*: Reports provide meaningful analysis on 100% of spend — purchase orders, nonpurchase-order invoices, and reimbursables.

Service Model: License and ASP

Compensation Structure: Customers may purchase seat licenses for the software or, if they prefer, can use Varian's ASP model.

Target Customers: Target industries include financial services, industrial services, health care, and the public sector. Varian's software is best suited for organizations that have annual revenue between $100 million and $3 billion.

Case Study: Whayne Supply, a 1000-employee Caterpillar dealership headquartered in Louisville, Kentucky, has hundreds of people across its 16 locations purchasing millions of dollars in mechanical parts, services, and supplies each year. Whayne is one of the few Caterpillar dealerships in North America with a centralized purchasing department at its headquarters that negotiates supplier contracts. But it still lacked quality, aggregated data that would reveal opportunities for even better negotiating leverage.

After using ProcureIT for one year, Whayne realized almost $2 million in savings. One area where ProcureIT plugged a hole was in the recovery of lost billings in the service department. Customers were not being billed for all parts, which was costing the company almost $640,000 a year. Whayne was able to link ProcureIT to its billing system to stop the leak. Another area where ProcureIT assisted Whayne was in contract compliance. The company was losing thousands of dollars each year because of off-contract spending. With ProcureIT in place to enforce purchasing policies, Whayne Supply saved over $200,000 in the first year. Finally, by eliminating manual purchasing processes, ProcureIT was able to save Whayne over $3.5 million by reducing the amount of time and materials used to request, approve, order, and receive items.

Verticalnet

Contact Information: David Kaplan, phone: (610) 695-2310, e-mail: dkaplan@verticalnet.com

Representative Clients: Cadbury-Schweppes, PepsiCo, Alcan, Caraustar Industries, Illinois Tool Works Inc., MasterBrand Cabinets, Wyeth, IKEA, Delta Air Lines, NBC

Scope and Type of Services Offered: A leader in strategic supply management solutions for Global 2000 companies, Verticalnet says it provides flexible software tools and expert services that maximize the value realized from sourcing initiatives. Verticalnet solutions enable opportunity definition, sourcing strategy formulation, and complete negotiation, contract, and performance management. Customers are said to gain unprecedented visibility across the full spectrum of strategic supply management activities, along with the business process tools to act on this insight. Verticalnet customers have the flexibility of selecting individual best-of-breed modules or a fully integrated suite; they can access solutions on demand or install them on their own servers. Either way, Verticalnet allows sourcing professionals to eliminate redundancies and wasted steps, streamline processes, and focus on higher value activities.

Dedicated to customer success over the long term, Verticalnet goes beyond software to offer deep sourcing domain knowledge, broad category expertise, and a full range of enabling services that include training, help desk, and real-time event support. Every month, Verticalnet customers complete more than 1000 sourcing events involving tens of thousands of suppliers. With each category sourced, these customers reduce costs and save time with repeatable best practices that drive sustainable value.

Key Strengths/Expertise:

- Full, integrated suite of supply management offerings (including spend analysis, e-sourcing, contract management, and performance management)
- A true software services hybrid that enables Verticalnet to focus on delivering value to its customers, rather than just trying to sell software or services stand-alone
- A true on-demand offering across the entire suite

♦ Advanced sourcing techniques (expressive bidding, advanced optimization, category-specific tools and services)
♦ Category expertise across the spectrum of direct, indirect, and services categories, with an emphasis on the most complex categories (transportation, packaging, commercial print, industrial MRO, etc.)

Service Model: Verticalnet offers both a hosted (ASP) and "on-demand" service model, depending on client preference and the nature of the project. About 80% of its customers have chosen the on-demand subscription model.

Compensation Structure: For software, Verticalnet offer perpetual license and maintenance or subscription models. Its consulting services are typically priced as a fixed fee or on a time-and-materials basis; however, Verticalnet also has gainsharing agreements for several of its advanced sourcing projects.

Target Customers: Verticalnet's target customers are large companies (typically $500 million in spend and greater) in manufacturing (primarily industrial, consumer packaged goods, and pharmaceuticals) and retail. It also has strong telecommunication and transportation services verticals. Its software solutions are in use across a wide range of direct, indirect, and services categories. Verticalnet also provides customized technology and service offerings targeted toward the transportation (all modes), packaging, commercial print, industrial MRO, and travel categories.

Case Study: All major airlines have faced a series of challenges in the past couple of years — economic downturn, terrorist-related fears, etc. Some, such as Delta, have been more creative than others in finding ways to cut costs. Implemented before these issues, Delta Air Lines' supply chain management organization set a goal in 2000 of $300 million in cost savings by the end of 2004 that turned out to be vital to the company as business weakened.

The key to success for Delta's lofty goal was strategic sourcing. After an extensive search, Verticalnet was chosen to help the company attack sourcing using a three-pronged approach:

1. Make strategic sourcing a company-wide initiative
2. Identify and standardize a best-in-class sourcing process
3. Focus on capability development

Deployed in 2001, Delta's e-sourcing initiative relied heavily on Verticalnet's solution for auctions and other key sourcing initiatives, ultimately leading to $400 million in savings and an ongoing ability for Delta to enforce a standard sourcing process globally and to maintain process and supply market knowledge. Today, Delta is considered to have the epitome of a world-class supply chain (source: Aberdeen Group, 2004).

Zycus, Inc.

Contact Information: 103 Carnegie Center, Suite 117, Princeton, NJ 08540, phone: (609) 799-5664, fax: (609) 799-6047

Representative Clients: General Electric, DuPont, Automatic Data Processing (ADP), Inc., Unilever, Federal government of USA (GSA Advantage), Bearing Point, Rogers Communication, Ingersoll-Rand, Wipro

Scope and Type of Services Offered: Zycus Spend Data Management™ (SDM) software suite is comprised of:

1. *AutoClass*: Spend Data Classification software
2. *AutoSpec*: Spend Data Enrichment software

Zycus SDM software supports the following solutions:

1. *Detailed Spend Visibility*: A spend visibility solution that is completely automated and offers a granular in-depth view into category spend is best architected on the current enterprise IT stack. Using auto-classification tools that plug into a data warehouse, an enterprise can solve the spend data quality problems that act as impediments to a detailed spend visibility solution.
2. *Item Master Enrichment*: A spend data enrichment solution that can rationalize multiple item masters into one single unified view using automated classification and enrichment capabilities, thus ensuring high-quality output, in a short time frame at a lower total cost of ownership.
3. *Purchasing Compliance*: With AutoClass software embedded in the requisition process, the e-procurement systems can guide buyers to preferred suppliers and contracts and can facilitate faster routings and approvals through appropriate commodity managers by helping find the correct commodity code at point of requisition.
4. *Catalog Search*: For e-procurement users challenged by low adoption due to search inefficiencies, auto-classification tools help categorize high-volume catalogues to a common and granular code such as UNSPSC.

Key Strengths/Expertise: Artificial-intelligence-based SDM software. Instead of relying on rules to identify patterns of terms, this algorithm mimics the brain and uses a neural network approach to predict output of future "transactions" based on past "sample" classifications.

1. *Seamless Integration*: Powerful scheduler features, exposed Java APIs provide SDM software with seamless integration capabilities with DataWarehouse and e-procurement tools, such as SAP BW, ARIBA, etc.

2. *Automated Spend Data Classification Software*: AutoClass can be installed "behind the firewall" and can run hands-free in client's environment.
3. *Deep Domain Expertise*: Deep domain expertise of the materials management group sharing over 150 man-years of experience across different verticals.

Zycus is a leading provider of SDM software that provides key functionalities of data classification and enrichment for sourcing and procurement applications. With a move to improving spend data quality as the foundation for maturing spend management initiatives, Zycus software is in demand at most leading procurement organizations today. Organizations that are building next-generation infrastructure for on-demand spend analytics and purchase performance tracking systems view software tools for spend data management as key to achieving their goals. Zycus Spend Data Management™ software products are positively impacting global businesses (such as GE, DuPont, and others) *today*, enabling the discovery of hidden savings opportunities.

Service Model: License model only. Three- or five-year term license and ASP.

Compensation Structure: Payment options are flexible and designed to fit individual products and solutions.

Target Customers: Fortune 1000 companies in industries including manufacturing, consumer packaged goods, beverage and food, oil and gas, retail, automotive, and other verticals.

Case Study:
Overview: As a part of global spend management transformation, DuPont aimed at adopting best practices in spend analysis. It decided to deploy an automated spend analysis system using best-of-the breed components. The primary considerations in this decision were

1. Ensure maximum savings discovery through deep-spend visibility to meet steep savings mandates
2. Ensure a robust infrastructure that allows for aggregation and analysis of spend from multiple systems across the globe consistently, accurately, and on a repeatable basis

Key Factors:

◆ Thirty-plus disparate SAP and non-SAP source systems
◆ Spend to be analyzed on a monthly basis and then move on to a weekly basis

♦ Aggregation and classification of both direct and indirect spend with very high accuracy of 80% and above

Missing Piece of the Puzzle: A spend data classification software that could integrate with SAP BW and cleanse and classify data to a uniform taxonomy.

Solution: Zycus AutoClass integrated with SAP BW–based Enterprise Sourcing Data Warehouse.
Benefits:

1. Enhanced return on investment from the SAP BW investment
2. Efficient category management
3. Accurate and granular classification of poor quality and multilingual spend
4. Ongoing tracking and monitoring of spend to measure realized savings

Appendix B
Supply Management Consultants

The following brief profiles of several leading vendors of supply management consultants are provided as a service, and the co-authors make no claims concerning the completeness or accuracy of the statements, which were provided by the vendors. In some cases, they have been slightly edited to remove marketing assertions or puffery. Some companies declined to provide profiles or failed to provide profiles by the deadline. It should be noted that this information changes constantly and often dramatically. Check the Web-Added Value™ Download Resource Center at www.jrosspub.com for changes and additions.

Accenture

Contact Information: Pat Byrne, Global Managing Partner, Supply Chain Management Service Line, Accenture, 11951 Freedom Drive, Reston, VA 20190, Web: www.accenture.com/supplychain

Representative Clients: Astra-Zeneca, Best Buy, Cable and Wireless, Commonwealth of Pennsylvania, Defense Logistics Agency, Dell, Deutsche Bank, DuPont, Gambro, Shell

Scope and Type of Services Offered: The professionals in Accenture's supply chain management service line work with clients across a broad range of industries to develop high-performance supply chains that enable profitable growth in new and existing markets. They combine global industry expertise and skills in sourcing and procurement, supply chain planning, manufacturing and design, fulfillment, and service management to help organizations transform their supply chain capabilities. Accenture works with clients to implement innovative solutions that align operating models to support business strategies, improve the effectiveness of pricing, leverage outsourcing to improve supply chain services, adopt radio frequency identification and other emerging technologies, and enhance the skills and capabilities of the supply chain workforce.

Key Strengths/Expertise: Accenture is a global management consulting, technology services, and outsourcing company with 110 offices in 48 countries. Its practice serves its clients, including nearly 60% of the Global Fortune 100, with deep industry and supply chain expertise, broad global resources, and a proven track record. Additionally, Accenture's Strategic Delivery Model industrializes systems integration, technology, and outsourcing services, enabling clients to generate savings that can be reinvested in the business and creating additional value for their organizations. Accenture achieves industrialization through its Delivery Center Network; its highly skilled, multidisciplinary teams; and its standard methods, tools, and architectures.

Target Customers: Accenture serves a range of public and private sector clients within its communications and high tech, financial services, government, products, and resources industry groups.

Compensation/Outsourcing Structure: Accenture partners with its clients to determine a deal structure that meets the goals and objectives of both parties. As a pioneer in the use of value-based arrangements, Accenture is currently working on multiple transformational engagements with innovative deal structures. It also will employ more traditional arrangements.

Case Study: Dell pioneered direct-to-customer and global build-to-order processes in high-tech: It never assembles a computer system until it has received an actual order. Until recently, however, Dell's supplier management processes typically relied on manual mechanisms, which limited its ability to scale global business, maintain an optimal balance between supply and demand, and react quickly to marketplace changes. In response, a new online factory-scheduling and demand-planning initiative was developed by Dell, Accenture, and i2, including:

- ◆ Reengineering key supply chain processes, particularly in the area of supplier collaboration
- ◆ Developing technical systems and software architecture based on Dell hardware and i2 software
- ◆ Implementing i2's Factory Planner, Supply Chain Planner, and Collaboration Planner in a build-to-order environment
- ◆ Building interface programs to connect the system with Dell's order management and manufacturing applications

Now in place in Dell's plants around the world, the program paid for itself five times over during the first 12 months of operation. At any given time, there is less than 4 days of inventory in the entire Dell operation, while many competitors routinely carry 30 days or more. In addition, automation has helped Dell improve response times across the supply chain by providing a global view of supply and demand at any specific Dell location at any time.

A.T. Kearney, Inc.

Contact Information: Thomas Slaight, Vice President, New York, phone: (212) 350-3130, e-mail: tom_slaight@atkearney.com

Representative Clients: Daimler Chrysler, ChevronTexaco, BellSouth, Gillette, Tyco, State of California, Volkswagen, Microsoft, Staples, GE Capital

Scope and Type of Services Offered: A.T. Kearney addresses all elements of the House of Purchasing and Supply Management®: Supply Strategy, Supply Organization, Sourcing and Category Management, Supplier Relationship Management, Operating Management, Performance Metrics, Knowledge and Information Management, and Human Resource Management. It provides consulting, technology, category management, and business process outsourcing services.

Key Strengths/Expertise: A.T. Kearney has a global presence to serve large and medium-sized corporate and governmental organizations. For the last decade, sourcing and supplier management services have been more than a third of its revenues. Kearney conducts the global best-practice benchmarking survey called Assessment on Excellence in Procurement every three years. It sponsors the supply management executive education program called the Center for Strategic Supply Leadership with the Institute for Supply Management.

Target Customers: Target customers are large and medium-sized corporate and governmental organizations in all industries in all regions of the world.

Compensation/Outsourcing Structure: A.T. Kearney provides a high return on its customers' consulting investment. It seeks creative compensation structures that are mutually beneficial to its clients and to itself. These may include but are not limited to time and expenses, gainsharing, investment, and joint ventures.

Case Study: When Jim Kilts became CEO of Nabisco in 1997, he had heard of Kearney, but had not been involved in a supply management project with the company. Nabisco had used Kearney to address two waves of strategic sourcing under its previous CEO. Kilts audited the Kearney results and then continued with the Strategic Sourcing Initiative (SSI) to address additional spend categories. Kilts appreciated the rigor of the Kearney approach and admired the success that its consultants had in obtaining tangible results working his new company's employees.

Three years later, when Kilts was hired by Gillette as the CEO hired from outside the company to accomplish a turnaround, one of the first things he did was to hire Kearney "to launch another SSI." Kearney was able to obtain sourcing savings at an accelerated rate using its new e-sourcing software (eBreviate), restructure relationships with long-time strategic suppliers, and rapidly build up supply management capabilities at Gillette. Kilts was so impressed with the new e-sourcing technology that he had a demonstration video prepared for his board of directors.

Calyptus Consulting Group, Inc.

Contact Information: George L. Harris, President, Calyptus Consulting Group, Inc., 76 Bedford Street, Suite 22, Lexington, MA 02420, phone: (781) 674-0041, fax: (781) 674-0038, e-mail: gharris@calyptusgroup.com, Web: www.calyptusgroup.com

Representative Clients: United Technologies Corp., Tyco, Microsoft, Bank of America, FirstEnergy, United States Postal Service, Bose Corp., U.S. Army Surface Distribution and Deployment Command, U.S. Federal Transit Administration

Scope and Type of Services Offered: Calyptus Consulting Group is a professional services company based in Lexington, Massachusetts specializing in the purchasing, contracting, and supply management areas. Calyptus offers supply chain management training and consulting services designed to help organizations improve their quality, supply chains, core competencies, and cost performance. In the private sector, it serves Fortune 500 companies with development of client-specific strategies and procurement training and consulting solutions that focus on and improve capabilities, performance, and goals.

Calyptus guides clients through supply chain assessments, contract compliance, and cost evaluation and assists with the ever-changing dynamics of managing supply chains. The company trains client staff and assists in implementation of improvement initiatives, including lean management and strategic sourcing. Solutions may include e-business, business process reengineering, usage control, training, policy and procedure development, lean management, and innovation and organization restructuring activities. Its government focus is in federal acqui-·sition, subcontracting, purchasing under government contracts, and purchasing improvement. Calyptus has conducted over 30 full-scale procurement system reviews and organizational assessments.

Training, consulting, and assessments are provided, with expertise across many industries, including manufacturing, defense/aerospace, software, financial services, consumer goods, personal services, chemicals and oil industries, and health care.

Key Strengths/Expertise:

- *Training*: Designed, developed, and conducted more than 60 different supply chain management training courses worldwide
- *Facilitation*: Facilitated more than 500 strategic sourcing teams in both direct and indirect spend categories
- *Consulting*: Developed sourcing strategies to assist customers in reducing costs in excess of $100 million per year

Target Customers: Calyptus typically works with Fortune 500 organizations and has significant experience in many different industries, as well as in the public sector. Calyptus is particularly adept in indirect spend categories.

Compensation/Fee Structure: Calyptus engages with customers on primarily a fixed-price per-project basis. In some cases where the work cannot be well defined, a client is engaged on a time-and-materials basis. Cost-saving projects have also been conducted on a contingency basis.

Case Study: For Otis Elevator, Calyptus completed a multiyear assignment that resulted in cost savings of $230 million. This engagement included developing a five-year supply management strategy, implementing annual improvement plans, facilitating more than 200 strategies and sourcing teams, training more than 1000 staff in strategic sourcing and quality management in eight languages, and providing documentation such as policies, procedures, and practices. Calyptus established a business-unit-specific tracking system and worked with the senior vice president and president of this business unit to monitor, track, and develop corrective action plans in order to realize the cost savings and improvement objectives. Calyptus also integrated Otis's plans with United Technologies Corp. Corporate Supply Management Goals.

Daniel Penn Associates, LLC

Contact Information: Antonio R. Rodriguez, President, Daniel Penn Associates, 151 New Park Avenue, Hartford, CT 06106, phone: (860) 232-8577, fax: (860) 586-0928, e-mail: info@danielpenn.com, Web: www.danielpenn.com

Representative Clients: U.S. General Services Administration, United Technologies Corp., Centocor, Inc. (a Johnson & Johnson company), Exelon Corp., Metropolitan District Commission (Hartford, Connecticut), PECO Energy Co., Acxiom Corp.

Scope and Type of Services Offered: Daniel Penn Associates provides management consulting services in the following areas of procurement:

- Strategic sourcing
- Spend analysis
- Supplier diversity
- Business process improvement
- Contract and negotiation strategy
- Procurement and ERP systems
- Acquisition strategy
- Electronic procurement initiatives
- Purchasing standards and procedures
- Procurement training
- Staffing and capacity planning
- Supply chain management

Key Strengths/Expertise:

- Senior-level, "hands-on" experienced consultants (20+ years)
- National and international in scope
- Government and private sector entities
- Minority business enterprise firm
- Delivers solutions that are practicable in implementation, innovative in thinking, and sustainable by internal staff

Target Customers:

- National and multinational companies in the manufacturing, financial services, and utility industries with revenues over $250 million
- City, county, state, and federal agencies with annual budgets over $400 million

Compensation/Outsourcing Structure: Daniel Penn Associates works on a fixed-fee or time-and-materials basis, with out-of-pocket expenses billed as incurred. For spend analysis and strategic sourcing engagements, gainsharing arrangements will also be considered.

Case Study: The U.S. General Services Administration has begun a program to review software purchases across all agencies of government, with a goal to consolidate and negotiate better pricing within common commodity groups. This initiative, which is called SmartBUY, includes commercial off-the-shelf software that is generally acquired using license agreements with terms and prices that vary based on volume. Daniel Penn Associates was chosen to help the government identify those commodities that will yield cost savings, to assist in developing strategic sourcing plans, and to support contract negotiation efforts.

Daniel Penn Associates consultants collected data from a number of federal civilian agencies, analyzed the spend, and recommended a targeted list of commodities that had potential for significant cost savings. Among the targeted commodities were office automation, network management, antivirus, database, business modeling tools, and open source software support. Initial estimates of savings to the government were in the range of $100 million per year.

IBM

Contact Information: John R. Sharman, Jr., e-mail: jrsharm@us.ibm.com

Representative Clients: British Petroleum, Alcoa, Motorola, Halliburton, Dynegy, DuPont, Syngenta, Proctor & Gamble, Bristol-Myers Squibb, International Paper, Coors

Scope and Type of Services Offered:

- ◆ *Transformation Services*: Strategy, process standardization, policy development, training, reorganization, key measures
- ◆ *Procurement Application Integration Services*: Ariba, SAP, PeopleSoft, Oracle, Perfect Commerce, Ketera, SAP, Emptoris, and Digital Union, to include application configuration, testing, deployment, training, risk mitigation, piloting, etc.
- ◆ *Strategic Sourcing Services*: Source for clients, source with clients, develop category sourcing strategies, develop category negotiation strategies, conduct request for information, conduct request for proposal, qualify suppliers, and perform advantaged pricing exercises — accelerated sourcing exercises that leverage existing IBM suppliers to the client's advantage

Key Strengths/Expertise: IBM's existing procurement commodity councils are used to actually source for clients (31 councils, 700+ people). IBM pricing is offered in select categories to IBM clients, which leverages IBM's $5 billion in spend. Category experts across a wide array of spend categories, with some of the top talent in the world, work on the client's behalf. Well-documented and tested tools and templates are available to accomplish everything IBM does on behalf of clients.

Target Customers: Fortune 500 companies

Compensation/Outsourcing Structure: Full and partial gainshare, profit risk model, time and materials, and fixed price

Case Study: IBM recently worked with a Fortune 100 global chemical and petroleum industry client to create a closed-loop procurement infrastructure that included multiple-category strategic sourcing. It put all of its profit at risk to participate in a gainshare program. The achievements of the combined IBM/client team significantly exceeded the savings objectives in some categories and exceeded the savings projections in all remaining categories. This effort allowed IBM to not just recover the profit it put at risk, but to overachieve and receive payment beyond the time-and-materials profit.

Appendix C

Supply Management Outsourcing Service Providers

The following brief profiles of several leading supply management outsourcing service providers are provided as a service, and the co-authors make no claims concerning the completeness or accuracy of the statements, which were provided by the vendors. In some cases, they have been slightly edited to remove marketing assertions or puffery. Some companies declined to provide profiles or failed to provide profiles by the deadline. It should be noted that this information changes constantly and often dramatically. Check the Web-Added Value™ Download Resource Center at www.jrosspub.com for changes and additions.

Accenture Procurement Solutions

Contact Information: Hap Brakeley, Managing Director, Accenture Procurement Solutions, phone: (617) 454-7315, e-mail: harry.h.brakeley@accenture.com; Jeff Zaniker, Partner, Accenture Procurement Solutions, North America, phone: (312) 693-6065, e-mail: jeffrey.c.zaniker@accenture.com; Charles Findlay, Partner, Accenture Procurement Solutions, Europe, phone: +44 (0) 207-844-5517, e-mail: charles.findlay@accenture.com

Representative Clients: Deutsche Bank, Lincoln National, Jones Lang LaSalle, Thames Water, BC Hydro, State of North Carolina, AT&T Prepaid, Sainsbury's, Dynegy, Accenture (Accenture's own internal procurement)

Scope and Type of Services Offered: Accenture Procurement Solutions delivers comprehensive procurement outsourcing services that improve bottom-line performance by reducing the cost of doing business. Accenture's procurement business process outsourcing service offering includes:

♦ Sourcing and category management
♦ Transaction processing
♦ Service management and reporting

Sourcing and Category Management: Accenture can save large organizations tens of millions of dollars on the cost of the goods and services they purchase. Through sourcing, contact implementation, and ongoing category management, Accenture Procurement Solutions manages both strategic and tactical purchases to reduce costs and improve efficiencies.

Transaction Processing: Accenture assumes responsibility for procurement-related transactional processes, such as order processing, accounts payable, and travel and expense processing. Transaction-processing services are delivered through Accenture's global delivery center network, tightly aligned with the most powerful enterprise spend management technologies.

Service Management and Reporting: Accenture can also assume responsibility for managing the procurement service, including defining and delivering compliance management processes as well as actively evaluating and managing the supply base.

Key Strengths/Expertise: Accenture Procurement Solutions offers high-performance sourcing-to-settlement services that deliver breakthrough savings on the total cost of goods and services, through:

♦ *Leading Sourcing Expertise*: 600+ sourcing and procurement clients across all industries and geographies, served by 7400 supply chain consultants, of which 2100 are procurement specialists
♦ *Robust Compliance Management*: Via leading processes and enabling technology that improve compliance by end users and suppliers, to increase the rate of on-contract buys
♦ *"Best of Both Worlds" Service Delivery*: Most experienced supply chain consulting practice and leading procurement integrator, combined with an extensive, low-cost global service delivery network and robust, multiclient utilities
♦ *Greater Flexibility*: A flexible front-end solution design and flexible service "on ramps"

Target Customers: Accenture Procurement Solutions provides end-to-end, sourcing-to-settlement services for all nonstrategic categories as well as select strategic categories. These source-to-pay services are offered to clients, in all industries, that are large enough to have an addressable spend base greater than $250 million.

Typical Length of Initial Outsourcing Engagement: Accenture prefers a minimum five- to seven-year arrangement.

Compensation/Outsourcing Structure: The compensation structure for Accenture's procurement outsourcing arrangements generally includes:

♦ A transition/transformation fee
♦ A base fee, for operating a specified scope of procurement services
♦ A contingent/gainshare fee, for attaining objectives (typically based on savings generated from in-scope goods and services)

Case Study: Lincoln Financial Group is one of the leading U.S. providers of annuities, life insurance, 401(k) and 403(b) plans, 529 college savings plans, mutual funds, managed accounts, institutional investment, and financial planning and advisory services. Headquartered in Philadelphia, Lincoln Financial Group reported 2004 consolidated assets of $110 billion.

As part of its ongoing efforts to become a high-performance business, Lincoln Financial Group strives to reduce costs and improve efficiencies wherever possible. Lincoln Financial Group decided to focus on reducing costs of purchased goods and services. Specifically, Lincoln Financial Group recognized the opportunity to achieve significant savings by outsourcing its procurement activities.

Under a five-year outsourcing agreement, Accenture is managing a full suite of procure-to-pay services for Lincoln Financial Group. This effort includes negotiating contracts with suppliers for goods and services and managing suppliers, procurement contracts, compliance, and online catalogue content, as well as processing orders, payables, travel, and expenses. It also includes application hosting and support, as well as operational reporting and analysis. Accenture is delivering these innovative services through Accenture Procurement Solutions, an Accenture business that provides procurement services to global enterprises and governments on an outsourced basis.

Ariba, Inc.

Contact Information: Shahriar Broumand, VP and General Manager, Ariba Managed Services

Representative Clients: Serves companies across North America, Europe, the Middle East, and Asia in the high-tech, airline, entertainment, and automotive industries, including Lucent Technologies

Scope and Type of Services Offered: Ariba Managed Services (AMS) provides a full range of procurement outsourcing services designed to help companies manage spend currently underleveraged by in-house procurement organizations. AMS offers full outsourcing services that provide complete management of specific functions within a procurement organization, including category management, strategic sourcing, and compliance management. The company also offers category and process-specific services related to specific commodities and tasks.

Key Strengths/Expertise: Ariba has deep commodity expertise gained through helping more than 300 of the world's leading global corporations that have collectively sourced more than $225 billion across a broad range of both indirect and direct spend categories using its products and services. Through a shared services model, Ariba applies its collective commodity expertise to help individual companies manage and leverage noncore spend and focus on addressing more strategic needs in core categories. Ariba delivers its services on an integrated end-to-end technology platform which allows companies to monitor, leverage, and keep spend management programs under control.

Target Customers: Large and medium-sized companies focused on reducing costs and generating savings.

Typical Length of Initial Outsourcing Engagement: Typical engagement is 5 to 10 years; however, 3-year "pilots" are also common.

Compensation/Outsourcing Structure: Flexible to include fixed-fee and gainsharing structures. The type of service selected dictates which fee structure is applied.

Case Study: A high-tech company with more than 40,000 employees worldwide, a decentralized procurement organization, autonomous regions and business units, and huge cost pressures engaged Ariba to reduce costs and increase value by taking over management of global indirect spend in 14 categories across North America, Europe, the Middle East, and Asia. Among the services Ariba provided are:

- *Spend Visibility*: Ongoing analysis of total spend.
- *Sourcing Management Services*: Manage the strategic sourcing activities to deliver significant savings.
- *Requisition Management*: Review, validate, and track noncatalogue requisition to improve accounting, reporting, compliance, and spend management.
- *Invoice Services*: Reconcile orders to procurement card statements (invoices) for catalogue requisitions. For noncatalogue transactions, manage blocked invoices by contacting end user, supplier, or accounts payable teams.
- *Catalogue and Supplier Enablement Services*: Manage all aspects of supplier enablement, catalogue creation, and ongoing content management. Suppliers are supported in all aspects of e-readiness, while clients receive customized catalogue views and seamless content updates for any required language.
- *Hosting Services*: Implement, support, and manage the Ariba applications, including help desk and call center services.

Since launching the project in 2000, the company has identified substantial savings and efficiencies and significantly advanced its spend management initiatives.

IBM

Contact Information: Les Keay, Americas BTO Procurement Partner, e-mail: les.j.keay@ca.ibm.com

Representative Clients: United Technologies Corp., Goodyear, Omron, Procter & Gamble, SYNGENTA

Scope and Type of Services Offered: IBM's BTO Procurement offerings provide for the transformation, integration, and operation of a client's source-to-pay operations. Its comprehensive (and flexible) menu of services includes:

- Strategic sourcing
- Procurement
- Accounts payable
- Travel and expense management
- Customer assistance
- Technology applications and infrastructure

IBM has invested in the source-to-pay solution that was created by the combination of best-in-class software (Emptoris and SAP), over 70 IBM patented processes, and a globally optimized delivery capability. The appropriate balance of activities and resources operating locally, regionally, and in low-cost global centers has been a proven formula for success.

Clients are supported by IBM's global procurement team for sourcing and operations, with a presence in over 100 countries. IBM's three-tier delivery architecture will:

- Provide nonstandard expertise processes, client-facing activities, and industry-specific activities from local expertise centers
- Consolidate standard nontransactional activities into regional centers
- Consolidate transactional activities in its low-cost global centers

Key Strengths/Expertise: IBM has been recognized as a best-in-class procurement operation *and* market-leading services provider. In addition to procurement consulting, it has been providing procurement outsourcing services since 1998. IBM acquired PWC Consulting, which brought IBM additional operations and customer relationships and consulting expertise, as well as industry-specific knowledge and expertise. The acquisition of KeyMRO, a French provider of outsource procurement services, in December 2004 provided IBM country-specific and regional capabilities while significantly increasing the spend management. The

IBM sourcing and commodity council communities are leveraged on a global basis for in-scope commodities, as appropriate.

Target Customers: While IBM has not limited the industries it is willing to pursue, it has found that the following industry segments are presently the most receptive to outsourcing of procurement:

1. Industrial products
2. Automotive
3. Consumer products
4. High-tech/electronics
5. Distribution/transportation

Typical Length of Initial Outsourcing Engagement: Most engagements are in the range of 5 to 10 years. To obtain the maximum savings, a minimum of 5 years is recommended.

Compensation/Outsourcing Structure: It is rare to find two clients that want the same deal structure. The goal is to help clients find the right balance between project risk and reward for both parties. Because of this, IBM has created three main pricing models that it uses as a starting point for discussions with clients:

 ◆ Operations fee model — *IBM will commit that savings levels will cover IBM annual fees*
 ◆ On-demand fee model
 ◆ Shared savings fee model

Case Study: United Technologies Corp.
   Description of Services: IBM is delivering procurement services for indirect materials for UTC, across several of its subsidiaries, under a business transformation outsourcing (BTO) agreement. UTC awarded the BTO contract to IBM to provide solutions for key challenges such as need for rapid, dramatic improvements in procurement effectiveness; need for effective control, monitoring, and leveraging of indirect spend of $4 billion; and inability to control highly decentralized indirect procurement environment ("everyone's a buyer") within independent business units.

 ◆ Lack of information about spend to monitor compliance and leverage corporate agreements
 ◆ Lack of common processes or systems

   Results: The UTC/IBM procurement outsourcing partnership successfully achieved bottom-line savings and attained the operating efficiency targets since 1998, with recent contract extension through 2008. Key benefits to date include:

- ◆ Orders and payments flow through common systems
- ◆ Maverick buying is low (Otis and Carrier, UTC divisions that allow IBM to track), less than 3%
- ◆ Close control and monitoring of spending, with full visibility and tracking for accountability
- ◆ On-hand inventory reduced or eliminated through tighter tracking and delivery controls
- ◆ Consolidated orders and leveraged price discounts

ICG Commerce

Contact Information: Kristen Knouft, phone: (484) 690-5159

Representative Clients: Avaya, Timken, Crown Cork & Seal, Nordstrom, Greif, Vought, Cooper Cameron, Qualxserv, Delta, Avon

Scope and Type of Services Offered: ICG Commerce is a procurement services provider committed to helping companies buy goods and services more effectively and more efficiently, to deliver significant, measurable savings to the bottom line. ICG Commerce makes an impact in three major ways. First, it applies technology and deep category experts to evaluate a company's needs and expenditures in each major buying category and perform a sourcing process that yields the best combination of price, product quality, and supplier service.

Second, ICG Commerce turns savings potential into reality by implementing and managing a technology-enabled transaction process that supports every step from request through invoice. Third, ICG Commerce effects continuing cost reductions by making spending visible for better control and by providing category specialists to maximize additional savings possibilities. The company has a comprehensive infrastructure that combines dedicated category experts, process specialists, and leading tools to deliver maximized results. It supports two primary service lines that can be tailored to meet each company's needs:

- ◆ Sourcing services
- ◆ Procurement outsourcing

ICG Commerce is exclusively focused on lowering costs and is the only company that addresses the entire procurement savings process.

Key Strengths/Expertise:

Experience: ICG Commerce has comprehensive, long-term outsourcing relationships with over a dozen companies. In addition, it is providing smaller scope procurement outsourcing services for another 90 companies worldwide.

Infrastructure: The company has built and refined a procurement center of excellence with the critical mass needed to deliver more effective and efficient purchase-to-pay services. It constantly evaluates procurement best practices, using leading quality improvement methods such as Six Sigma to drive service-level improvements.

Focus: ICG Commerce is exclusively focused on helping companies improve procurement performance. It has no competing business priorities and no other motives for controlling a company's procurement expenditures.

Target Customers: ICG Commerce is proactively targeting customers with annual revenues in the $1 billion to $8 billion range across all industries; however, the company accepts and serves both smaller and much larger customers.

Typical Length of Initial Outsourcing Engagement: ICG Commerce's outsourcing engagements typically run from five to seven years in length.

Compensation/Outsourcing Structure: ICG Commerce's pricing is a fee-for-service model with an initial implementation fee and then an ongoing monthly services fee based on the agreed-upon scope of work. Portions of its fees become variable to adjust for large fluctuations in transaction volumes and/or project-based work that is requested to support one-off initiatives.

Case Study: ICG Commerce is providing comprehensive procurement outsourcing services for a $4 billion telecommunications company. The company's objectives for outsourcing included increasing the amount of spend under management, reducing costs to procure indirect goods and services, proactively managing the supply base globally, and increasing the return on its technology investment.

ICG Commerce was selected to provide comprehensive strategy-to-settlement services for seven global commodity groups and transaction processing using Ariba for all indirect commodities. These services have included:

◆ Utilization of e-sourcing and traditional sourcing techniques to "identify" savings
◆ Enablement of suppliers through custom and prebuilt catalogues
◆ Development and implementation of a procurement-focused change management program
◆ Implementation of a savings tracking and compliance program
◆ Implementation of an ongoing category management program to drive continuous improvements, monitor the market, and improve supplier performance

ICG Commerce seamlessly transitioned the company to an outsourced model which allowed the company to focus on core competencies and growth in less than six months. Over the last 12 months, ICG Commerce has met or exceeded all service level agreement and savings targets, driving a significant return on investment.

Source Notes

Most of the information in this book is derived from personal experiences of the four authors. Information is referenced below if it is derived from another source or if in the opinion of the authors readers may want further description of the source.

The co-authors would like to thank April E. Asquith, reference supervisor at the Needham (Massachusetts) Free Public Library, for her assistance in locating hard-to-find reference materials cited here.

Chapter 1

1. David Kearns and David Nadler, *Prophets in the Dark*, HarperCollins, 1992. Used as a general source for this reference.
2. Doug Smock interview with Tom Stallkamp, December 2004.
3. Doug Garr, *IBM Redux: Lou Gerstner & the Business Turnaround of the Decade*, HarperBusiness, 1999. Used as a general source for this reference.

Chapter 2

1. Story by Doug Smock in *Purchasing*, April 5, 2001 (see archives at www.purchasing.com).
2. Story by Doug Smock in *Purchasing*, September 6, 2001 (see archives at www.purchasing.com).

Chapter 3

1. Jack Welch with John A. Byrne, *Jack: Straight from the Gut*, Warner Business Books, 2001, p. 200.
2. Shelley Stewart interview with Glen Meakem, February, 2005.

Chapter 4

1. Interview with Bo I. Andersson in January 2001 while Doug Smock was chief editor of *Purchasing* magazine at Reed Business Information-US. For more information, see February 22, 2001 archives at www.purchasing.com.
2. Interviews with toolmakers in the late 1990s when Doug Smock was editorial director of *Modern Mold & Tooling* at McGraw-Hill.
3. Doug Smock interview with Kent Brittan, November 2004.
4. "The Unsung CEO," *Business Week*, October 25, 2004.
5. Marshall L. Fisher, "What Is the Right Supply Chain for Your Product?" *Harvard Business Review on Managing the Value Chain*, 2000, p. 127.

Chapter 6

1. SAS Procurement Executive Roundtable, 2002 and interviews with R. Gene Richter.
2. Louis V. Gerstner, *Who Says Elephants Can't Dance? Inside IBM's Historic Turnaround*, HarperBusiness, 2002, p. 244.
3. Defining the Procurement Organization — 2004, Center for Advanced Purchasing Studies (CapsReserach.org).
4. Peter F. Drucker, *Management Challenges for the 21st Century*, HarperCollins, 1999, p. 9.

Chapter 7

1. James Carbone, "Reinventing Purchasing Wins Medal for IBM," *Purchasing*, September 16, 1999 (www.purchasing.com).
2. "Intel Leads on RosettaNet," www.globalpo.com.

Chapter 9

1. John P. Kotter, *John P. Kotter on What Leaders Really Do*, Harvard Business School Press, 1999.
2. For an excellent review of Katzorke's program at Cessna, see Susan Avery, "Cessna Soars," *Purchasing*, September 4, 2003 (www.purchasing.com).

Chapter 10

1. Comments made by Gene Richter at purchasing conferences sponsored across the United States by SAS, Cary, North Carolina, in 2002.
2. "Reinventing Purchasing Wins Medal for IBM," *Purchasing*, September 16, 1999 (www.purchasing.com).
3. Michael H. Moffett and William E. Youngdahl, *Jose Ignacio Lopez de Arriortua*, Thunderbird, The American Graduate (now Garvin) School of International Management, 1998.

4. Robert A. Lutz, *Guts: The Seven Laws of Business That Made Chrysler the World's Hottest Car Company*, John Wiley & Sons, 1998, p. 26.
5. Ibid., p. 36.
6. Ibid., pp. 37–38.
7. Jeffrey H. Dyer, "How Chrysler Created an American Keiretsu," *Harvard Business Review on Managing the Value Chain*, 2000, pp. 61–90.
8. Interview with Doug Smock, February 2005.
9. Interview with Doug Smock.
10. Jeffrey H. Dyer, "How Chrysler Created an American Keiretsu," *Harvard Business Review on Managing the Value Chain*, 2000, pp. 61–90.
11. Robert A. Lutz, *Guts: The Seven Laws of Business That Made Chrysler the World's Hottest Car Company*, John Wiley & Sons, 1998, p. 39.
12. Interview with Doug Smock, December 2004.
13. Robert A. Lutz, *Guts: The Seven Laws of Business That Made Chrysler the World's Hottest Car Company*, John Wiley & Sons, 1998, p. 53.
14. Interview with Doug Smock at the Detroit Auto Show.
15. Robert B. Handfield and Ernest L. Nichols, Jr., *Supply Chain Redesign*, Prentice Hall, 2002, p. 344.
16. Interview with Doug Smock, December 2004.
17. Interview with Doug Smock, February 2005.

Chapter 11

1. Speech by Nabil Sakkab at the European Research Conference 2002 organized by the European Commission to mark the launch of its Sixth Framework Program for Research. P&G led a workshop on industry experience in collaboration with BASF and CEFIC (the European Chemical Industry Association).

Note: Most of the information in this chapter is based on interviews by Doug Smock with staff members of P&G in Cincinnati and over the phone. Articles about P&G's procurement strategies by Smock appeared in *Purchasing*, November 4, 2004 (www.purchasing.com) and *Modern Plastics*, December 1, 2004 (www.modplas.com).

Chapter 12

1. Eugene E. Wilson, *Slipstream: The Autobiography of an Air Craftsman*, McGraw-Hill, 1950, pp. 67–68.
2. Cary Hoge Mead, *Wings Over the World*, The Swannet Press, 1971, p. 81.

Note: Most of the information in this chapter came from interviews by Doug Smock at UTC in late 2004 and 2005. The discussion in this chapter on the indirect outsourcing program implemented with IBM was also based on recollections of co-author Shelley Stewart, Jr. and an article by Anne Millen Porter that appeared in *Purchasing*, June 15, 2000 (www.purchasing.com).

Chapter 13

1. Robert A. Rudzki, "Leading Strategic Change," *Supply Chain Management Review*, January/February 2001.

Chapter 15

1. Shelley Stewart interview, February 2005.
2. Gwendolyn Whitfield, "Supplier Diversity and Buyer Behavior: Does Organizational Culture Really Matter?" unpublished at the time of interview by Shelley Stewart.
3. Keynote address at the 2004 Annual Conference of the Institute for Supply Management.
4. Interview with Doug Smock, November 2004.
5. "Leading Supplier Diversity Initiatives," Procurement Strategy Council/2002 Corporate Executive Board. General reference.
6. Project Support Memorandum, April 2002. General reference.
7. "Maintaining MWBE Relationships in Adverse Economic Environments," Procurement Strategy Council/2002 Corporate Executive Board Initiative Snapshot, February 2003. General reference.
8. "Creating Supplier Diversity Programs in the Financial Services Industry," Procurement Strategy Council/2004 Corporate Executive Board Key Findings, March 2004. General reference.
9. Shelley Stewart questionnaire to several companies mentioned in this section, February 2005. General reference.

Chapter 16

1. Comments by Naren Gursaheney, Senior Vice President of Operational Excellence, at a Tyco Webcast with investment analysts, February 2005.
2. "Low Cost Country Sourcing — An Executive Overview," Ariba, September 2003.
3. Ed Frauenheim, "Dell Drops India Call Centre," November 25, 2003 (www.silicon.com).

Chapter 20

1. Bob Rudzki interview with Jim Pearson, Vice President, A.T. Kearney, Inc., March 2005.

Index